Objectively Speaking

Ayn Rand Interviewed

Edited by
Marlene Podritske
and Peter Schwartz

LEXINGTON BOOKS

A division of
ROWMAN & LITTLEFIELD PUBLISHERS, INC.
Lanham • Boulder • New York • Toronto • Plymouth, UK

LEXINGTON BOOKS

A division of Rowman & Littlefield Publishers, Inc.
A wholly owned subsidiary of The Rowman & Littlefield Publishing Group, Inc.
4501 Forbes Boulevard, Suite 200
Lanham, MD 20706

Estover Road
Plymouth PL6 7PY
United Kingdom

British Library Cataloguing in Publication Information Available

Library of Congress Cataloging-in-Publication Data

Objectively speaking: Ayn Rand interviewed / edited by Marlene Podritske and
Peter Schwartz.
    p. cm.
Includes index.
ISBN-13: 978-0-7391-3194-7 (cloth: alk. paper)
ISBN-10: 0-7391-3194-X (cloth: alk. paper)
ISBN-13: 978-0-7391-3195-4 (pbk.: alk. paper)
ISBN-10: 0-7391-3195-8 (pbk.: alk. paper)
ISBN-13: 978-0-7391-3196-1 (e-book)
ISBN-10: 0-7391-3196-6 (e-book)
1. Rand, Ayn—Interviews. I. Podritske, Marlene, 1948– II. Schwartz, Peter, 1949–
B945.R234A5 2009
191—dc22

2008045442

Printed in the United States of America

⊗ ™ The paper used in this publication meets the minimum requirements of
American National Standard for Information Sciences—Permanence of Paper
for Printed Library Materials, ANSI/NISO Z39.48-1992.

Objectively Speaking

Contents

Part 3: On Television and Radio:
Ayn Rand in America's Living Rooms (1959–1981)

Preface

Ayn Rand expressed a reluctance to grant interviews, concerned that complex ideas could be easily misunderstood and serious discussion limited due to the "in-a-nutshell" constraints of live programming. Further, the growing popularity of the talk-show format (complete with audience participation and an often confrontational host) was replacing the one-to-one interview she preferred. This change had the potential to make appearances more argumentative than informative. As an invited guest, she welcomed the opportunity to present her ideas but believed, justifiably, that this setting was often an ineffectual, if not dishonest, venue for intellectual discussion. As she remarked to Johnny Carson during her second appearance on *The Tonight Show* (see chapter 26), when he commented on this adversarial interview strategy, "I'm always glad to discuss ideas, but not to debate them."

When she did agree to appear, however, she was always a lively, fully-engaged participant, defending her views unyieldingly, against all challenges. Her intellectual consistency over time and in a multitude of contexts is in full evidence in this collection. Her unrehearsed responses to these interviewers—from the skeptic to the sycophant, the antagonist to the advocate—ring with the same unequivocal coherence and conviction that define her written work. Here is Ayn Rand in extemporaneous, impassioned interaction—clarifying, teaching, admonishing, supporting, correcting.

Ayn Rand's intensive interview schedule during the 1960s was initiated by the interest on the part of professors and students in her philosophy of Objectivism, as articulated in her 1957 novel, *Atlas Shrugged*. Later, her new nonfiction works elaborated on the principles of that philosophy and stimulated many of the remaining interviews. But whatever the original motivation, her appearances typically developed into wide-ranging discussions offering insights into social phenomena, lessons on the arts, autobiographical details, and commentary on political and cultural personalities.

The underlying structure of the book is chronological. Part 1 includes: her first known interview, at age 27; her excerpted responses from a heavily editorialized article; and her initial radio interview, with a rather ill-prepared host.

Part 2 is a selection from two series recorded intermittently at Columbia University, between 1962 and 1966, and represents the most active period of her public appearances. A panel of professors and students would query Ayn Rand on specific principles of Objectivism and their application to "living on earth." Both series were rebroadcast at various times throughout the United States and Canada, making the exact sequence of the extant tapes unclear. Therefore, the interviews in this section logically lent themselves to classification by topic rather than chronology. Different interviews on the same subject (e.g., education) were combined and material from one interview that was clearly more appropriate to another topic was moved.

Part 3 is devoted to interviews from both general and specialized media, beginning with Mike Wallace in 1959 and concluding with her final public appearance in 1981 with Louis Rukeyser. Fittingly, the book's epilogue belongs to Dr. Leonard Peikoff, her heir and the one who knew her best, as he fondly recalls, in a 1999 radio interview, his thirty-year personal and professional association with Ayn Rand.

These interviews are essentially structured conversations. My task was to eliminate the repetitions, grammatical errors, and self-corrections that are common in extemporaneous speech but which often lead to confusions or awkwardness in print. Extraneous material was deleted and interviewers' lengthy preambles to questions were shortened.

I found that without the oral and visual cues of intonation, expression, and gesture, particular emphases and connotations could be lost to the reader. Therefore, the occasional exchanges that relied heavily on these conversational signposts were reformulated to make them clearer in print, while the integrity of both the question and the response was maintained. I sought to minimize editorial alterations in order to preserve the natural flow and flavor of dialogue as much as possible. The reader is cautioned to be mindful that these interviews are not necessarily Ayn Rand's final, considered arguments on any point; they are not meant to stand as her official statements and they have been edited without her oversight. Coeditor Peter Schwartz completed the final editing for redundancy, clarity, economy, and accuracy.

Although Ayn Rand denied any interest in being a "teacher," when she did assume that role, she took pains to be a great one, as is evident in many of these interviews. She insisted on the defining of terms as a prerequisite to any kind of meaningful, focused discussion. Always clear, logical, and patient, she sought to elevate her questioners' own thinking skills. Her occasional flashes of anger were never directed at those she believed were struggling to understand, but were reserved for those who intentionally sought to misconstrue her words.

A wonderful illustration of her understanding of the teaching process occurred in a 1967 radio interview (not included in this book) when she described a lecture she had recently given at Columbia University. It demonstrates her ability to communicate ideas and stimulate intellectual inquiry—the proper role of a teacher. Her obvious satisfaction with the experience relies not on the audience's agreement with her views, but on the response of active minds to the logic and rationality of her presentation.

> I was invited by a young professor to address students studying business economics. About 400 people crowded into the classroom to listen to my topic, "What is Capitalism?" What I presented certainly was not a hesitant, uncertain, or compromising view of capitalism. I was presenting an extreme and unpopular viewpoint. Yet that audience sat in enthusiastic attention through the whole hour. When I say enthusiastic, I mean that they responded at the right moments with the proper reactions. Therefore, I knew that they were hearing me. The most fascinating part was the question period. It was quite obvious from the questions that most of the students were not in agreement with my viewpoint. Yet they were interested; their minds were active. They were asking polite, appropriate, intelligent questions. They were responding to my moral certainty. They did not have to agree with me. But what they obviously needed and responded to was the sight of a speaker who was intellectually certain of her case, and was able to give them reasons for any statement. They wanted to hear reasons, and responded remarkably.

These interviews, spanning six decades, were selected to provide the broadest scope of topics from both mainstream and niche media, with a gamut of interviewers from the famous professional to the anonymous amateur. Interviews available in anthologies or as reprints (such as her *Playboy* interview) and those dealing with very localized issues were excluded (as, of course, were those of copyright-holders who did not grant permission to use their material).

In 1975, when challenged about her opposition to "women's lib" by *The Christian Science Monitor*, she explained, "I'm against that for the same reason I'm against racism. I am against classifying anyone on anatomical, physiological grounds. What makes you human is your mind, and that is in your control; that's what you are to be judged on."

And that is what Ayn Rand is to be judged on. This collection attests to the interest in that mind over time and across a sea of backgrounds and perspectives. For the full, panoramic view of her ideas, read her books. But for sparkling, thought-provoking snapshots of one of the world's most innovative thinkers in action, read these interviews.

Marlene Podritske
Kent, Connecticut
March 2007

Acknowledgments

Compilation and Introduction Copyright 2008 by the Ayn Rand Institute. All rights reserved.

"Speaking Freely" Copyright 1972 by Edwin Newman. Used by permission.

"Russian Girl Jeers at U.S. for Depression Complain" *Oakland Tribune* 1932. Used by permission of ANG Newspapers.

"Russian Love Life" *Boston Post* Sept. 6, 1936 Courtesy of Boston Public Library

"The Woman of Tomorrow" Interview by Nancy Craig July 13, 1949 By permission of WABC-AM

Nineteen Radio Interviews "Ayn Rand on Campus" 1962–1966 WKCR (Columbia University) Used by permission.

Mike Wallace interview from "Mike Wallace Interviews" WNTA-TV, Feb. 25, 1959. By permission of Mike Wallace.

Ayn Rand Interviews, The Tonight Show with Johnny Carson, August and October 1967. By permission of Carson Entertainment.

"An Interview with Ayn Rand: For the New Intellectual" with James Mc-Connell May 15, 1961. By permission of University of Michigan.

"Day at Night" Television Interview, March 1974. By permission of Publivision, Inc.

"Focus on Youth" Garth R. Ancien November 1976 By permission of Garth Ancien

"The Raymond Newman Journal" 1980 By permission of Raymond Newman

"Louis Rukeyser's Business Journal" 1981. By permission of Louis Rukeyser.

"Recollections of Ayn Rand" from "The Leonard Peikoff Show," 1998. Edited and by permission of Leonard Peikoff.

1

BEGINNINGS: A RUSSIAN ÉMIGRÉ'S FIRST INTERVIEWS (1932–1949)

"Russian Girl Jeers at U.S. for Depression Complaint," *Oakland Tribune*, 1932

[In Russia,] American motion pictures are cut, and propaganda against the rich is inserted.

EDITOR'S NOTE: This is the first published interview of Ayn Rand. She is described as a Hollywood scenarist who had just sold her story "The Red Pawn" to Universal Studios. The title above is the headline of the newspaper article, in which she, as a Russian émigré, is asked about the harsh conditions of the Depression in America. Her extended reply follows.

"For three years Americans have been complaining of a depression. They don't even know what it is.

"In Russia there are no definite tax laws. You may pay taxes for 1932, and then in 1933 you may pay additional taxes for 1932 all over again, if the government is a little bit short. Small private businesses are taxed lightly when they 'break even,' but when they show a profit, the taxes are readjusted so as to give nearly everything to the government.

"The 'high-priced executive' in Russia does not have the physical comforts of the laborer in America. [In Russia] several families live in one home and, in industrial districts, from five to seven people live in one *room*. The government allots the space each inhabitant may occupy. Husband and wife may have a total stranger thrust into their room at any time.

"For food, there is gruel—heavy and filling, but not doing the digestive tract much good. At times I have eaten cakes made of ground carrot greens, coffee grounds and acorns. Once enough money is saved to buy a dress or a pair of shoes, the government must give permission for the purchase. You stand in

3

line for hours, waiting to get what is wanted at the stores. The purchase of a pair of stockings is an event. There are no fashions and no fashion magazines. In one city, a factory turned out thousands of yards of cloth in just four different patterns, and on the streets you saw women, in groups of threes and fours, all wearing the same kinds of dresses.

"Only the very wealthy own motor cars, and these cars are second-hand. It is dangerous to ride in one anyway, because the poorer people throw things at you. American motion pictures are cut, and propaganda against the rich is inserted before the pictures are shown. The Russians even shoot additional scenes with people who do not resemble the [actors] in the pictures [and] who launch into diatribes against the rich."

• 2 •

"True Picture of Russian Girls' Love Life Tragic," *Boston Post*, 1936

Most American girls have never . . . considered that love needs leisure and that the gracelessness of [Russian] living . . . impoverishes love until it is as starved and unbeautiful as a plant denied sun and air and water.

EDITOR'S NOTE: This is from a newspaper article comparing the "unhappy existence of Soviet women" with that of "free New England maidens and wives." Ayn Rand's first novel, We the Living, *had just been published, and she was asked by the interviewer to concretize the differences between Soviet Russia and the United States through an examination of the personal and working lives of women. Her replies, excerpted from the lengthy article, are reproduced here as one continuous presentation. The awkward title above is the newspaper's own.*

"Let's draw companion pictures of the young Russian woman at work and in love, and . . . her American sister.

"Take Olga. She lives in a three-room apartment—she and her sister and her father and her mother. They have no bathtub, and their bathroom is the crudest and most unsanitary. . . . Olga wears the coarsest of cotton underwear and weary, dreary black cotton stockings.

"She gets to her office at eight in the morning, walking because she hates to fight as hard as necessary to go in an unpleasant bus. The first thing she does is read the wall newspaper. This is a paper, pinned to the wall each day, in which any of her fellow workers may make any kind of criticism they wish to—of her, or of anybody else working at the same office. If Olga dresses a little better than the others, if she dresses not so neatly as the rest, if she is

5

suspected of being more interested in her boyfriend than in the Soviet Union, if she does not seem 'socially minded,' if she is suspected of lacking zeal for Communism—there is her name. . . .

"All day long she works. Dry bread and dry fish may be her noonday lunch. Most of the time, anyway, Olga is hungry, and always she is malnourished. Five o'clock arrives. But Olga doesn't go home. Some nights she donates several added hours, free of pay, to the Soviet Union. And other nights, she goes to political meetings, where she must make speeches on political subjects and listen to the speeches of others.

"Finally she goes home to a dreary, bleak supper. A little bread perhaps. Horse meat or some other meat fried in linseed oil with onions. And after late dinner, she has to get out her books and read to keep politically informed, for if she comes to her workers' examinations and does not know her politics, she will lose her job.

"Olga has a boyfriend, but she has little time for him. The state claims most of her working hours and all of her strength. But the Soviets tell her she is free. 'Free for what?' she would like to ask.

"[Then] there is Miss Kitty Cotton, a secretary in Boston. She leaps out of bed at eight o'clock sharp, dashes into her shower-bath and puts on silk underwear, sheer silk stockings and a saucy frock, whose original was a Paris model. She runs for the bus, after coffee and orange juice and toast, which her mother has all ready for her. Or maybe, after breakfast, the boyfriend waits with his roadster. She reaches the office at nine—by a daily morning miracle. She works till noon. Then she has a very nice lunch of an ice cream soda, a sandwich and a piece of cake. When she is feeling rich, or when the boyfriend takes her out, she has lobster or chicken salad, French fried potatoes, dessert and coffee. She goes back to her office and spends a busy day, writing down the letters her boss dictated to her that morning.

"Five arrives. She dashes home. Into glorious party clothes. Fresh bath, lipstick, powder, perfume and a wonderful new dress, a darling little model which cost only a trifle over $10, for Kitty is a good shopper and there are bargains in her birth city of Boston. Well, the boyfriend is honking. And away goes Kitty to spend a grand evening. . . . Dinner, and a drive and maybe a dance somewhere out in the country at a pleasant roadside tavern. . . .

"For the most part, these young Miss Kittys are thankful. But to their greatest blessing of all, they hardly give a thought. That is, their privilege of having a private life. Of seeing the boyfriend alone at dinner, or entertaining him alone on the porch or in mother's parlor, cleared for courting.

"Kitty, the American girl, can have a private life when [she] is in love. But Olga, the Russian girl, has no private life nor ever may while the Soviets are in power. For these gentlemen say that the state is all-important and the individual of little moment. Thus Olga's courtship and Olga's marriage is a senseless, hurried and dreary affair.

"Most American girls have never given a thought as to what political unhappiness and distress can do to private lives. Nor have they, probably, considered that love needs leisure, and that the gracelessness of [Russian] living . . . impoverishes love until it is as starved and unbeautiful as a plant denied sun and air and water. I have seen the most beautiful love sadden and sicken and perish. I have seen marriages that might have been happy, had they been granted a little room at home for the living of lives of decent seclusion, end tragically and miserably. . . .

"In the United States a married woman can suit herself about whether she works outside her home or remains in it to take care of her house and her family. In Russia a married woman who does not work is assessed an unemployment tax. It costs her money to remain at home and try to give her children personal care. This results in the majority of city children being brought up as little gamins, while their mothers work long hours in a factory or office or store to help support them.

"In these United States of ours, we working women may fear we will lose our jobs. That is one fear we all have, to some degree at any rate. But when the job is gone, we don't feel at the end of our resources. We still can go out and get another. I know this well, for in my first years in this country I worked as a waitress, as a saleswoman from door to door, as an assistant wardrobe woman in Hollywood, as a scenario writer, as a worker at a bewildering number of jobs. And when fired, I always landed somewhere else, eventually.

"But in Russia the terrific fear of the young girl worker is the fear of losing her job. Once it is gone, it is almost impossible for her to get another job, since under the collectivist state, the government is the only employer. And if the government has discharged you, it is rather unreasonable to expect the same boss to take you back again. The same boss seldom does.

"And so leisure, home life, parties, pretty clothes, private and personal opinions, the freedom to go about to pleasant places when you are young and in love and hoping to be married—all these must be sacrificed by the working girl in Russia today. . . .

"I am glad to be an American today, and not sorry I have ceased to be a Russian citizen. Our institutions over here may not yet be perfect, but I, having had experience with many of the older countries, believe that here we women have the opportunity to live happier lives than anywhere else in the world."

• 3 •

"The Woman of Tomorrow," *WJZ Radio*, 1949

By the time I was nine, I had decided that writing stories would be my profession.

EDITOR'S NOTE: This interview, on a New York City radio show called "The Woman of Tomorrow," took place following the release of the movie version of The Fountainhead.

Interviewer: *Our guest today is Ayn Rand, author of the best-selling novel* The Fountainhead, *which has had some of the highest sales in the history of modern publishing. It has been printed in twelve languages, and although it came out in 1943—six years ago—it is still in great demand. Miss Rand, that must make your publisher, Bobbs–Merrill, very happy.*

AR: So they tell me. And it pleases me very much, because twelve different publishers rejected the book as being too intellectual for the general public. They said it would not sell. Only Bobbs-Merrill had the courage to publish it. It's a curious thing about the book—it wasn't an immediate best-seller. It grew slowly. Much of its success was due to word-of-mouth recommendations. And it wasn't until two years after its publication that sales reached their peak.

Interviewer: *I attended a screening the other night of the Warner Brothers' movie production of* The Fountainhead. *It's a beautiful story of a man who had the courage to stick to his ideals. I think I'm one of a very small group of people who haven't yet read the book. Does the film follow the book faithfully?*

AR: The film is extremely faithful to the book, not only in story, but in spirit.

Interviewer: You wrote the screenplay, didn't you?

AR: I did, which, as you know, is unusual. When Henry Blanke decided to produce the film, he insisted that the author do the screenplay. Incidentally, he is one of the few artistic producers in Hollywood today. *The Fountainhead* was my first screenplay; I went to Hollywood in 1943 to write it. And in between the first version and the final shooting script, Hal Wallis of Paramount asked me to do two other screenplays—one called *Love Letters* and the other, *You Came Along.*

Interviewer: Did you have anything to do with selecting the cast?

AR: Only in a consulting capacity. I had always wanted Gary Cooper as Howard Roark. He has an artistic fitness for the role. When Mr. Blanke asked me who my ideal choice was, that's what I told him. At the time, Gary Cooper was not with Warner Brothers. He had, however, read the book and was interested in it. He went to Warner Brothers and asked for the part, not knowing that I had recommended him.

Interviewer: Have you been living in California since 1943?

AR: Yes. Previously I lived in New York, and as soon as I finish my new novel, I'll return there.

Interviewer: Oh, you have a new book in the writing. Is it anything like The Fountainhead?

AR: Not in superficial detail or setting, but it is like *The Fountainhead* in theme and spirit—only much stronger. Its theme is individualism, but from an entirely different angle. It's a story that glorifies the American industrialist and shows that industrial achievements are as much a product of the spirit— that they take as much courage, independence and integrity—as works of art. The background of the story is the railroads and the steel industry. I hope to have it published by the end of 1950.

Interviewer: Was your writing career something you picked at an early age?

AR: From the time I was six years old, I was always inventing stories. By the time I was nine, I had decided that writing stories would be my profession.

Interviewer: *When you wrote* The Fountainhead, *did you plan it as symbolic of certain struggles and problems of the times?*

AR: That's a question that many readers have asked—whether my characters are copies of real people in public life or not human beings at all, but symbols. Neither alternative is true. I advocate Romanticism, which emphasizes the great, the unusual or the beautiful in actual human life—as opposed to the Naturalistic school, which presents the sordid side and claims that it is depicting "life as it is." I think there has been too much of the sordid, and of the commonplace, in art. The public is very tired of this approach because it offers no inspiration. We have had so many pictures about commonplace people, about criminals, about degenerates. At the moment, I can't think of any recent pictures that present an inspiring or heroic type of human being. I have a feeling that *The Fountainhead* will mark the return of fine Romantic pictures to the screen.

Interviewer: *You've said that your husband serves as your editor. I noticed that you dedicated* The Fountainhead *to him.*

AR: He is the first person to hear everything I write, and his criticism has always been correct and valuable. His viewpoint is the same as mine, but he has always been objective about my work. When I start to write a book, the characters become members of our family. For the seven years that I was writing *The Fountainhead*, we lived with Howard Roark, Dominique Francon and Gail Wynand. Those characters were actually more real to us than the people we knew. And even after the book was finished, they remained in the family for two years. (In fact, I came to the point that I had to shut them out by conscious effort in order to start on my new book.) I hope that now, with the release of the movie, the characters will become as real to other people as they have been to my husband and me.

2

ON CAMPUS: AYN RAND TALKS WITH FUTURE INTELLECTUALS (1962–1966)

· 4 ·

Objectivism versus Conservatism

The conservatives do not want laissez-faire. They merely want
fewer controls than do the liberals.

*EDITOR'S NOTE: The interviews that make up Part 2 were aired on Columbia
University's radio series, "Ayn Rand on Campus," from 1962 to 1966.*

Interviewer: *Our topic this evening is the Objectivist view of conservatism. But
would you first give a brief rundown of Objectivism for those listeners who haven't
heard you before?*

AR: With pleasure, except that I ask you to remember that it really will be
brief. I will give you Objectivism's essential position in the four main branches
of philosophy: metaphysics, epistemology, ethics and politics.

In metaphysics, Objectivism holds that existence exists, which means that
reality is an objective absolute unaffected by, and existing independently of, any
perceiver or any perceiver's feelings, wishes, hopes or fears. In epistemology,
Objectivism holds that reason is man's only means of knowledge and his only
guide to action. By reason, we mean the faculty that identifies and integrates
the material provided by man's senses. In ethics, Objectivism holds that man
exists for his own sake, that he must neither sacrifice himself to others nor sacrifice others to himself and that his highest moral purpose is the achievement
of his own happiness. In politics, Objectivism stands for laissez-faire capitalism,
which means the separation of state and economics; as a corollary, we hold that
men must deal with one another as traders, exchanging value for value, with no
one being told that he must sacrifice for the sake of others or of the state.

15

Interviewer: Many people seem to feel that Objectivism is merely another form of conservatism. What is the difference between the two?

AR: I am emphatically not a conservative, nor is Objectivism a conservative philosophy. To begin with the positive, I describe myself as a radical for capitalism. I mean "radical" in the original, respectable sense of the word: *fundamental.* Objectivism starts from fundamental premises, which are diametrically opposed to those of today's conservatives.

Interviewer: Could you outline the premises of conservatism with which you disagree?

AR: "Conservative" is as loose a term today as "liberal," and most people who use it keep the meaning intentionally vague. There is no firm definition. Therefore, what I say does not necessarily apply to each individual who calls himself a conservative. I am speaking of the dominant trend and of the general impression people have of conservatism. By commonly accepted usage, a conservative is someone who opposes the welfare state and supports capitalism. In fact, however, most conservatives do not stand for free enterprise, but for various degrees of a mixed economy.

More basically, as far as one can determine what conservatives hold, too many of them tie their political views to religion. They claim that mysticism—a belief in God—provides the justification for rights, freedom and capitalism. Nothing could be more disastrous to the cause of capitalism—and nothing could be more opposed to Objectivism, which holds reason as the sole means of validating any idea or action. Tying capitalism to faith means that capitalism *cannot* be justified in reason. A conservative who claims that his case rests on faith declares that reason is on the side of his enemies—that one can oppose collectivism only on the grounds of mystical faith. To the extent that anyone accepts this argument, he is forced to reject capitalism—if he is a man who wants to be rational. Therefore, these alleged defenders of capitalism are pushing potential sympathizers to the exact opposite side.

Interviewer: Do all those who call themselves conservatives use only mystical, religious grounds for justifying free enterprise? Aren't there some, at least, who justify it on rational grounds?

AR: Yes, there are some. They are usually called "libertarians," with Professor Ludwig von Mises and Henry Hazlitt as their best exponents. Such so-called conservatives are defenders of capitalism on a non-mystical, scientific basis. They do not advocate a mixed economy, and are much better than the typical conservative. Unfortunately, since no clear intellectual lines are drawn, even people of this kind are quite willing to collaborate with the mystical types. Because conservatism is not sharply defined, it includes people of all shades of opinion. My main objection to any movement of that sort is that it is futile. It is disastrous to one's own cause to allow oneself to belong to an undefined group, or to collaborate with other groups, without any clear identification of basic principles or basic points of agreement.

Interviewer: Wouldn't you say—as they probably would—that these collaborators just believe it is more practical to make changes more slowly, since the welfare state can't simply be abolished immediately?

AR: There are two different issues here. The first is: What is your basic political goal? Only with that foundation can you then discuss the second: How do you implement it in practice? The question of whether you want to abolish all controls at once or only gradually has nothing to do with the question of what your goal is. For instance, Objectivists do not argue that we can get out of today's mess overnight. I have always said that a process of decontrol is required. The ultimate goal is complete free enterprise, but it has to be achieved gradually. To achieve it overnight, by fiat, would be a) impossible, and b) dictatorial. One cannot solve social questions that way.

But my disagreement with conservatives is over the issue of *ends*. The conservatives do not want laissez-faire. They merely want fewer controls than do the liberals. The conservatives never give any precise guidelines for choosing the particular controls they want eliminated. By what standard are those selected? Where do you draw the line? Those questions are left in a total fog. But as to their ultimate goal, the conservatives advocate a mixed economy.

Interviewer: You were talking about a wing of conservatism that you called "libertarian." Are there other differences that Objectivism has with the libertarians, besides the fact that they are willing to collaborate and be identified with conservatives?

AR: Yes. But since libertarians, too, are a loosely defined group, the differences will vary from individual to individual. In a general sense, though, our main difference with the libertarians lies in the fact that they are concerned primarily with economics and politics. Objectivism is primarily not a political-economic movement, but a philosophy. We derive our politics and economics from a certain philosophic framework, without which we would not advocate the particular ideas we do. But the libertarians hang in mid-air, in effect, with no foundation for their positions. Their philosophic principles, from which they allegedly derive their views, are full of contradictions and differ from one libertarian to another. We disagree with them at the root, even though we may agree with many of their political-economic views.

Interviewer: If you were consulted by someone who had just turned twenty-one and was going to vote in the next presidential election, what would you tell him?

AR: I can answer you only as of this moment, because there are so many confusions and contradictions in politics now that you cannot tell from day to day which political candidate will take what position. There have been so many who have reversed their views or have made them so vague that one cannot really be certain what they would say in their next speech. We really have to be careful. At present, I would advise a young man of twenty-one to go out and concentrate not on the presidential election, but on the primaries.

The first issue is whether we will even get a meaningful choice of candidates. If the history of 1960 and all the preceding elections is repeated, there will not be much point in a young man's voting. I would still advise him to vote, but his vote will make no real difference because he will have no real choice. There is only one chance at present of getting a real choice, and that is represented by Senator [Barry] Goldwater. Therefore, I would advise a young man today first to do everything he can, politically, to help nominate Goldwater as the Republican candidate. I disagree with Goldwater on many things, particularly his domestic policies. He is an advocate of a mixed economy, although he endorses far fewer controls than any of the other candidates. His is not a satisfactory political philosophy, but it is so much better than what is held by the rest of the field, that he is certainly worth supporting.

But where I agree with Goldwater most is on his foreign policy, the best example of which was in his speech on the Nuclear Test Ban Treaty. The position he took there was practically perfect. What he advocated, and the reasons he gave, were so logical that he demonstrated, as he has in the past, that in foreign policy he is fundamentally on the right road. I may disagree on certain details and formulations, but in essence Goldwater recognizes an issue no other politician or potential candidate seems to: America's right to self-interest and self-esteem.

Everybody else is eager to subordinate America to any country on earth. Modern politicians seem to recognize the self-interest of every little tribe in every corner of Africa or Asia, and are willing to abet the most blatant forms of racist nationalism. But they do not recognize the possibility that the United States has any legitimate national interests. The United States apparently is treated as one gigantic sacrificial victim, to be destroyed for the sake of every other nation on earth. Goldwater, by contrast, recognizes that America has a right to assert its self-interest and that it has earned its self-esteem. This position reflects Goldwater's best aspect.

Interviewer: Would you say that one of the points of agreement between conservatives and Objectivism is in foreign policy?

AR: Not all conservatives. Some of them are very much for "internationalism," of the one-world, United Nations kind. Quite a few of them are sympathetic to the U.N. or to the idea of sharing American resources with the rest of world through foreign aid. Not all of them are as clear-cut on this as Goldwater.

Interviewer: Are there any prominent conservatives who support this kind of "internationalism"?

AR: [Richard] Nixon does, for instance. I'm not sure you can call him a conservative, but he is accepted as one. He is quite an "internationalist." I don't know the position of [George] Romney or [William] Scranton. Of course, they are supposed to be liberal Republicans, which makes the question even more complicated.

Interviewer: Do you see any other similarities between conservatives and Objectivists today?

AR: None—and I wouldn't even call the foregoing a similarity. When you discuss political ideas and the prime political groups, you have to define them in terms of fundamentals—not details, not consequences, but basic causes. Conservatives contradict themselves from measure to measure and from day to day. Some of their policies are derived from the premise of free enterprise. Others come from the exact opposite, from a collectivist premise. Therefore, I do not want to lend them a consistency they don't deserve by saying that Objectivists have anything in common with them.

The best you could say is that conservatives might take a position we also would take—but only with regard to narrow issues. In the same respect, there are issues on which Objectivists would side with the liberals. There aren't many, but on certain occasions, I have found myself agreeing with the liberals. They, too, may advocate the right things, but for the wrong reasons. For instance, on the question of prayer in public schools or the separation of church and state, Objectivists are certainly in closer agreement with the liberals than with the majority of so-called conservatives.

Interviewer: How serious is the issue of religion in the conservative philosophy, as presented, for example, by National Review, *which is a favorite rallying point for college students on the right?*

AR: Do you mean how seriously do the *National Review* people take it? Or how seriously does it endanger capitalism? If you mean the first, they take it *very* seriously. They place issues of religion above any other consideration, philosophical or political. For instance, the editors of *National Review* published an article some time ago in which they called Reinhold Niebuhr—who is notoriously liberal in his political views—a conservative. The reason they gave is very interesting and very eloquent, philosophically. They said, in effect, that he believes in the innate depravity of man. He believes that man is an imperfect being, who must not aspire to solve his problems by means of his own reason. Niebuhr's low view of man—his conviction that man is fundamentally unable to deal with reality—represents the kind of metaphysical humility that is the essence of a conservative. That was the gist of the article, which I think conveys the typical *National Review* position on the relationship between mysticism and politics. They take their mysticism seriously. As to the second question, this conservative approach is obviously an enormously serious threat to capitalism, as I've already indicated.

Interviewer: How would you advise an Objectivist to act in the political arena, besides casting a primary vote for Senator Goldwater? Are there any candidates worth supporting?

AR: Since the candidates today are so inconsistent, the only thing an Objectivist can do is keep his own principles clearly in mind. He should judge each candidate on the basis of those principles, and then support the candidates or the measures that he can justify philosophically. But he cannot be committed to the total policy of any one candidate, because no one today in politics is that consistent. What the Objectivist should do in politics is advocate the right ideas. His political interests should be primarily educational. Elections are only the last step, the final result of the ideas that dominate a culture. He should not confine his activity to election years, because elections are actually won or lost throughout the year—during any time except November. By the time you come to an election in November, you are cashing in on the truth or falsehood of what has been advocated and accepted up to that point. In the political arena, the Objectivist should concern himself with "propaganda," in the best sense of the word—i.e., enlightenment, education, spreading the right principles.

Interviewer: *Then you would advise the young Objectivist to work for the party of his choice and try to change its views to some extent?*

AR: Only when and if it is possible to do so without endorsing any views diametrically opposed to his own. He can work within organizations, or he can work privately on any scale open to him; it all depends on the circumstances. But he must advocate his ideas without ever compromising them, without ever sanctioning the wrong ideas or candidates and without ever accepting the dreadful modern fallacy that a pragmatic, unprincipled attitude is practical. He must never support his own opposites. If he does, he will achieve only the destruction of his Objectivist goals.

• 5 •

The Campaign against "Extremism"

To be a moderate is to advocate a moderate amount of statism, a moderate amount of injustice, a moderate amount of infringement of individual rights. Surely, nobody would call that a virtue.

Interviewer: At the [1964] Republican Convention, the issue of "extremism" was raised. How would you define that term?

AR: The burden of definition rests on those who introduce that word. The trouble with the word is precisely that it has no definition—that none has been given and none *can* be given. If you want my general description, it is a smear-tag. It is a term that was introduced exclusively for the purpose of smearing.

Interviewer: Do you think the term can ever be used validly?

AR: No. There is no such word as "extremism" in the dictionary, but there is the word "extreme." It is defined as a great or unusual degree of some quality or characteristic, one that is farthest removed from the average or the ordinary. Clearly, "extreme" refers to measurement, to degrees. Therefore, you cannot use the word with moral connotations; you cannot claim that an extreme is either good or bad. Measurement per se has no value significance. Such significance is acquired only from the nature of that which you measure—and it is an absurdity to claim that an extreme degree of anything, regardless of its nature, is evil. Yet that is what the term "extremism" does. It is used exclusively as a smear, to imply that an action or an idea is evil merely because it is extreme. That is intellectually improper. The word is used to accuse somebody without evidence or definition. "Extremism" is like a swear-word you attach to someone as a label, to avoid the necessity of identifying why you are attacking that person or what you are accusing him of.

Interviewer: Do you think that people who use the term intend to refer, not to moral issues, but only to "extremism" in political action?

AR: I don't. What would "extremism in political action" mean? "Political action" itself is a very loose generality. Take me as an example of an extreme advocate of freedom. What would my "extremism" consist of—that I do not compromise on the principles of freedom, that in all political issues I defend individual rights? And then the "extremism" of a believer in dictator-ship would consist in his taking every possible action to enslave people and to violate rights. Would it be logical to say that he and I are equally to be condemned, merely because we each take an extreme, uncompromising stand on our particular views? Obviously, the term has no meaning. No one could say that in political action you must never take an extreme position. It is the nature of your position, not your consistency in advocating it, that warrants support or condemnation. But the term "extremism" implies the opposite. It is an attack on consistency—on *any* kind of consistency. Yet can you really consider consistency per se immoral?

Interviewer: During the Republican Convention three major groups were labeled as "extremists": the Communist Party, the Ku Klux Klan and the John Birch Soci-ety. Should these be classified together as groups with bad principles that use extreme actions to implement them?

AR: That accusation was one of the most contemptible examples of pub-lic smearing—of an attempt to *institutionalize* smears—that we have ever witnessed in politics. What possible connection can there be among those three groups? The Communist Party and the Ku Klux Klan obviously have a fundamental attribute in common: the use of violence. Both groups reject individual rights and believe in their "right" to use force against others. Both are guilty of outright murders.

Has the John Birch Society done anything comparable? The Birch So-ciety is an ineffectual, confused group—which, incidentally, is the reason it was picked for this particular smear. I do not want to be forced into defending this organization; it has many dubious attributes, though it is not exactly evil. But it is not particularly significant, and no major accusations against it have been validated. Whenever the question was asked—at the convention and in

the press generally—"What is the evil of which the Birch Society is guilty?,"
all we were told was that it had libeled President Eisenhower. (Actually it was
alleged that the president of the society, as a private individual, had libeled
Eisenhower, and the society itself has regularly repudiated that libel.) All
right, even if we grant the charge, libel is an offense—but it is certainly not in
the category of evil that characterizes the Communist Party or the Ku Klux
Klan. Nobody has yet been able to say why the Birch Society is lumped with
those two clear-cut evils. Yet it is precisely this package-deal that reveals why
the very term "extremism" is suspect. Its sole, obvious purpose is to smear
anyone with whom the "moderates" disagree.

*Interviewer: It seems to me that the bad guys are now the "extremists," and the
good guys are the "moderates." Could you tell me what a "moderate" is?*

AR: No, and neither could anyone else—and that is the reason for those labels. The modern method of attack is to introduce into our language tags and
labels that have no precise definition and are used as smear-words. What does
"moderate" mean? Like "extreme," it is a term denoting measurement. Moderation per se cannot be a virtue, because it means a lukewarm, middle-of-
the-road, compromising attitude. In regard to principles—particularly moral
or political principles—moderation is a vice, not a virtue. Now, moderation
in one's diet may be a virtue, but that is not the issue here. When people
call themselves moderates, ask yourself: "Moderate—about what?" Since the
basic question today is freedom versus statism, or individual rights versus
government controls, to be a moderate is to advocate a moderate amount of
statism, a moderate amount of injustice, a moderate amount of infringement
of individual rights. Surely, nobody would call that a virtue.

*Interviewer: Are the moderates different from the liberals? Do the latter advocate
a "liberal" amount of injustice and a "liberal" amount of infringement of rights?*

AR: So it seems. I think "moderate" is only a new word for "liberal," because
the terms "conservative" and "liberal" are so shopworn today that they have
lost all meaning. Nobody pays attention to them any longer. Therefore, the
smear-brigades need new terms, and they are trying to introduce "extremists"
and "moderates" to replace conservatives and liberals.

*Interviewer: When Governor [Nelson] Rockefeller and other liberal members of
the GOP initiated this attack upon the "extremists" of the right, their charges were
played up and legitimized by the news media. I wonder how this affects people's
attitude toward the press?*

AR: The effect is disastrous. If you observed the resentment by the Republican delegates against the press, you saw the result. The press is not entirely on the side of the liberals but, like every other segment of the population today, it has no clear-cut intellectual standards or convictions. It merely follows any aggressive leadership. If the so-called liberal establishment—if such exists—launches a smear-term, the press picks it up simply to have something sensational to say. The result is the kind of distorted, one-sided presentation of the news that we get today.

Interviewer: Do you think the press is merely picking it up or actually adding to it? Let me give you some examples. After the Republican Convention, the New York Herald Tribune *said in its editorial page, "The Republican Party now does face a clear and present threat from the know-nothings and purveyors of hate and the apostles of bigotry." The* St. Louis Post-Dispatch *said, "The Goldwater coalition is a coalition of southern racists, county-seat conservatives, desert rightist radicals and suburban back-lashers." Jackie Robinson said, "I would say that I now believe I know how it felt to be a Jew in Hitler's Germany." These are apparently the voices of the "moderates."*

AR: These are well-selected examples. We have to take notice of this fact—of the fact that the most vicious, irrational, "immoderate" statements are being offered by the "moderates" in the name of moderation and fairness.

Interviewer: This is especially true if we agree that the worst crime anyone has ever accused the John Birch Society of is slander or libel.

AR: But there is more to this injustice. Why were the members of the Birch Society picked as the representatives of the right? Observe that it is the liberal press that has made them famous. It is the liberal press that has over-publicized them, out of all proportion to their actual importance, and is now using them as a straw-man, or scapegoat, to smear anyone who might agree with any one idea that some Birchite has expressed. The aim of this technique is to create a package-deal of guilt by association. The Birch Society is known predominantly for being conservative, which is loosely taken to mean a defender of capitalism. By picking this least representative and least significant organization of the political right, the liberals are smearing anyone who agrees with any part of the Birch Society program. They are labeling such agreement as equivalent to an embrace of the Birch Society as such. This disgraceful performance is made possible only by the absence of intellectual direction or consistent ideology on the part of the right, which impotently puts up with such tactics. It is made possible only by the sanction of the victims. The smearing is so shameful that some sort of concerted public protest against it should have taken place long ago. If it has not taken place, then the public deserves what it is getting.

Interviewer: *Is there anyone else, then, the press should pick as a representative of the right, if the John Birch Society is not appropriate?*

AR: Certainly not. Handling ideological issues by means of personalities is a statist method. The idea of naming movements after living persons originated in Soviet Russia; the first record of an "ism" made out of a name is "Trotskyism." Since then, we've had examples of smear tactics like "McCarthyism," and now a similar attempt is being made with "Goldwaterism." You must never choose an individual as a representative of a school of thought; you must always discuss *ideas*. If the country were divided into groups with clear-cut ideologies, then you could judge an individual's ideas by reference to the group to which he belongs. But no such thing exists in a free country. Therefore, you could not say that the right consists of "Goldwaterites" or of "Birchites"—or of "Randists," for that matter—or of any one particular person's views. You have to evaluate every movement and every individual in terms of ideas, not in terms of persons.

Interviewer: *It seems that the press is avoiding this approach.*

AR: It is. But this is a culture-wide problem—and its source is the universities and the disintegration of modern philosophy. The members of the press bring with them the intellectual equipment acquired in their college years. They are not original thinkers; they represent the general cultural trend. For decades, the universities have been indoctrinating people with the tenets of modern philosophy—with epistemological irrationalism, with moral subjectivism, with a whole complex of ideas designed to prove one thing: that we can know nothing. Students are taught that nothing has a specific identity, that definitions do not matter, that concepts are a product of arbitrary social convention. With this intellectual equipment, men are helpless to deal with political abstractions, or abstractions of any kind. Having been taught that ideas are impractical because they do not apply to reality, they fear above all to commit themselves to any specific statement of ideas. Observe that when you talk in terms of personalities, you talk in terms of intellectual package-deals. Saying that you are for Johnson or for Goldwater does not tell us why. What particular ideas do you advocate? What views do you object to? If you were obliged to name your ideas, you would have to possess a clear understanding of ideological terms. You would have to think precisely—which the overwhelming majority of people today are afraid to do. The habitual reference to personalities and package-deals is an escape from the necessity of dealing with clear-cut abstractions and principles.

Interviewer: For people in public life, what is the best line of defense against these smear tactics?

AR: The basic defense is never to use undefined terms. Never give currency to, nor enter into debates about, such issues as "extremism." Define your terms very clearly, and never sanction any package-deals and smear-labels. Since I can't cover the issue exhaustively here, I will suggest an article of mine titled " 'Extremism,' or the Art of Smearing" in *[Capitalism: The Unknown Ideal]*. There, I cover every aspect of this issue, including the epistemological methods that make the spread of smear-words possible. Anyone who wants to protect himself against unwittingly sanctioning his own enemies should read that article.

Interviewer: Are you saying that Goldwater, in effect, brought this on himself by using "extremism" without defining it?

AR: Definitely not. The term has been in use for at least the last five years—since well before the convention. And Goldwater has attempted, by every proper means, to fight the use of the term. I highly approve of the statement in his acceptance speech—for which he is being attacked—that "extremism" in defense of liberty is not a vice. One can at most regret that he didn't spend another paragraph to make his point a little more explicit. But he clearly stated that he rejects unthinking labels, and he reminded the country of the real meaning of the word "extreme." He was certainly rejecting the "extremism" smear-tag.

Interviewer: At the convention, Governor Rockefeller gave a speech during which he was loudly booed. You've stated that the booing was a reasonable response on the part of the delegates. Would you clarify that?

AR: Rockefeller's speech was as demagogic and hate-filled a statement as anyone has made at any convention. He was accusing the Goldwater faction of issuing anonymous threats to bomb his campaign office—while he was denouncing "extremism" in politics. He was condemning the Birch Society for making unproved accusations—for engaging in libel—and he was committing that very offense himself, with self-righteous hatred written all over his face. He was accusing the majority of the delegates of the most vicious, unproved crimes. How did he expect them to respond—by sitting there calmly and applauding? Incidentally, I got a fan letter from some young man in Chicago, who wrote that he had been a visitor at the Republican Convention when Rockefeller spoke. He had had no intention of interrupting, until the "moderates" started applauding some of Rockefeller's more inflammatory insults, at which point this young man started booing. I am certain that his reaction represents the psychology of the other attendees there. They would not have booed had the "moderates" not expressed intense approval of the slurs being hurled at Goldwater's followers. Under the circumstances, his followers were right.

Interviewer: Do you think that the vicious attack against Goldwater and the right by the "moderates" reflected genuine beliefs on their part, or a pragmatic attempt to destroy a political opposition?

AR: If you want to use that description, the attack was a pragmatic attempt to destroy by smears. It was the behavior of cornered people, who had no more arguments, who had raised no issues during the pre-nomination campaign, who had offered nothing except attacks on conservatism—and who now were spitting their last insults. It was a demonstration of the bankruptcy of the "moderates," who had no ideas to defend and no ideas to which they objected. It was personal smears substituting for ideology.

Interviewer: Does this mean that you think the "moderates" will lose their battle?

AR: If you're asking whether they will lose the upcoming election, nobody can predict that. It depends on how well Goldwater conducts his campaign. I think he has a good chance to win, but that is not a certainty. However, the tactics of the "moderates" is a sign of their ideological bankruptcy. No matter which way the election goes, they have demonstrated that they have nothing to offer intellectually.

Interviewer: Do you think that the liberal Democrats suffer the same intellectual bankruptcy as do the liberal Republicans?

AR: Yes, certainly, because both parties' liberals are on the same premise: welfare-statism and the mixed-economy of the left. It is a premise that is rapidly collapsing.

· 6 ·

The "Robber-Barons"

The so-called robber-barons *created* the wealth they are accused of having stolen. The accusations against them are the worst intellectual injustice in the whole history of capitalism.

Interviewer: The industrialists of the nineteenth century are often vilified as capitalist exploiters—as robber-barons. What are your views of these men and the charges made against them?

AR: If a man from Mars—a man with, let us say, an objective, uncorrupted intelligence—looked at the economic history of the nineteenth century, he would conclude that the so-called robber-barons were the greatest benefactors of mankind ever. They brought the greatest good and an impossibly high standard of living—impossible by all historical precedent—to the country in which they functioned. They were men who took chances on ideas and who, at their own risk and on their own initiative, created vast new wealth. They did not use force; no one was compelled to work for them, to buy their products or to deal with them in any way. What, then, was their crime? The crime of possessing productive genius.

They were called "robbers"—because they had the ability to generate their own wealth. This confusion between production and robbery is necessary in order to sell men on statism. If one makes no distinction between political power and economic power, between force and production, then of course one would accept statism and condemn the producers. But we must keep our terms clear—and this is where we have to begin the discussion. Before anyone can rob, there has to be something to *be* robbed. Before anyone

31

can loot, there has to be material wealth. The so-called robber-barons *created* the wealth they are accused of having stolen. The accusations against them are the worst intellectual injustice in the whole history of capitalism.

Interviewer: Many historians and social commentators have pointed to the development of America's railroad industry in the nineteenth century as an example of how uncontrolled capitalism leads to the growth of arbitrary power, the corruption of government and many other evils. Is there any truth to these allegations?

AR: There is no truth whatever, but there is a very important confusion here. We must distinguish between the industrialists who operate on a free market and the kind who operate with government help. Since the United States was never a fully free, capitalist country, but merely the freest in history, there was government interference in the economy from the beginning. The interference was minimal, though, and was not able, at first, to hamper the magnificent progress of this country.

There are two ways to get rich—and only two. One is to produce wealth and to trade with others by voluntary agreement, to mutual benefit; the second is to acquire wealth by force. To acquire it by force, one must be either an actual criminal or a legalized criminal—that is, a man who uses the power of government to obtain special privileges not possessed by his competitors, and thus gains wealth by legalized force. Both kinds of industrialists existed in this country from the beginning. But the crucial point is that all the evils popularly ascribed to capitalism in the nineteenth century were actually a result of government intervention in the economy. They were committed by those businessmen who were not free-enterprisers, who did not function by competition on a free market and who rose not by merit but predominantly by government favors.

The best example is in the history of the railroads. The railroad that aroused the greatest public resentment, with some justice, was the Central Pacific of California, now known as the Southern Pacific. The government in the nineteenth century gave subsidies to the Central Pacific and to another private railroad, the Union Pacific, in order to create the first transcontinental line, to be built simultaneously from both ends of the continent.

In both cases, the main motive of the railroad owners was to acquire the subsidies, not to build a railroad. Further, there was as yet no economic need for a transcontinental railroad, since there was not enough freight to justify private investment. But the government—employing propaganda similar to today's, with such rationalizations as "the prestige of the country"—decided to build a railroad by giving subsidies to private groups. This is a classic example of a mixed economy, wherein a businessman rises not by sound economic judgment, but by government pull. The builders of this transcontinental railroad had an advantage that no private competitor could match: they had government funding. As a consequence, the Central Pacific held a monopoly in the state of California for about thirty years. In addition, it bribed state legislators to pass laws forbidding the entry of any competitor into California. To be exact, the law forbade any competing railroad to enter any California port, and since most of the freight traffic came through the ports, no railroad could survive in California without access to the ports. Several attempts were made by competing companies to break the monopoly of the Central Pacific, and of course they failed. Thus protected, the Central Pacific engaged in truly immoral economic practices. It changed freight rates arbitrarily, every year, charging whatever the farmers had produced and leaving them practically nothing as profit and barely any seed for the next crop.

Who is to blame in this case? The popular fallacy, spread with the help of the old statist-collectivist intellectuals, is that private industry is responsible. *The Octopus,* the famous novel by Frank Norris which denounced the railroads, was based on the activities of the Central Pacific and was the foundation for the pervasive hatred of railroads. But who was the actual villain? Not the free market, but the government—originally by providing federal subsidies, and then by providing a state grant of monopoly status, which delivered the public into the railroad's power and permitted it to engage in various abuses. A coercive monopoly can be established only by an act of government—and the history of the Central Pacific is a classic example. It was the government that was ultimately guilty of the abuses—but it was the free market that took the blame.

The problem was not the result of dishonest legislators. No legislator who is given arbitrary power can be either honest or dishonest in exercising it. The dishonesty lies not in the person, but in the institution. When a government holds arbitrary control over the economy, it will necessarily act unjustly, because it will be using force in favor of one group of people at the expense of others.

The proper lesson in regard to the subsidized railroads should have been that government power creates only injustice and distortions in the economy—and should be revoked. So long as the government retains such power, abuses have to take place, with each control leading to more disastrous controls. But that was not the conclusion drawn; to this day, people have not grasped that lesson. Whenever anything goes wrong in some industry, it is capitalism that is blamed. Yet if you investigate, you will find without exception that the source of the evils is government intervention, not free enterprise.

Interviewer: Could you define the term "monopoly," as you use it here?

AR: In a strict sense, "monopoly" means an exclusive privilege to act in a certain capacity or to deal with a certain product. In that sense, everyone holds a monopoly on his own work. But as the term is usually used in politics and economics, it means a *coercive* monopoly—that is, to an exclusive right to a certain field of activity, from which all competitors, present and future, are barred. No company in a free market can establish such a monopoly, because the freedom of the market brings in new entrants. In the nineteenth century, many attempts were made to corner the market in various commodities; invariably, they ended with the failure and the bankruptcy of the man who had tried to establish a private monopoly.

A coercive monopoly can be instituted only by law—only by a special government privilege granted to one producer and barring all others from a given activity. The public utilities are a classic example, in that no competitor can legally enter the field. All the evils popularly associated with monopolies are in fact a result of such coercive monopolies. If you look into their history, both here and in Europe, you will find that coercive monopolies have never been created by the collusion of businessmen in a free market. They have always been the product of an act of government.

Interviewer: If coercive monopolies are created by government, how do you explain the fact that government then turns around and passes anti-monopoly laws? What are these laws directed against, if the government is the creator of the monopoly?

AR: Such laws—the antitrust laws—are directed against the ablest and most successful members of industry. These laws are the instrument of government control over all business. They are, as every lawyer knows, such an undefined, and indefinable, mess of contradictions that every businessman in the country can be prosecuted as a criminal at any time, at the discretion of the government. The moment someone goes into business, he breaks some antitrust law or other. The laws are so contradictory that if he complies with one, he simultaneously breaks another. The antitrust laws have granted the government the arbitrary power, which the last two administrations have certainly been using, to crack down on any industrialist, not for the purpose of "protecting competition"—which is a contradiction in terms—but for the purpose of establishing control over business.

"Free competition" enforced by law is a contradiction in terms. The only means of protecting competition is a completely free market. When government controls are imposed, they work to the advantage of any entrepreneur with government pull. Any man who cannot compete on merit runs to the government and invokes the antitrust laws against his abler competitors. The net result of these laws has been only the protection of mediocrity and the destruction of ability and success.

Interviewer: In November 1965 a blackout of the entire Northeast prompted government efforts to curb the so-called monopolistic power of public utilities. You wrote in Atlas Shrugged: *"The plane was above the peaks of the skyscrapers when suddenly, with the abruptness of a shudder, as if the ground had parted to engulf it, the city disappeared from the face of the earth. It took them a moment to realize that the panic had reached the power stations—and that the lights of New York had gone out." I thought that your work was not supposed to be prophetic, but it seems to have turned out that way. Could you discuss the public utilities, such as Con Edison, which people are now calling "robber-barons"?*

AR: This passage from *Atlas Shrugged* has been quoted by many people. I received letters and wires right after the blackout, and I still hear that people talk about how prophetic the novel was. I did not want it to be prophetic. I actually wanted it to help *prevent* itself from becoming prophetic. But so far, while it *is* helping, I am afraid that one cannot stop a trend that quickly, and many of the things in *Atlas Shrugged* are coming true. Although I intended them for a more distant future, some of the fictionalized events are happening already because our main cultural trend is still in the direction of statism and collectivism. It can still be reversed. But if the trend does continue, the kind of disasters I describe are unavoidable.

The blackout in New York is a good example of the fallacy of the "robber-baron." Right after the blackout, there was a hue-and-cry to expand government's power and to blame Con Edison and other private companies for the catastrophe. Yet the blackout occurred because all the utility companies in the East, and in Canada, were tied together in a so-called grid system, which was initiated by the government. Before the blackout, there had been discussions for a long time about the government's proposal to tie the whole country into a similar grid system. The plan was to extend regional utility systems into a national grid, in which all power producers would be linked together—on the principle that the stronger ones would carry the weaker. This was supposed to be the only way to enable smaller regions to get power from the more populated, more productive parts of the country. The justification offered was, in effect: "We must all help each other, and if something breaks down in one part of the utility system, the power of the rest of the system will save it."

This is a perfect example of collectivism, better than you could present in fiction. When something goes wrong in one place, it carries the whole system down with it—and that, symbolically and literally, is the essence of collectivism. Instead of collective security, the result is that one flaw destroys everybody. In the case of the New York blackout, it took several weeks to determine where the flaw started. Con Edison and the other semi-private companies were considered guilty before any trial. Government officials used the disaster as an excuse to plead for greater powers, even though it was the government that totally controlled the operation of utilities. What finally happened? After a few weeks of investigation, it was found that the initial breakdown that caused the blackout originated in Canada—*in a government-owned utility.* Nothing much has been said about this issue since, and I doubt whether people will grasp the lesson to be learned from all this.

Interviewer: Businesses frequently say that in order to keep up with their competitors, they must seek out government largesse of one kind or another. What would be the proper attitude for a moral entrepreneur to take?

Quite frequently we hear the cry from capitalists that everyone else is doing it, and that to stay in business, they must compete for government largesse of one kind or another. What would be the proper move for the moral capitalist when facing the "robber-baron" today? Even in the nineteenth century, what would have been the proper move?

AR: If you are talking about government contracts, there are lines in which a businessman cannot exist without them. Therefore, seeking such contracts today cannot be held against him. Actually, the worst form of state interference is not government contracts, but government favors and special privileges. The only thing a moral businessman can do today is to fight for all he is worth, intellectually and philosophically, against government controls. He has to fight for a return to a freer economy and, eventually, for the establishment of totally free economy. He may not see it in his lifetime, but fighting for the ideal is the only road open to us. The battle was lost on philosophical grounds, and can now be won only on those same grounds—through a moral defense of full, laissez-faire capitalism.

· 7 ·

Myths of Capitalism

A coercive monopoly has never existed, either in the United States or anywhere else in the world, without the intervention of government.

Interviewer: It has been stated that although capitalism gave the world a higher standard of living for a steadily increasing number of people, it turned the world inside out. Personal loyalties gave way to financial relationships. The wealthy man ceased to be the patron of his poor neighbor, becoming instead a "mass man," very often with no purpose in life other than self-aggrandizement. How would you answer this charge?

AR: I wouldn't take the charge too seriously, because it rests on a package-deal and uses terms that need to be translated into their actual meaning. To begin with, if a wealthy man is to be considered in charge of his poor neighbors, he has to have power over them—which means that he has to live in a feudal system. Therefore, what the author of this accusation implies, but lacks the courage to say openly—because if he did, it would be rejected instantly—is that he prefers feudalism to capitalism. Now, when he says that the capitalist becomes a "mass man," that is another slanted comment. If that term is translated, it simply means that every man works for the widest market possible, and that his economic future is determined by the value of his product and by the free individual judgment of those who want to trade with him. When you object to a "mass man," it means that you object to the fact of a free market. It means you object to the fact that every man can deal with as many men as care to deal with him, and that he has to offer his products or services to a mass market. A free market does not mean that the total mass of people will buy a given product—only that those who want to, have a chance to.

Secondly, what is meant by the claim that somebody's "loyalties" are being upset? Obviously it refers to some dogma that the whole of society is supposed to accept and from which nobody can deviate. That again is an idea conceivable only under a medieval, feudal system. One of capitalism's great advantages is that there are no loyalties, or values, prescribed by the state or by the community. Everyone chooses his own, and the person who chooses rational ones is the person who will succeed. What the accusation tries to disguise is that under capitalism every man stands on his own. He is free to choose his own values, including his occupation, and to go as far as his ability and ambition carry him. Therefore, if you translate the accusation into an exact, concretized image—if you ask what it means in actual reality—it is paying the greatest compliment possible to capitalism. It is criticizing capitalism for its *virtues*, not its flaws. The implicit viewpoint of the author is quite clear—he is a medieval collectivist, who resents the freedom and the individualism possible only under a capitalist system.

Interviewer: During the turn of the last century, great industrial combinations were formed, such as U.S. Steel, American Can and General Electric. Can a capitalist society function if these monopolies are allowed to grow?

AR: The error in your question is the belief that a free market leads to monopolies. This is one of the widespread fallacies inherited from Karl Marx, who claimed that capitalism by its nature results in an economy run entirely by a few monopolistic concerns, with everybody else reduced to the state of proletarians. If you observe the development of capitalism, you can see empirically that this is not true. But to make the point fully clear, we must define "monopoly." When people use that term, they mean a *coercive* monopoly—that is, a business which pre-empts a certain line of activity by barring any competitor from entering that field. A *non*-coercive monopoly, where one company provides a service that no one else does, cannot in any way be considered a social evil. Because in that sense, every one of us is a monopolist. Every man has certain goods or services to offer which are his exclusive production and which other people cannot provide.

A coercive monopoly has never existed, either in the United States or anywhere else in the world, without the intervention of government. It takes an act of government to grant a special privilege, such as an exclusive franchise, to some company, and to prohibit all others from that field. If a few large companies, by combining, can offer better goods or services at lower prices than anyone else, one would have to say: more power to them. It is then to everybody's advantage to deal with that one combined firm and not have to deal with ten less efficient firms. However, no matter how efficient such a voluntary monopoly was, it would be under constant threat of competition from the moment it let down its standards of efficiency. It could be a monopoly only so long as it produced better and cheaper goods than anyone else. A competitor could enter the market with a new idea, a new invention, and undersell the leading company at any moment. In order for that company to *bar* an able competitor, it would need some government action behind it. This never happened with the companies you mentioned. The combinations they formed were voluntary and proper. There is no moral or political justification for prohibiting combinations of that kind, because it is ultimately the free market that decides whether or not they will succeed.

Size as such is not a guarantee of economic power. To cite a fairly recent example, U.S. Steel almost held a monopoly for about ten years in the steel market, until the rise of what was then called "little steel"—newer and smaller companies, specifically Republic Steel and National Steel. In the early 1930s, they were the first to come out with metal alloys. To avoid losing its market, U.S. Steel had to change its mode of production and introduce new research. This is what happens to large companies if they do not maintain the value of their products. Any large company, or combination of companies, can be destroyed in a free market by any competent newcomer. Bigness is no threat to the economy.

But what kind of monopolies *are* beyond the reach of competition? Public utilities, electric companies, telephone companies—all of which were created by the government. For example, during World War II, the federal government forced two telegraph companies, Postal Telegraph and Western Union, to combine into one government-protected monopoly. You will find that whenever a large business controls an entire field exclusively, it is by government intervention. Both history and theory demonstrate that coercive monopolies are not the product of a free market. For further details, I refer you to ["Common Fallacies About Capitalism," in *Capitalism: The Unknown Ideal*], which offers additional sources to read on the subject.

Interviewer: In a laissez-faire system, isn't there a possibility that a large, rich monopoly could overcharge, and simply force out any emerging competitor by lowering prices drastically for a short time?

AR: That's the allied fallacy—the price war. No, it couldn't happen. Or rather, price wars did happen, but they could not succeed, for a very simple reason. Again, concretize what would happen in practice. If a large firm wanted to get rid of competition in that way, it would have to sell its product at a loss for a while in order to force the competitor out. Once the competitor was gone, the large company would have to raise its prices in order to recoup its loss. But new competitors could then enter the field and undersell the large company by just a little, which would represent a large profit for them, since they would not have any losses to recoup. The big company would then have to start undercutting *them*, and the process would go on into infinity—which would not happen, of course, because the large company would go bankrupt.

Interviewer: But aren't there industries in which it is too costly for competitors to arise? For example, if just one company ruled the steel industry today, it would require too much of a capital outlay for a new competitor to establish itself.

AR: Your own premise is exactly why this would not happen under capitalism. If it is an industry that requires a large outlay of money, as you describe, it would take a very long time for a company to drive out a competitor. Once the large company began the process, long before it had driven out even the first competitor, the investment market—the bankers who invest in new ventures—would be making plans to finance the future competition. Precisely because the large company would need a long time to succeed with its strategy, the future competition would have plenty of time to make its plans. In practice, events would never get to that stage. No company wise enough to hold a large part of the market would embark on a policy of this kind. And if you study economic history, you will see that no market position was ever won by means of such price wars. Whenever they were tried, they usually either petered out or ruined both parties involved.

Interviewer: Would you say that the high tariffs in the United States during the last quarter of the nineteenth century led to the great mergers in many industrial fields?

AR: No. There were various economic reasons, but tariffs were not directly responsible. But an interesting aspect of tariffs is that they were one of the early government interferences in the economy—and were prompted, not by labor or by the liberals, but by business. It was businessmen who favored tariffs, and in so doing, they were committing economic suicide, as we can see today. Later, every other economic group adopted the same tactics, and began to seek legislation favoring its interests. But under laissez-faire capitalism, the government would have to take its hands off the economy altogether and could not enact laws in favor of *any* group—neither business, nor labor, nor anyone else. The question under laissez-faire is not: "Whom should government favor?"

Rather, capitalism is a system in which government has *no* power to intervene in the economy and in which it serves only as a policeman.

Interviewer: *Do you think that the public utilities are what is called a natural monopoly?*

AR: No, and that's a very misleading term. The only legitimate referent of "natural monopoly" is what I mentioned earlier—a company doing all the business in a given field because it is doing it so well that no competitor can do it better and none try to enter the field. Let's say you have a small town that can support only one drugstore. You might call that one store a "natural monopoly." But if the population grew, that one drugstore could not then keep others from entering the area and competing. Thus, if by "natural monopoly" you mean a particular situation in which no more than one business is required to cover the market, then that happens constantly. And there is nothing wrong with it.

However, if you mean that there are certain lines of activity, such as public utilities, that have to be in the hands of one company—that is not true. Companies can compete in those areas—and *did* compete at one time. If, however, they find that competition does not pay under certain circumstances—such as when the presence of two telephone companies in one area results in too many communication difficulties for the customers— then the two companies would merge. They would become more economically profitable, which means: more efficient, which is better for everybody. But there is no *a priori* rule by which you could say that a particular line of business has to be run by a single company.

Interviewer: *In your article "Notes on the History of American Free Enterprise"* [*in* Capitalism: The Unknown Ideal], *you criticize government land grants to the railroads. How could the railroads have otherwise acquired the land on which they built?*

AR: To begin with, only some railroads obtained those land grants. A railroad could, and should, have acquired land in the same way any business acquires any property: by buying it. A good example of such a railroad was the Great Northern, built by J. J. Hill without any land grants or any federal help.

Interviewer: *From whom did it buy unsettled land?*

AR: If you mean so-called public land, the proper principle was adopted by the Homestead Act, through which a man could acquire unsettled land by working it for a certain number of years. If the principle of free enterprise had been followed, the railroad companies would have obtained the land either by using it for a few years or, if necessary, by paying the government. Strictly speaking, though, I do not think it is proper to consider ownerless land government property. The government in that case is really only the custodian, who should establish the rules by which private ownership can be acquired. "Public property" in this context is a fiction; it is not possible to put into practice, and it results only in bureaucrats' disposing of such property by giving it to whichever "aristocrat-of-pull" they happen to favor. But that is a separate question.

If you are asking how the railroads should have acted with respect to private land—they should have purchased it. They should have gotten private loans. Those that did, like the Great Northern, were the railroads that had the best economic history. Most of the others got themselves into terrible financial trouble and even went through bankruptcies sooner or later. If you look at the history of railroads, you will observe that the most successful railroads were the ones that had the least government help.

Interviewer: Are financial or industrial panics essential to a capitalistic system?

AR: No. Again I refer you to an article ["Common Fallacies About Capitalism," in *Capitalism: The Unknown Ideal*]. That article demonstrates in great detail that major depressions and panics are the result of government interference in the economy—specifically, government manipulation of credit and money. That was the cause of the Depression of 1929 and of all the preceding, lesser ones. Once more, it is capitalism that is taking the blame for the evils created by its opposite: statist intervention.

· 8 ·

The Political Structure of a Free Society

This country is not a democracy. It was established as a republic, which means a system of free, representative government, limited by the principle of individual rights.

Interviewer: *We usually think of capitalism as an economic system, and a republic or a democracy as a political system. Do you agree?*

AR: That is correct. But capitalism should really be called a political-economic system because every economic system depends on a certain kind of political structure. It is impossible to speak of a political system independently of economics, or of economics independently of politics. A political system is a set of moral, political and economic principles, expressed in a country's laws and institutions, that set the terms of the relationships among men in a given area. The way men conduct their economic lives depends on the kind of laws that exist in their society. And conversely, a government cannot implement any laws except by material means—that is, either by regulating or by protecting a country's economic system. After all, a man's ideas as such cannot be ruled; a man is free to think inside his own mind even under a dictatorship. What he is not free to do is to put his ideas into action. And economics is the major field of human activity in which men translate their ideas into practice, by engaging in material production to satisfy their needs of survival. No political system can exist without a relationship to the field of economics. The basic question is only whether that relationship is right or wrong.

Interviewer: *And what should their relationship be?*

43

AR: In a proper, rational system, man should be free, politically and economically. The function of the government should be only to protect individual rights, which includes property rights—that is, to protect man by eliminating force from human relationships. In a free society the government should protect property and should protect contractual agreements against unilateral breach, or fraud. But the field of economics should be separated from the field of politics, in the same way and on the same principle as the separation of church and state. Government should not be allowed to interfere with human production and trade. The government should function only as a policeman, protecting against anyone who wants to resort to physical force.

Interviewer: *What should be the political system of a capitalistic society? A republic? A democracy? And is a constitution needed?*

AR: The only structure appropriate to a free, capitalist society is a constitutional republic—specifically, the type established in principle by the American Constitution. This is a system devised to limit the power of the government to its one proper function: the protection of individual rights. If men are to be free, the system of laws under which they live must be objective. Men must know in advance what actions are prohibited by law, and why. If a country existed as a republic but without a constitution, there would be no definition of the basic principles on which that country functions and no definition of the kind of laws that may or may not be passed. The government would, in effect, be playing it deuces wild. Anybody could attempt to enact any kind of law. That would be complete political chaos.

A constitution is necessary in order to define not only the basic principles of a country, but the means of their implementation, including the types of institutions that will keep a country free. It is not enough to agree on principles. Holding the right political principles does not tell you automatically how to put them into practice. It does not tell you what institutions must be established to preserve freedom—to prevent loopholes that a statist or any power-luster could use to seize control. The job of keeping a country free is very complicated, and a constitution is indispensable.

"Democracy" is an inappropriate term to apply to a free country. Its original meaning is: "unlimited majority rule," i.e., the principle that a majority has the right to pass any law it pleases and the right to dispose of the minority in any way it wishes. A democracy is a form of government in which the state may take any action whatsoever, with the sole standard of right or wrong being a majority vote, a counting of noses. A democracy is thus incompatible with the constitution. The best examples of democracies are the city-states of ancient Greece, where the majority had the authority to impose a death sentence upon someone if they disapproved of his ideas. The fate of Socrates illustrates this. He was condemned to death because a majority of the citizens believed that his ideas were subverting the youth of Athens. He refused to escape, although he had the chance. He declared that while his fellow citizens were wrong in their decision, they nonetheless had the right to vote away his life. This is a ghastly example of the sanction of the victim—and a perfect example of the nature of a democracy as a political system.

In political thought, a democracy had always been considered a morally improper and politically impractical form of government. You will find in "The Federalist Papers" references to the fact that democracies always had a short life and a violent death, meaning that democracies necessarily degenerate into tyranny.

This country is *not* a democracy. It was established as a republic, which means a system of free, representative government, limited by the principle of individual rights. It means that the majority may vote, but only within a strictly delimited sphere. It means that the majority cannot vote away the rights of any individual. It means that the power of government is constrained, in that there is a line beyond which it cannot go. All that the government may do in regard to rights is protect them; it may not infringe them. That is in essence the nature of a proper republic, which was the concept on which this country was formed.

Today of course, the colloquial meaning of "democracy" is simply general suffrage in a free country. But that is a sloppy and dangerous usage, which confuses the political issues and gives people the impression, if they don't think carefully, that this country is based on unlimited majority rule. Nothing could be further from the truth.

Interviewer: Does a representative democracy cure any of the flaws in democracy, or merely lessen them?

AR: It *worsens* them, if anything. A system which is based on unlimited majority rule, but which delegates that power to the chosen representatives of the citizens, would be worse than one in which the power lies in the citizens' direct vote. In a large country a majority would not be likely to agree on some vicious legislation, whereas a small body of representatives, unguided and unlimited by any restricting principle, would. That is the pattern of a tyranny. These representatives, in the name of the alleged majority, could establish complete statist rule and yet be consistent with the principle of unlimited majority rule.

Interviewer: Could you outline the principles underlying decisions about who ought to vote and what they ought to vote for? Should there be limitations on universal suffrage? Should people vote on specific laws?

AR: Let me take your last question first. Certainly, people cannot vote on specific laws. There could not possibly be agreement among two hundred million people on the wording of some law. Nor would they be qualified to make such judgments. The actual wording of a law is enormously important, and is a job for specialists. To allow people to vote on every law would be democracy at its worst.

As to universal suffrage, since all citizens are equal before the law, they all should have the vote—with only one important qualification: they should be mentally competent to vote. Therefore, age and knowledge matter. An illiterate should not be permitted to vote, and neither should a child. There can be many different theories on how to establish an individual's competence; that is an issue of implementation, which is open to discussion. But there is no question that a vote must be taken seriously, and that the voter has to be mentally able to do so. Literacy tests are enormously important here, though I doubt the efficacy of most of them. Better standards should be found for determining the intellectual competence of the voter. But the essential fact of competence must be established. Otherwise the process of voting and the idea of representative government become meaningless.

Interviewer: Should any sort of property considerations be included in the granting of suffrage?

AR: That is a technical question, on which I have no firm conviction. Some people believe that the ownership of land, not just any property, should be a condition of voting, in order to keep a country free. I am not sure that the case for this has been fully proven. But I do think that a good argument could be made for a certain amount of property as a qualification, because that would be one way of demonstrating the responsibility of a citizen. However, I am open on this question.

Interviewer: Which rights does the government possess over the people?

AR: The government—or any organization—has *no* rights. A "right" is a concept that pertains only to the individual. There is really only one right, which is so fundamental that all other rights are merely derivatives and re-statements of it: the right of a man to his own life.

A right is a moral concept that defines and sanctions a man's freedom of action in a social context. It pertains to what is good for man in relation to other men. On a desert island, you would still need morality, but you wouldn't need rights, because there would be no one to infringe your freedom of action. It is only in a society that the question of rights arises. And the basic issue is: Does one man have the right to dispose of the life of another? Once you have established that a man is the owner of his own life—that his life is his to dispose of and does not belong to anyone else—you then have the base from which all other rights are derived. If a man has a right to his own life, then he has a right to take all those actions that are necessary, by his nature as a rational being, to sustain and protect it. In order to prove that a certain action is in fact a right, you have to prove that it is required by man's nature.

If it is a right, it is equally applicable to all human beings. Therefore, the first question to be answered in deciding what is or is not a right is: Does the claimed right apply equally to all men or not? If it does not, it cannot be a right. For instance, when some men today assert "economic rights"—when they claim they are entitled to a minimum sustenance to be provided by others—they are obviously denying the concept of rights. In order to provide such unearned support to one man, you would have to exact slave labor from another man. Nothing that infringes some men's rights for the benefit of others can, in logic and in morality, be a right.

Interviewer: What position should government take in protecting the rights of the individual?

AR: The basic way one man can violate the rights of another is by initiating physical force against him. Government is required to protect the individual against such force. When there are disputes among men, the government has to be an arbiter who settles such disputes according to objective principles, in order to prevent anyone from resorting to violence. In cases of crime or foreign attack, it is the government's obligation to protect men from the aggressors who are using physical force. Those are the basic functions of a proper government, which acts solely to protect individual rights.

Interviewer: You've said that the government should protect the individual. Should it also protect an assemblage of individuals, such as a union?

AR: Yes and no. A union, or any group, cannot have any rights other than the rights of its individual members. If somebody attacks a union by force, the government should protect it. What is being protected, though, is the individual rights of each member. But to protect a group as such is to support by law some actions of that group against some of its individual members who may disagree with it. That, of course, is a direct contradiction.

Interviewer: Do you think that the income tax amendment is a contradiction to the Constitution?

AR: Yes, because it gives an enormous undefined and arbitrary power to the government.

Interviewer: If the progressive feature of the income tax were removed, would there still be a contradiction?

AR: I object to the income tax as such, on principle. Now, I do not advocate abolishing it as the first reform on the way to a free society. The situation is much too complex today to begin with that. But as the public's knowledge improves and moves toward the endorsement of a fully free society, sooner or later one of the reforms that will have to be passed is the abolition of the income tax.

Interviewer: What would you recommend as an equitable and feasible type of taxation to finance government? Would you favor some kind of lottery?

AR: You are really asking what I would support in an ideal, laissez-faire system. The imposition of any kind of tax is a violation of individual rights, in that the government is initiating force to seize a man's property. All forced taxation contradicts the principle of a free society. It is much too early for this issue to be an immediate concern, but as a distant goal of the free society toward which we should aim, I would recommend a voluntary system to finance government. A proper government, one that adopts the role of a policeman, is obviously needed by the citizens of a country. And that which man needs, he will pay for willingly.

The great contradiction in this issue lies in the fact that centuries of an authoritarian tradition have led people to accept the idea that government is a dispenser of favors. This comes from the time when government was regarded as the owner of the citizens. An absolute monarch, for instance, owned his subjects—their work, their property and their lives. Any services he rendered the country in terms of governing had to be given for free, since he was simply dispensing favors to those he owned. This concept has never been revised, even in light of the emergence of the first really free country in the world: the United States of America. But if government is an agent and a servant of the citizens, not their ruler, then it has to be paid. Services are not donated for free. They should be tied to a form of payment, as is the case with the exchange of services among private citizens.

Of the various possibilities, a public lottery is one of the means that have been used successfully in minor instances, but offhand I would say that it would hardly be a proper way to finance the government of a large country. I suggest—only as a pattern, not as a definitive solution, because it's much too early to think of one—the imposition of a certain insurance fee tax (if you want to call it a "tax") on the signing of contracts. Since most of the business of industrial society is conducted on a contractual basis—every credit transaction, for example, is a contract—there is an enormous chain of agreements resting on the government's power to enforce a contract if it is broken by one of the parties. Enforcement is therefore a service that every man signing a contract desperately needs and should pay for. Your payment could be a very small, constitutionally established percentage of the financial amount involved in your contract. You would then have the right to call upon the law if the contract is violated. You would not be forced to pay for this insurance, but without it you could not go to court to seek legal enforcement. You would thus be free to avail yourself of the government's services or not. This is one possibility.

There are many difficulties with such an idea, but they are difficulties of precise implementation. I refer you to an article of mine ["Government Financing in a Free Society"] in *The Virtue of Selfishness*, which explains how one could contribute freely to the support of government's proper functions. Needless to say, a voluntary system would not work today, when the government's functions have grown beyond all proper bounds and when ninety-nine percent of the government's undertakings are ones to which nobody would or should contribute willingly. In a free society, however, where men need the services being provided by government, they would readily pay for them.

· 9 ·

The American Constitution

*In order to undermine the Constitution, it has been necessary
to rely on the contradictory or vague elements in it. The destruction of our political system has been achieved by means of
certain ambiguous clauses.*

Interviewer: What would you say is the most valuable political system?

AR: Valuable—from what standpoint? Since political systems are man-made
and a matter of human choice, the question should be: "What is the *right*
political system?" And the answer is: capitalism, of course—total, laissez-faire
capitalism, which means a separation of state and economics.

*Interviewer: To what degree do the principles of our Constitution coincide with
the principles of a free, laissez-faire society?*

AR: They coincide to a major degree, apart from certain contradictions.
Unfortunately, the Constitution was to some extent a compromise among
various factions who composed it. The consequences have been disastrous,
and we are paying for those errors to this day.

One major contradiction in the Constitution is the power of eminent
domain, which is a strictly statist principle. It is being used today in the disgraceful urban-renewal program. It gives government the right to seize any
property it wishes, provided there is "just compensation"—a vague term that
leaves open the question: Who determines what is just? This power is now
being used not even for any alleged "public purpose," but for the benefit of

some private individuals at the expense of others—for the benefit of private builders subsidized by the government and armed with the power to destroy anyone's property rights by invoking eminent domain.

A wider and worse contradiction involves the clause giving the federal government the power to regulate interstate commerce. The commerce clause is too brief and too general, and has led to the exact opposite of the original framers' intentions. It was intended mainly to prevent individual states from setting up trade barriers, which would have created thirteen frontiers between states. But it has now come to be used for the opposite purpose—to restrain trade and business and, consequently, all freedom. It is such a broad grant of power that there are those who claim, with logic, that it gives the government the authority to regulate anything. Even if you do nothing but sit in your room, you are still affecting interstate commerce by means of the goods you do not buy—if anyone wants to stretch the meaning that far (and attempts have been made to do just that). The destruction of economic freedom in this country has occurred predominantly through the commerce clause.

Of course, the very worst contradiction was the tolerance, if not the sanction, of slavery—which was not overtly permitted but was, in effect, ignored by the Constitution. This issue led to a civil war, and remains an unresolved problem. The result of any contradiction is to undercut the rest of the document or the body of knowledge to which it belongs. It is therefore tragic—and should serve as a lesson to all those inclined to favor compromise—that the American Constitution, which was overwhelmingly based on the right principles, was undercut by such contradictions as its writers permitted.

Interviewer: *Can a free enterprise system exist under our present Constitutional setup?*

AR: Today the Constitution is predominantly ignored and evaded; there is only a very thin remnant, which people observe more or less by inertia. Besides, since even in the Constitution's original state, certain contradictions existed, they had to lead to further contradictions and to a certain type of lawlessness in practice. Therefore, today's Constitution with all its different interpretations—made possible by its original contradictions—is in an untenable position. What we need above all is to clarify and reaffirm the original Constitutional *principles*, and remove the contradictions.

However, even in its imperfect state, the Constitution is the document that permitted this country to achieve its incredible progress. It is an unprecedented document, and its results are likewise unprecedented in history. We can be certain that its basic principles—particularly the idea of the Constitution as a limit on the power of government—are valid and should be followed.

Can capitalism exist under the present Constitution? No—but neither can *any* system. Nothing can exist under a contradiction. But it would not be too difficult to eliminate the contradictions.

Interviewer: In view of what has happened to the Constitution, do you think that any document, no matter how strictly written, can be effective in limiting government's power if there is a determined effort to expand that power?

AR: There are two aspects to your question. If you are asking whether a written document can guarantee compliance with its terms, and automatically protect a society from any group wishing to destroy that document—then the answer is no. Nothing can establish a system that will work regardless of the philosophical knowledge of the citizens. No document will protect a country when and if men do not choose to think about the principles required to protect their freedom.

But assuming a country with the proper intellectual foundation, a written document is necessary to limit the power of government. It is an objective point of reference, in case of any doubts as to what type of laws can and cannot be passed. It is precisely the eroding of the American Constitution that proves my point. In order to undermine the Constitution, it has been necessary to rely on the contradictory or vague elements in it. The destruction of our political system has been achieved by means of certain ambiguous clauses, as I've mentioned. To this day, when Congress passes blatantly unconstitutional laws, the Supreme Court stretches the meaning of the Constitution further and further in order to validate these laws. But the very fact that the Court is obliged to stretch the Constitution—rather than simply to ignore it—is the best proof that a constitution is necessary and does work.

If you study the history of the violation of our Constitution, you will see that the process began when small, dubious infringements were accepted. If the electorate were more enlightened, politically and philosophically, the Supreme Court would not have been able to endorse such breaches. The people would have objected the first time an unconstitutional law was approved.

Interviewer: One of the great innovations of the American political structure was the federal system, under which the powers of government were distributed between a central government and local units. What do you think of such a system?

AR: A federal system is both consistent with and required by a free society. This is issue of implementing the right principles. If you establish a free society, you have to protect it from arbitrary encroachments by men who may want to seize power. A free society cannot rest merely on the good intentions of its public officials. The freedom of a country cannot be dependent upon the intangible and unpredictable matter of a particular official's moral character; that would not be freedom. You must set up a political structure in such a way that whether a man is moral or immoral, he does not have the legal power to subvert the institutions of a country and to destroy its freedom. The structure of checks and balances, of which people have made a meaningless bromide today, is crucial for that purpose.

The system defined in the Constitution was originally conceived to prevent total power from falling into the hands of any group of officials or any single institution of the government. The purpose of dividing power among federal, state and local entities was precisely to delimit the power that any *one* official or *one* institution could exercise, and to set up counterweights to that power. If, for example, the federal government wanted to control or enslave the country, it would have to go against the interests of the state or municipal governments. At each level of power there would be institutionalized opposition to the ambitions of any branch that might want to exceed its Constitutional authority. The division of power among the various levels of government was thus devised—and devised very skillfully by the writers of the Constitution—in order not to allow the exercise of power to hinge upon the moral character of particular officials.

Today, of course, nothing is left of this structure. It was undercut long ago, and in order to re-establish it a great many laws and encroachments by the federal government would have to be repealed. For an enlightening discussion of this subject, I recommend a book called *The God of the Machine* by Isabel Paterson, written in 1943. It analyzes the importance of the checks-and-balances system and the division of power in a more profound manner than any other book I could name.

Interviewer: *In that connection, should each state be given a certain minimum level of representation in the national legislature, as opposed to a system in which there is representation only in proportion to population?*

AR: It is absolutely essential to have state representation, as apart from the individual citizen's representation. Under checks-and-balances, local government serves not as an ally, but as a deliberate antagonist of the central government, as a constraint on its power. The responsibilities of both have to be balanced in such a way that each prevents the other from an unconstitutional usurpation of power. Now, what or whom are you balancing? Men live in certain localities. In a large country, the federal government is at a great distance from its citizens. An individual citizen, residing in a given area, cannot exercise direct control over the federal government, and it is impossible for him to spread his ideas to such an extent that he would influence a majority of the country. How then can the citizen have a certain, proper influence on the conduct of the central government? Only through a series of steps flowing downward from the central government to local governments, with each step moving closer to, and thus enhancing the influence of, the individual citizen. Therefore, geographical location becomes enormously important. The government has to be structured so that local citizens exercise direct power over their local authorities. Above them, there are county authorities, then state authorities, then regional and federal authorities. In other words, you need a hierarchy that ultimately rests on the actual place of residence of the citizens who are going to vote and direct the course of the country.

Citizens as such do not represent a political unit. To have a country, two elements are needed: men and geography. A country is always limited by its geographical boundaries, and the men who live in it are then its citizens. But a country is not a collection of men floating in space. The gypsies who travel all over the world could not be considered a nation; they are individuals, but they have no geographical location. They are nomads. Therefore, they are not yet an element of a political structure. The proposal to limit all political voting districts to "one man, one vote," as it is called, is in effect an attempt to destroy all political structure and to reduce the country to a nomadic population, ruled directly by the central government. It is one of the most dangerous proposals in this country. It is a direct road to a "democracy," in the original and worst sense of the word—i.e., unlimited majority rule. It would leave the country in the power, and at the whim, of any majority of the moment.

If your purpose is to protect individual rights, you need a series of semi-sovereign states and localities, each governed by its local population and united into a wider entity, which is the United States.

Interviewer: Along this line, would you favor the filibuster, which also limits majority rule?

AR: That is a small, technical question. I'm not sure that a filibuster is the proper means of opposing unlimited majority rule. I would be in favor of the right to filibuster only on the principle that one must not gag debate in a parliamentary form of government. The legislators should have the time to discuss proposed legislation. However, it is also true that a filibuster could go on forever. The question of how to lay down the rules so as to give ample time for debate, yet not allow it to degenerate into sheer obstruction, is thus a purely technical one. It is not too important, because legislatures should be limited by the Constitution, not by any tricks that may be pulled on the floor of Congress to prevent or hasten the passage of a particular law. What *is* important in this regard are the Constitutional principles that name the kind of laws Congress may or may not pass.

Interviewer: Do you think the way we choose the Supreme Court, by presidential nomination, is right? Does it give too much power to the judiciary and too much influence to the presidency?

AR: That's a difficult, technical question. In principle it is not a bad system, because it was designed to make the judiciary independent of the direct popular vote—that is, independent of any shifting majority of the moment. This was not an impractical idea. However, it is an example of why no system can survive the absence of philosophic consistency on the part of the citizens. For instance, it used to be an unwritten law that, as a proper, moral check on the president's arbitrary whims, the justices should be selected from representatives of both parties and that they should have distinguished legal careers. This was not a constitutional provision, but it was a proper, unwritten law. Observe how often it has been broken. Presidents have progressively been appointing justices, not on the grounds of merit, but as a means of furthering political alliances and dispensing political rewards. I think the worst appointments in this respect were by Kennedy. He chose relatively young men, who might become distinguished jurists forty years from now, but are not in that category today.

Interviewer: Who should determine the constitutionality of laws?

AR: In an ideal society, it should be the job of the Supreme Court. But I think the Constitution should be a little more explicit about the areas in which the government does or does not have the right to take action.

Interviewer: You spoke about the fact that the Supreme Court has been unreasonable in stretching the Constitution of the United States. What extra limitations, if any, would you put on the Supreme Court now?

AR: It isn't with the Supreme Court that you have to begin. If you want to indulge in theoretical utopia-building, the following limitation should be written into the Constitution: "Congress shall pass no law which contradicts other laws, or which is so unclear that no two Congressmen or private lawyers can agree on what it means." The present state of the Supreme Court is not entirely the Court's fault. Today's Congressmen, being at the mercy of the next election and in total ideological chaos, have been careful to pass the kind of non-objective laws they hoped would please everybody. The passage of vaguely worded laws, which will not antagonize anyone, has been a growing trend over the past decade. Ultimately, though, somebody has to decide what such laws mean. Congress has been dumping these laws on the Supreme Court, which has, in effect, been *forced* to legislate, because Congress has failed to do so. In fact, there have been complaints from Supreme Court Justices, making this very point. Therefore, if you want to correct the present situation, you would have to start by establishing stricter provisions for the enactment of objective laws.

· *10* ·

Objective Law

Tyranny requires non-objective laws. No matter how severe a form of government you might have, if its laws and its edicts are objective, it is not a tyranny.

Interviewer: What exactly is the function of law in society?

AR: The proper purpose of law is to establish the principles of conduct governing human relationships in a society. Specifically, it is to establish the principles that respect individual rights by preventing citizens from infringing one another's rights. The concept of law is inextricably tied to the concept of rights, without which no rule of law is possible. In this context, it is interesting that the concept of law originated in ancient Rome. It was a very limited, very primitive concept, in that only Roman citizens were supposed to have certain rights. This was definitely an improper idea philosophically. But the significance is that, for the first time, man conceived of such a thing as a principle pertaining to some individuals that had to be respected by all men in a given society. It was a principle pertaining to the definition, and the protection, of individual rights in society. That is why the root of law is in ancient Roman civilization.

Interviewer: What is the difference between objective and non-objective law?

AR: This is one of the most important issues today. "Objective" means definable—graspable by a rational consciousness. An objective law, therefore, defines what is forbidden and what the penalty is. An objective law is one that a man can understand and apply, so that before committing an action, he is able to know whether it is a crime and what penalty he incurs by committing it. A law-abiding citizen should be able to apply the law as guidance for his own social actions.

A non-objective law, on the other hand, is one without specific definition. It may have as many different interpretations as there are men. Under non-objective law, a citizen cannot tell what is permitted or forbidden. He cannot tell what the punishment will be for violators. A non-objective law is left strictly to the interpretation of the authorities—usually judges, and under dictatorships, commissars. It is in fact indefinable. The best example is anti-trust legislation, under which a man cannot tell what is allowed or not, and may commit a crime without knowing that he is doing so.

Interviewer: A popular legal doctrine holds that the law is whatever judges say it is, and that legislative enactments are merely sources used by judges to help them in establishing the law. Do you believe that this is a primary cause of the present state of non-objective law?

AR: It is not the cause; it is one of the primary manifestations. If I am not mistaken, it was Justice Oliver Wendell Holmes who originated that doctrine—and he has had the worst philosophical influence on American law. The doctrine is a statement of pure non-objectivity. It is a formula for tyranny. If the laws are whatever the judges say they are, I don't see the purpose in having any laws at all. Whatever the judges, or others authorities, decide at any given moment determines what happens to the citizens. This doctrine is not a formulation of a principle of law—it is the negation of the very concept of law.

Interviewer: The proliferation of non-objective law and the increasing amount of government control seem to have occurred together. Is there any significance in that fact?

AR: Yes. Tyranny requires non-objective laws. No matter how severe a form of government you might have, if its laws and its edicts are objective, it is not a tyranny. It does not have arbitrary power over the citizens. In all history there has never been a system that combined a strict, objective code of rules and governmental tyranny. The essence of tyrannical power is *arbitrary* power. And the only means to arbitrary rule are non-objective laws—such as *ex post facto*, or retroactive, laws, under which an action that was legal when you took it is later declared illegal and you are punished for it. That is typical non-objective law. Such laws, incidentally, are explicitly forbidden in the Constitution, and yet are being practiced on a wider and wider scale today.

Interviewer: *One justification sometimes offered for non-objective law, particularly in the realm of economic regulation, is that market phenomena change so quickly that the government must have a certain amount of flexibility. Is there some merit in this argument?*

AR: Quite the opposite. It provides the best illustration of why there should be no government controls on the economy. You can state as a principle that when a law cannot be formulated objectively in some realm, it is a sign that *no* law should be formulated there. If an issue cannot be objectively made into law, then there is no reason that the decision of one man—that is, a judge or a bureaucrat—should be superior to the decision of another man—that is, a private citizen.

This topic brings us back to the question of the purpose of law. Since the laws of a free society—which are the only ones that can properly be called laws—exist to protect individual rights, it is up to the law to define how the principle of rights is to be applied in cases where there appears to be a clash of rights. Where no objective definition can be given, though, it is a violation of rights to pass the decision-making power to some authority. Where no specific violation of somebody's rights can be defined, no violation exists and there is no justification for legislating in that sphere. This is the fundamental argument against all government control of business, and is the reason such control can never be practical or moral.

Interviewer: *Would you say that there are cases in which a judge's individual discretion would have to enter—for example, when he must decide whether a child should be removed from the custody of abusive parents?*

AR: Yes, but only with respect to details. The general principle must be defined by law; the concrete application may be left up to the judge. For instance, the judge couldn't decide arbitrarily that he wants to take the child away from the parents and place him in an institution. The law would have to define the scope of the judge's powers. Then, in each case, latitude may be given to the judge, providing it is clearly limited and defined. If he has to consider the best interests of the child, the law would have to define exactly what factors make up those best interests—such as the moral character of the parents or the financial support they provide—and what the judge may take as proof of proper or improper character, et cetera. Another example is the law's provision for sentences of not less than and not more than a certain number of years. Here too the judge can be allowed latitude, since a given crime can be committed under so many different, perhaps mitigating, circumstances. But again, such discretion must be exercised under objectively defined rules and within objectively defined limits. For instance, you couldn't leave it up to the judge to decide whether a pickpocket should be jailed for a month or executed.

Interviewer: In law we must hold the citizen to the standard of a rational man— of a man who possesses free will and is able to control his actions—before we impose punishment. But what about children, and people who are insane? Obviously we wouldn't hold them to the same standard, or would we? Also, would you comment on the use of the plea of temporary insanity?

AR: A child or an insane person cannot be held responsible for his actions in the way that a normal adult is. In the case of an insane person, one would have to incarcerate him or put him out of circulation to prevent him from committing further crimes. But one could not impose on him a punishment intended only for, and deserved only by, the man who is conscious of his actions.

The issue of temporary insanity is very tricky. If the science of psychology, which at present is nothing but a jumble of contradictory hypotheses, were to reach the stage where objective principles could be defined, it would then be up to a psychiatrist to establish what constitutes a state of real insanity, and then what constitutes the phenomenon of temporary insanity. Temporary insanity does exist—for instance, when a man under the stress of violent emotion loses control of himself and commits some crime he would not have committed with conscious premeditation. Such a state of mind does constitute a certain mitigating circumstance—but not always, because the question then arises: What did the man do to himself psychologically to reach a state in which he loses complete conscious control and becomes temporarily dangerous enough to commit murder? Here, the question of moral and legal responsibility is much more complex than in the case of actual psychosis. And the answer would in part depend on scientific knowledge that is not available at present. Thus, a plea of temporary insanity has to be allowed to some extent, since it does occur. But the technical means of determining when that state is present, and when the plea is proper or improper, is too complex at present. I would not venture even a hypothesis in that realm, because we have too little knowledge.

Interviewer: In a society such as ours, with its plethora of laws and regulations, is it ever proper for ignorance of the law to be used as an excuse?

AR: In principle, you could not make ignorance of the law a justification, because it is too subjective. Anyone could claim that he didn't know the law—and if he wanted to break it, he'd make sure that he didn't "know" it. But today our legislatures are running hog-wild in the opposite direction, making it impossible for anyone to know the law firsthand. I think the corollary of the principle that ignorance of the law is no defense, is the obligation of legislators to make their laws objective and intelligible, so that everyone is able to know what the law consists of. A lawyer should be required only for serious, complex matters—not for every step of a citizen's life, as is the case today.

Interviewer: Certain seemingly legitimate actions are now prohibited to the entire population because society feels that otherwise some people might engage in clearly criminal activity. What do you think about preventive laws?

AR: Preventive law belongs only in a dictatorship. It is a strictly statist concept. You say that "society feels . . ."—but there is no such entity as "society"; it is simply a group of individual men. And there is no right on the part of some people to decide, by guessing someone's future intentions, what other people may or may not do. More than that, you do not hold down the total population, including the best of your citizens, to the levels indulged in only by the worst. If we carried this approach to its consistent extreme, we would have a legal curfew forbidding everyone from leaving his house at night because some small minority of people might indulge in crimes under cover of darkness. This would be a pure example of preventive law. And there is no conceivable justification for it.

Interviewer: What should be the guiding principle in determining what punishment is appropriate to what offense?

AR: The principle should be established by means of hierarchical order. In devising a proper penal system, one begins by arranging crimes in order, from the most minor to the very worst. Let us say, for example, you start with a pickpocket and end with a murderer. The severity of the crime is judged by the extent of the harm it inflicts on people. Next, you establish the minimum and maximum penalties that can be imposed. Then every other crime is ranked within that hierarchy—which is approximately how most legal systems do in fact establish penalties. The severity of the punishment matches the severity of the crime.

Interviewer: I'd like to raise some epistemological ramifications of law. Even if a law is objective, we still have the problem of establishing the specific facts—of determining whether a particular act falls under the law or not. Could you comment on this problem in law, perhaps in relation to the question of capital punishment?

AR: This is a very difficult question. In a practical sense, the main purpose of the law is precisely to establish rules of evidence, so that if people are harmed, they do not settle their conflicts by personally resorting to force. In a civilized society, the citizens delegate to the government the power of retaliatory force—that is, the power of defending them on the basis of their right of self-defense. This power has to be delegated to the government in order to establish objective rules of evidence, which cannot be left to the discretion of every individual. Of course, the rules of evidence cannot be established with total infallibility. Even when you have identified the broad principles, there are too many complexities in applying them to a given case.

With respect to capital punishment, as a matter of moral principle, I approve of it in cases of first-degree murder. If someone has committed murder by conscious, deliberate intent, he deserves to forfeit his own life. But the issue of objective proof enters here. I think a good argument could be made, with which I am inclined to agree, that because errors in proof are possible, capital punishment should be outlawed—not out of moral consideration for the murderer, but to prevent the rare instance of an innocent man's being convicted. It is better to sentence nine actual murderers to life imprisonment than to execute one innocent man.

Interviewer: What ought to be the response of a businessman caught between two non-objective laws? For example, he is accused of under-pricing his competitors and of being a monopoly.

AR: Such a businessman has no recourse, except to use the best lawyer and the loudest public relations man in the country—neither of which type exists for this purpose, as far as I know—in order to publicize his situation and to demand redress on principle. Unfortunately, the businessman in such cases usually seeks some kind of compromise. He accepts whatever the government prescribes and his lawyer tries to make the best deal possible with the bureaucrats.

Instead, businessmen in that position should fight by making the issue as public as possible. But today all of them are afraid and, in a certain sense, you can't fully blame them. They claim that anyone who takes a strong stand would be deserted by his fellow-businessmen, and could not succeed in opposing the government alone. Well, that is true in some respects, but not in others. A man who firmly declares that he intends to fight on principle would be the one whom the bureaucrats would leave alone, because a public debate on the principles is precisely what the bureaucrats could not withstand.

Interviewer: You said that non-objective law is a step on the road to dictatorship. Do you think that President Kennedy's threats against the steel industry a few years ago were an extension of non-objective law into a realm where no actual law even existed?

AR: I certainly would say so. During the so-called steel crisis, President Kennedy attempted to penalize the steel industry for not accepting his economic guidelines in settling a union contract—when he had no authority at all to regulate collective bargaining or to promulgate any such guidelines. That was a blatant example of non-objective law in action. Kennedy initiated all sorts of intimidation tactics, openly invoking the antitrust laws against the steel companies. He was coercing a particular group, because it had displeased him, merely by threatening that he had a body of non-objective law which he could use at his arbitrary discretion. Today, President Johnson is establishing pricing guidelines, to which nobody is strongly objecting. He is doing quietly what Kennedy had done in a dramatic and noisy manner. The precedent, once established, is now being carried on without much protest—which is another of the disastrous consequences of non-objective law.

The Role of a Free Press

News coverage today consists in slanting a story according to the mood, not of the people or even of the government, but of the so-called intellectual establishment.

Interviewer: *What do you think is the function of the press in a free society?*

AR: In the broadest sense, the press means all media of communication—newspapers, magazines, books, radio, television. It includes every method by which men spread ideas and information. The press is the profession that communicates knowledge. This may be journalistic knowledge, about the news of the day, or wider knowledge, which is provided by books, particularly nonfiction works, textbooks, et cetera. It is the spread of knowledge—the spread of ideas—that is covered by the term "the press." When we speak of freedom of the press, we mean the freedom of all these professions.

Interviewer: *What ethics applies to a reporter covering some event?*

AR: Anyone who communicates anything should perform the exact function he says he is performing. For instance, a book of fiction should be fiction, and not a thinly veiled report of real events. By the same principle, a newspaper reporter who is supposed to be communicating actual events must have objectivity as his first ethical absolute. He has to convey facts without any slant or personal viewpoint. The only philosophical viewpoint that should be present is the one most rare today: the commitment to objectivity.

Interviewer: In a recent best-selling novel about Washington politics, Capable of Honor, *Allen Drury presented a horrifying account of how journalists can distort facts. To what extent do you think the press obscures vital issues?*

AR: To the full extent of Mr. Drury's novel—and then perhaps some more. It is an excellent novel, incidentally, and I recommend it to everyone's attention. Mr. Drury is a very talented, realistic novelist. The picture he presents in that novel is extremely accurate. The story is horrifying, but what is more shocking is that one reads it without particular astonishment. Drury, as a good fiction writer, merely depicts the essence of what is going on, but his book reads almost like plain, objective reporting. All the journalistic biases he presents are observable by us in daily life—in the newspapers, on the radio, on television. We are so used to one-sided, distorted news that I think we would be shocked if we had a truly objective voice among today's journalists. That novel sums up the situation better than any abstract discussion could. It has great value because it is horrifying to see the whole picture, in the way that fiction condenses the meaning of events. You can then look for documentary evidence all around you, and you will see the accuracy of Mr. Drury's presentation.

Interviewer: Is freedom of the press an absolute? For example, should a reporter be allowed to reveal everything? Is it ever his duty to conceal something?

AR: Freedom of the press *is* an absolute. If there is anything that should not be made public—and that would include only libel of private individuals or military secrets—a reporter should not mention the subject at all. It's interesting in this connection that when you testify in court, you take an oath to tell the truth, the whole truth and nothing but the truth—and I emphasize here the issue of the *whole* truth. A half-truth, in many issues, is more misleading than an outright lie; it is more of a distortion. Therefore, if a reporter cannot reveal the whole truth in a given issue, he should not touch that issue at all.

News should be carefully delimited so that classified information is not discussed in the newspapers at all. The question, of course, is what information should be classified. And I would say that only military matters, including certain, strictly delimited technical matters, should not be revealed by the press. I mean such issues as the number and type of armaments this country is storing, or how an atomic bomb is made. These are, properly, military issues. They are not political or ideological ones, and there is no reason the citizens need that information.

But there can be no justification for keeping other matters, such as diplomatic policies, secret. If it is a free country, the citizens have to make the choice of what policies they wish the country to pursue, and if non-military political information is hidden from them, on what basis can we have an informed electorate? Here, as is true of every other aspect of political life today, there is too much stretching of government power, and the category of classified information now covers much more than purely technical military matters.

Interviewer: It's kind of interesting that it's precisely military secrets and military data that for a while you could go to the library and look up, whereas the basis for policy decisions often is closeted.

AR: That is always the case in a semi-free country, which is what we have today. Once objective principles have been rejected, it is left up to any bureau of the government to decide how it wants to interpret certain laws, including laws about classified information. So you'll find that military information that should be kept secret can be gathered piecemeal from various publications. But the content of fundamental political policies is hidden from the very public in whose name these policies are allegedly undertaken.

Interviewer: In pursuing a story, should a reporter keep digging for information, making his own judgment as to what should be classified?

AR: No, because information that should be classified will not be available to a private citizen's digging. But in all other issues, it is the moral responsibility of a reporter to present the full truth to the best of his knowledge and ability. In the past, a great many governmental abuses were exposed by the energy and integrity of a reporter who unearthed the facts and made them public. Pursuing the truth should still be the policy in journalism but, unfortunately, it is not.

Interviewer: Should a newspaper provide a forum for columnists whose views are directly opposed to its own editorial policy?

AR: Certainly not. That is a preposterous idea, which comes from mixing the realm of government with that of the private individual. To begin with, even in an institution like broadcasting, where government has taken control over the airwaves, the idea of granting "equal time" to all sides has not worked. It is impractical and it is morally not fully justified. It is an impossible attempt to make a fundamentally unjust principle work fairly. In broadcasting, the attempt may have a semi-plausible justification, in that if government is supposed to represent all people, then all viewpoints have to be given an equal chance.

However, this does not apply to private institutions or private property. There is no reason on earth why the owner of a newspaper has to give an opportunity for expression to those who oppose his own viewpoint. He is giving a weapon to his own enemies. Such a policy can lead only to the kind of cynicism and lack of intellectual integrity that we see in most communications media today. If a publisher is asked—officially or simply by cultural pressure—to allow "equal time" to his adversaries, it means that we are functioning on the premise that ideas are not to be taken seriously, that no one can know the truth and that we are all just subjectivists expressing our own prejudices. If so, one man's prejudice is as good as another's, and nobody can have any serious convictions. A man of integrity, who takes issues seriously, believes that his viewpoint is right and that he has to defend it in his own newspaper or magazine. He cannot be asked to give voice to that which he considers mistaken or evil. A private publication must be responsible for its own viewpoint and must have the integrity of maintaining it consistently. It has no obligation—in fact, it would be immoral—to give voice to its own enemies.

Interviewer: Would it be immoral for a business to advertise in a publication with an anti-capitalist editorial policy?

AR: Yes, of course. It would be immoral if the owners of the business advocated free enterprise. Those who are opposed to free enterprise—and there are certainly enough of them today—are free to express their views by their own means and at their own expense.

Interviewer: You have said that our knowledge of why we are in Vietnam and exactly what is happening there is sketchy, to say the least. Do you feel that this has been the result of news management by the government or of a failure on the part of the press?

AR: Both. The press today is enormously influenced by the government. It is not fully controlled, but neither is it fully free. Therefore, there is a certain element of news-suppression when it comes to anything incompatible with the government's policy. On the other hand, news coverage today consists in slanting a story according to the mood, not of the people or even of the government, but of the so-called intellectual establishment.

The reporting of the news from Vietnam is therefore disgraceful on two counts. First, you cannot really get a clear picture of what is going on there. Such reports as you do get are mostly slanted against the United States' position—if there is any—and for the Vietcong's, at least indirectly. Second, this is made possible by the fact that the government has no clear-cut policy in Vietnam. Even if the press wanted to give an account of what our objectives are in this war and what there is for us to gain, it could not do so. The press has published statements by President Johnson and other top government officials, but none of them makes any sense. None is clear enough to give anyone an idea of what the war is all about. Thus the press is helpless both in regard to the position of our government on the war and in regard to the unprincipled, chaotic state of ideology in general today. That state has made the Vietnam issue into a jumble of misinformation and senselessness.

Interviewer: What do you think about freedom of the press versus the right of a defendant to a fair trial? Many people see a conflict between the First and the Sixth Amendments of the Constitution, and therefore advocate the British system, which suppresses information about criminal cases once legal proceedings are under way. Do you think such information should be withheld, either voluntarily or by law?

AR: No. This idea is enormously dangerous. The entire American system of jurisprudence is based on the principle of a public trial. Once you establish the idea, for any reason whatever, that the public should not have access to information about a trial, what is to prevent the same principle from being applied to political cases? What is to prevent a defendant from being railroaded in a case in which the jurors may be prejudiced, or in which the conduct of the trial may be otherwise highly improper? The defendant would be left at the mercy of those closely involved in the case, with the public having no information until it is too late. Nothing in principle would then prevent a secret, "star-chamber" proceeding.

One of the things that keeps jurors, judges and all others in line—so that they at least attempt to display some kind of objectivity and integrity—is the fear of public opinion. If men have shaky integrity to begin with, then the fear of public exposure is a proper protection for the man on trial. It is true that if you remove that protection, some monstrous criminal who is obviously guilty, such as Lee Harvey Oswald, might be given more "benefit of the doubt" by the jurors; but since the evidence is overwhelmingly against him, he would still be convicted. Who, then, would suffer under a secret system? Someone accused of a crime for which the evidence is not as clear-cut, or someone whose trial is subject to political pressures. If his case is not allowed public discussion, he would be left at the mercy of whatever legal procedures the government, at its discretion, chose to follow. Publicity is the best protection for innocent men. And it certainly does not violate the rights of the guilty—if someone has in fact committed a crime, on what grounds can he expect his action not to be publicized?

There is another dangerous issue here, however. In a statist system, like Soviet Russia's, crimes against private citizens are treated very lightly, and *over*protection is given to the "rights" of plain criminals. The opposite attitude is taken toward so-called crimes against the state, which in Russia are openly called political crimes, and in a mixed economy involve semi-political issues. Whatever the government defines as such a "crime" is punished very severely. This is the area in which individual rights are most infringed and where the individual is left without any protection.

Obviously, in a free country the exact reverse should be true. There should be no such category as "crimes against the state," and with respect to crimes against individuals, the law should be very severe. Every objective procedural protection should be given to the accused, in case he happens to be innocent—but not to the extent that is advocated today. Today it is almost impossible to convict a criminal. Yet in proceedings involving administrative agencies, the rights of accused individuals are violated daily, without any protection at all. This is part of the same principle.

Interviewer: *What about allowing the defendant to request that information about his trial not be given out, if he feels that this will be prejudicial to him? And what about, instead of making all trials fully public, releasing all information immediately after a speedy trial, so that no one's rights are compromised?*

AR: To answer your second point first: publicity after the fact is too late. In a case where an injustice has been done, the public may protest, but it is really too late. The man has already been convicted, and the appeals court will not be influenced by public opinion, at least not to the same extent that the original court would have been.

As to your first point, I am not sure what the implications might be. Certainly, what you propose is better than simply hiding all cases from the press. But it is a kind of compromise, because you do not know what use a guilty defendant might make of it. And to give a man the right to shut off information is very dubious.

The more serious issue here is the moral status of the press. If the press were objective, there would be no concern about any danger to a possibly innocent man who is unduly attacked before a trial. "Yellow journalism" has always existed, and there will always be sensation-mongering newspapers that attempt to exaggerate the accusations in some cases and to do injustice to the defendant. But in the freer periods in this country's history, the "yellow press" did not have much influence on the public. The ones that did have influence were the papers of better standing—the ones that were more intellectual and more responsible—even if they had smaller circulations. Therefore, if the press adopted civilized standards of objectivity, there would be no wide threat that possibly innocent men, with inconclusive evidence against them, would be judged guilty before trial. It is because the press is not objective that remedies to achieve a "fair trial" are being proposed. But they only make the problem worse.

Interviewer: We have confined ourselves pretty much to the printed word. Does all this apply as well to the electronic media?

AR: Yes, of course. The same principles apply, and the same defects exist in the news coverage on radio and television—perhaps a little more so, because the electronic media have the disadvantage of being under government control. They face greater pressure to conform, under threat of losing their licenses, and therefore have a greater fear of expressing independent viewpoints. The tendency has been toward a sickeningly dull, middle-of-the-road conformity, in which original, independent views are getting rarer and rarer. An overwhelming majority of the media have reached that gray level of mediocrity which usually characterizes the press in a country that has censorship. We don't have censorship today. But too large a part of our communications media, particularly on the air, is reaching for the safe level of conformity.

Interviewer: Do you think that there is any greater objectivity in the electronic media than in the print media?

AR: I would say less. Some of the most outrageously slanted statements have been made during political elections. Since the electronic media, particularly television, have a greater influence on immediate, journalistic events than on longer-range issues, they have an enormous impact on elections. It is here that the lack of objectivity and fairness has been obvious for quite some time. There are exceptions, but I am speaking of the general trend.

Interviewer: Do you think that there are inherently proper contents for particular media? For example, since radio and television can provide more immediate news, should newspapers confine themselves to more in-depth analysis? And should television offer more programs of information rather than strictly entertainment?

AR: I challenge any attempt to set a policy of that kind for any medium of communication. There is no principle by which one could establish such rules. There are so many different ways you can approach the issue of news communication that no general policy can be established, even voluntarily, let alone through government enforcement. To use your own example, television does give you immediate coverage, but it is necessarily brief. There is an enormous need for in-depth analysis on television—and I don't mean the kind of boring, slanted, timid documentaries that are being produced as specials today. I think there would be great demand for serious discussions of political events on television, as well as in newspapers. But such policies should always be set by the particular newspaper or television station. Nobody can prescribe a universal rule, because there is room for many approaches.

Interviewer: Do you think that the generally low quality of public-affairs presentations on television is a result of government regulation?

AR: Yes. The single major cause is the fear of the government's power at license-renewal time. Although government officials have repeatedly stated that they don't exercise any control, this is obviously an impossible claim. When government has the arbitrary right to refuse to renew a license, an official would never have to bring any overt pressure on the owner of a radio or television station. All he would have to do is communicate indirectly that he prefers a certain viewpoint to be stressed, and his preference would acquire all the power of outright censorship. This is really censorship by disapproval, and a given official may not even be personally guilty of it. His associates—or even total strangers, among the assorted lobbyists and pull-peddlers in Washington—could exercise the same intimidating pressure in his name, and nobody, including the victim, would ever check. All they would need to do is to spread a rumor that some bureaucrat—who may know nothing about this—prefers that a station adopt policy A rather than policy B on a given question. That would be sufficient to achieve compliance. You could not even accuse the affected stations of cowardice. When their very existence is at the mercy of a commission's arbitrary power, it is built into their mode of operations that they give in to pressure, explicit or implicit. They are perpetually in danger, and the only way they can operate is by playing it safe and not antagonizing anybody. And that means never expressing any clear, forceful or independent opinion.

Interviewer: It is claimed that the scientific facts of the electromagnetic spectrum necessitated government control over the airwaves. That is, if two channels were broadcast on frequencies too close to one another, there would be chaos. Do you think this rationale is, or ever was, valid?

AR: Certainly not. The government should have acted as an arbiter to define and protect property rights in the airwaves; it should not have assumed ownership over them. If channels were limited and operators could jam one another, the government should have created an objective set of rules by which ownership of given frequencies would be established, on a simple first-come-first-served basis. If you use a certain frequency for a number of years, it becomes yours. The government should have been protecting property rights, instead of suspending them.

Today we don't even have the excuse of a limited number of airwaves, because there are many more television frequencies available—like the ultra-high frequencies—than there are applicants for ownership. But people want to take over an established frequency, and are bidding for somebody else's license to a station rather than exploiting the unlimited new medium of ultra-high frequencies.

But more fundamentally, every value that men use exists in a limited amount. This is true of every mineral, it is true of food, it is true of real estate. The mere fact that a certain commodity is rare does not entitle the government to assume ownership of it. If you want the entire population to have access to that rare commodity, the best way to do so is to make it private property and put it on the free market. If the owner of a given broadcast frequency cannot make proper economic use of it, the force of competition will make him sell that property to someone who can. He is wasting a very valuable asset, and those who can make better use of it will be in a position to buy it. I've written an article ["The Property Status of Airwaves," published in *Capitalism: The Unknown Ideal*] about this, and I suggest that those interested in this question read it.

Interviewer: Why should ownership of airwaves be on a first-come-first-served basis? Why shouldn't ownership go to the one who makes the highest bid, or promises to provide a better form of programming?

AR: You are implying that the government is. the owner of the airwaves, since one bids to buy something only from its owner. But I challenge that premise. The airwaves as such cannot be used without the work, the ingenuity and the capital of the broadcasters. Mere potentiality does not constitute the value of the airwaves. The value is created by those who actually make use of that potentiality. Therefore, there is no reason for the government to assume ownership of some frequency and sell it.

But your second suggestion implies an even worse principle—that the government is somehow qualified to pass judgment on the moral or esthetic or philosophical value of programs. Even if there were some standard by which it could make such judgments, the government would be the very last entity to have the *right* to do so.

Now, if one wanted to return to free enterprise—and I wouldn't expect this to be one of the early reforms—the government might have to sell the existing stations to the highest bidder, because the present licensees are actually exercising a privilege without paying for it. In exchange for their licenses, they take no economic risk in operating a station. Being a "public service" has financial value to license-holders, because they do not have to pay for the right to use a certain wavelength. As in every case of getting something for nothing, though, there are strings attached. The result of those strings is the timid, obedient state of the radio and television industry today. If we adopted laissez-faire, there might have to be a sale of this alleged public property, which government never had the right to take in the first place. To return to freedom, one would have to sell the current stations to private owners, perhaps to the highest bidder. But it's really a premature concern; we won't come to that reform for quite some time.

Interviewer: Back in the Kennedy administration, Newton Minnow characterized television as a "vast wasteland," and pressured broadcasters to produce "educational" and "public service" programming. What kind of motives would you ascribe to him to explain the government's sudden interest in education?

AR: To discuss the motives of any given individual you would have to know him personally. But if you ask more generally about the policy of a government official in this case, the answer is obvious. Don't you think that government officials have as much desire to appear in large close-ups on television as any movie star? Only more so. The movie star, though, has some actual value to offer. If more free time were given to political and news broadcasts, every government official with good public-relations men could hope to get free television time to air his face and his views—or lack of them—to the whole country. The government of a mixed economy like ours has a vast interest in making the country as "politics-conscious" as possible. By that, I don't mean educated in actual ideas, but simply exposed to the immediate influence of any official looking for public support. Therefore, the government's vested interest in more political broadcasts is quite obvious.

Interviewer: It seems to me that a newspaper's lack of objectivity comes from the reporter's personal prejudices, rather than from an attempt to carefully steer a middle-of-the-road course. In television, however, it seems that the major goal is simply not to say anything that might offend anyone. Do you think there is this type of dichotomy?

AR: You mean a dichotomy between print and electronic media? No, I think the two present variants of the same problem. I don't think that the source of the problem with newspapers is the prejudices of the individual reporter. The trouble with the press today is the same as that with every other profession. The culture of a country is influenced by its predominant philosophy. The result of the philosophy that people—including journalists—have been taught for generations is the tendency toward the gray, the timid, the non-committal, the middle-of-the-road.

On the one hand, men are taught that there is no such thing as objectivity, that there is no such thing as knowledge, that none of us can be certain of anything. On the other hand, you have a government that tries to assume more and more power, that claims to rule by consensus, that rewards the compromiser while penalizing the non-conformist. The two realms reinforce one another, and both act to reinforce the incentive of all media to stay in the middle. The government's control over radio and television is, of course, more immediate and more forceful than its indirect influence on the print media. The electronic media will therefore reflect this conformist tendency a little more acutely and with fewer exceptions. But the basic cause is the same throughout the press—and throughout all other professions. It is the culture's dominant philosophy, which comes from the universities, that determines the kind of ideas people will hold, and therefore the kind of actions they will take and the kind of politics they will endorse.

Interviewer: Would you say then that the "vast wasteland" in television, of which Mr. Minnow speaks, reflects the general state of our culture?

AR: Very much so. I agree with Mr. Minnow in only one respect—that television *is* a vast wasteland. But my remedy is not the one he suggests. My remedy is philosophical and it would start with changing the epistemology and esthetics classes taught in our colleges. It would *not* consist in cutting out a few cowboy and private-eye shows—which are sometimes very entertaining, though not this season—and replacing them with interviews of politicians and more slanted documentaries. Mr. Minnow was right in criticizing the culture, but he is the last one entitled to do so, because he, as a government official, is the product of that culture and is contributing to all its bad features. The wasteland starts in college and is enforced by government. One is the cause, the other is the effect. But Mr. Minnow, as an effect of the very philosophy that is creating the wasteland, cannot hope to find a solution by asking for more power—that is, for more of the same poison that produced the wasteland in the first place.

Interviewer: To what extent do you think that the failings of modern journalists are the result of the training they receive in the field of journalism?

AR: I am not well acquainted with what goes on in departments of journalism. I would say that in every profession, the general trend—always allowing for exceptions—is made by the kind of training young people receive in college. And look at today's results: the non-objectivity, the imprecision, the general sloppiness which extends even to grammar. The quality of journalists' writing is disgracefully low. When such deficiencies exist on such a wide scale, one has to attribute them to the kind of training the reporters receive in schools of journalism.

Interviewer: Do you think that recent examples of government involvement in the communications industry, such as the new satellite company COMSAT, are a natural outgrowth of the premise that government owns the airwaves?

AR: Of course. Such proposals as COMSAT are perhaps some of the most dangerous signs of future trends. It isn't even a government institution, but the worst phenomenon of a mixed economy: a combination of private interests—private favorites, in effect—and political power. This is what I call "the aristocracy of pull." A private group acquires the advantage of a government-granted monopoly and government funding, in order to exercise a degree of power with which no strictly private entrepreneur can compete. The only protection we have is that any endeavor organized by pressure groups attracts mediocrities, and the organization collapses through the weight of its own incompetence. The pull-peddlers can provide broadcasting, but it would usually be so bad that, as long as the country is even semi-free, a small, private broadcaster will take the audience away. But as a principle, this combination of government and private power is the worst symptom of a mixed economy. It represents, in fact, the principle of fascism.

Interviewer: I think a very clear example of what you just said happened in England recently, with the so-called pirate stations taking away the BBC's virtual monopoly of the airwaves in England.

AR: Yes, exactly. It's a development I was very interested in and happy to read about. It also happened in other European countries. This is a sign of men fighting for freedom, and a sign of the power of freedom—of rising on merit—as against government monopolies.

Interviewer: What would you prescribe for someone who wants to be well-informed? How should he go about selecting the most objective sources in the communications media?

AR: I have no advice to give. It's almost hopeless because there are no publications I would care to recommend. The only thing you can do is learn to read between the lines. In other words, follow whichever newspaper you regard as the most reliable and then watch the inner logic of the articles. This approach may not give you the knowledge of what really happened, but it will at least give you an indication of when the report is slanted. In any type of slanted reporting, you will find contradictions and evasions. Just at the point of the story where you want to know what happened, you will notice that the journalist writes around the issue. He tells you all the insignificant details—but not the essence of what happened. By that sign, if you read very carefully, you will know that you have not gotten the full story. That's the best I can suggest. Unfortunately, we don't have objective, reliable sources of information today.

· 12 ·

Education

Public education instills social conformity and obedience, not independence. . . . It is only a private system that can inculcate reason.

Interviewer: *What in your view is the essence of education?*

AR: Education means the development of a man's mind to enable him to deal with the facts of reality. In all living species, the young have to be taught their means of survival by their elders. If you have ever watched cats or birds, you will observe that the mother teaches the kittens to hunt or the birds to fly. In each species—at least among the higher animals—the parent teaches the young the particular skills required for survival. This process certainly applies to a human being, whose means of survival are the most complex, and are also volitional.

Man's basic tool of survival is his mind—his rational faculty. To become a full adult and survive on his own, an individual needs two things: a knowledge of the facts, at least up to the point acquired by his elders; and, more important, the knowledge of how to use his mind to acquire more facts. Man is the only species able to transmit and expand his knowledge from generation to generation. Animals can transmit to their young only the same limited skills with which they are endowed by nature. They cannot transmit knowledge. Man can.

The crucial question is *how* man acquires knowledge. He does not automatically know what is true or false. He does not automatically know how to validate his conclusions by making them consonant with the facts of reality.

The ability to acquire knowledge, which means: to reason, is not innate. Man is born only with the *capacity* to think, but he has to discover how to use that capacity. He has to discover the laws of logic—the rules by which he can validate his knowledge and determine what is true. The basic purpose of education, beginning with the infant and on through college, is to train a young man in the use of his mind. He must be given certain fundamental facts already acquired by mankind, so that he does not have to start from scratch, like a savage in the jungle. But above all, he must be taught how to acquire knowledge. When a man graduates from a university, therefore, he should know the essentials in the particular field in which he is majoring, and he should know how to take that knowledge further. He should know how to think.

This is precisely where modern education has failed dismally. Not only does it not provide the student with basic facts, but it is devised—almost as if on purpose—to negate his thinking ability. If today's young people are not neurotic when they enter college, they have a good chance of becoming so by the time they leave. The entire anti-rational trend in the philosophy of education today is designed to paralyze a man's conceptual mind.

Interviewer: Do you believe that the objectives of education, as you've outlined them, can be achieved in a public educational system?

AR: They cannot. Objectivists are thoroughly opposed to public education, and to any form of forced public activity. The current state of our public schools is an indication of why the use of force is so disastrous.

There may of course be exceptions in specific schools, but as a system, public education instills social conformity and obedience, not independence. If education is in the hands of the state, then the teachers, in order to be honest, will tend to support the system within which they work. They will tend to endorse the ideas of statism—of obedience to the state. It was Spinoza who made this same observation about state-run schools. It is only a private system that can inculcate reason. In private schools—as in all private undertakings—the idea of independence, of self-reliance, of rationality is stressed. Again, there may be exceptions among particular teachers, but this is what private education, by its nature, leads to.

Interviewer: How will the children of the poor be able to cope with the demands of our technological society, since their parents will not be able to afford the private schools?

AR: To begin with, if it weren't for the public school system and other statist encroachments on the economy, private education would not be as expensive as it is today. Furthermore, competition in private schools would have the same beneficent effect that it has in all other activities. The need for schools would create the supply. Since schools and teachers would have to compete in achieving excellence, education would gain both in quantity and in quality. There would be more and better-equipped schools, available to more and more people.

There will always be situations in which parents are too poor to educate their children. In such cases, those children must rely on the charity or the self-interest of others. In a free—which means: prosperous—society, a great deal of money is voluntarily invested in education, as our history has shown. Most of today's great private universities were created by private individuals and are still being supported by private funds. It is obvious that men are interested in fostering education as a charitable activity. When and if a society has private funds available, those funds will supply an education to those who may not be able to afford it but who are eager to obtain it. That is, if parents have a child who is not particularly interested in school, there is no use in educating him. Such a child may go through the motions of attending school, and even college, but will come out as ignorant as when he started, perhaps even more so. But an intelligent, ambitious child will be able to find private assistance, in the form of scholarships or of private instruction.

But a more reliable motive than charity is the rational self-interest of the men involved in a highly technological society. The answer to the problem is contained in the very statement of the problem. A technological society requires a high degree of skills and specialized knowledge, without which businesses cannot be run. It is in the interest of the industrialists to have an educated work force. You can observe how this motive operates even today. Most businesses, particularly the large, specialized ones, hire graduates for well-paid, responsible jobs and spend company time in teaching them things they may not have learned in college. Companies run specialized schools to train future employees, not for any mawkish, altruistic reason, but for a very proper, selfish reason: they need skilled employees. Unlike our public schools, they do not try to forcibly educate the reluctant or the unpromising ones. But those who are ambitious and eager to learn are given their chance. This is another instance of mutual trade to mutual profit. In all free relationships among rational men, their interests do not clash. If there is a large need for a certain kind of skill, those demanding it will provide the facilities for developing it.

Interviewer: Would an Objectivist read such philosophers as Kant, Marx and Camus, given that their views are so divorced from reality?

AR: Do you mean to imply that Objectivism has a proscribed list of books, as the Catholic Church has? There is no rule about what an Objectivist, or any rational man, should or should not read. One's reading depends on one's purpose. If you are interested in philosophy, if you want to study ideas and their history, then you certainly would read these writers. You would particularly read Kant, who is enormously significant in a negative way—as a destroyer of reason. If you want to learn about some of the worst philosophical ideas and their consequences, Kant is the first philosopher you should read. Also, you can learn a great deal about philosophical problems and about the kind of pitfalls involved in solving those problems. Kant is the single most skillful philosopher in taking advantage of philosophical pitfalls and in corrupting man's thinking.

Now, Marx is not really a philosopher. He is important only in that he has had a great political influence on the present century. But a few centuries from now he will be only a historical rarity. He is of no great philosophical significance. Neither is Camus, who is a minor philosophizer. Kant, however, is a major figure.

Interviewer: What caused the flight from reason that we see in education and in modern culture?

AR: The flight from reason was a result of philosophy. What caused it? A great many things. But if I had to name one particular cause of philosophy's consistent attempt to escape from reason, I would say it is ethics. So long as mankind's dominant ethics was altruism, it had to lead to irrationalism in metaphysics and epistemology. Altruism could be accepted only by an act of faith; no philosopher has ever been able to justify altruism in reason. And it is here that Kant is very significant.

Kant is the most influential philosopher today, and even the schools that allegedly oppose him are actually variants of Kantianism. They have accepted one or another of Kant's basic premises and have carried them to their logical extreme. Kant admitted, in advance of presenting his philosophical system, what his purpose was. He openly declared that he wanted to save the morality of altruism from the danger represented by reason. This is not just an implication of his. He stated explicitly that if reason were allowed to triumph in philosophy, the morality of altruism would perish. Therefore, Kant had to devise a philosophy that would seem to invalidate reason—which he succeeded in doing better than any other philosopher (if you accept his basic system). If your goal is to undercut the validity of reason, then Kant's method is the most expert and the most cunning. Of course, the goal cannot really be accomplished, but Kant is the champion in coming as near to it as anyone.

But to return to the question, the main—though not exclusive—cause of the revolt against reason is man's adherence to the morality of altruism.

Interviewer: In what ways can the development of intellectual independence be aided in a person's grade-school education?

AR: By several means. The main one—which is the opposite of the approach taken by so-called progressive education—is for students to be taught basic, absolute facts, rather than techniques of "expressing" themselves before they have actually learned anything. In order to be taught to think, a young person has to be presented with facts, within the context of his knowledge and of what he can deal with mentally. Further, these facts must not be given to him as arbitrary dogma; they have to be demonstrated. Facts should be presented to a child as if they were being presented to a philosopher—namely, with full supporting evidence. If a teacher makes any assertions, he should prove his case. He should say *why* he is asserting something, so that the child is trained in how to distinguish fact from hypothesis, or fact from belief. He should be taught the rudiments of how to ask the appropriate questions and how to validate what he accepts as a fact.

I would introduce logic in high school and, possibly in a rudimentary form and without formally naming it as logic, even in grade school. I would certainly require that all teachers be experts in logic, and that they never be guilty of fallacies or confusions in dealing with grade-school pupils. Disasters are caused on that level by a teacher's arbitrary assertions and contradictions.

Interviewer: Earlier you spoke of the "laws of logic." What are they?

AR: These are the three classical laws. It's really one: the Law of Identity, which claims that A is A. But it has two corollaries: the Law of Excluded Middle, which is known as Either-Or; and the Law of Contradiction, which states that A cannot be non-A at the same time and in the same respect. Those are the three laws of logic formulated by Aristotle. There are many derivative laws, but they are merely applications. These three cover the base of logic.

Interviewer: Is it ever fair to indoctrinate, particularly in the formative years? For example, should Americanism be taught to students so that they learn to appreciate the American system?

AR: "Indoctrination" is a very loose term. If your question is: "Should children be taught American history?"—certainly they should. Should they be taught history objectively, in a non-slanted manner, in terms of essentials and in a manner that the teacher can justify logically? Certainly. This is education, not indoctrination. If, however, you mean: "Should a slanted view, presented according to the teacher's personal interpretation, be introduced?"—then, certainly not. It is important for the teacher to know, and to communicate, the difference between interpretation and fact. It would be quite proper for a teacher to present his interpretation, if he labels it as such, and to tell the children what he bases it on. Interpretation is part of the teacher's job—provided it is objective and he does not offer interpretation as fact.

Interviewer: Concerning the learning process itself, why do equally reasonable and intelligent men come to opposite conclusions given the same data?

AR: First of all, this does not happen often, but it certainly does happen in complex issues. The explanation lies in the fact that no knowledge is ever acquired outside a context. In order to understand a given set of data, a man has to refer it to the context of his previous knowledge. He must integrate it with what he knows, or discover that it contradicts what he knows. Since no two people have exactly the same amount of knowledge or the same frame of reference—and more: since no two people will focus on a subject with the same degree of interest—they may come to different conclusions from the same evidence on a very complex or technical issue.

However, if they wanted to reconcile their differences, which might take a long time, one can say with certainty that by methodically checking all their reasons and all their premises, they would ultimately reach the same conclusion. The only possible exception is in cases where the evidence is truly inconclusive, so that neither person could reach a firm conclusion. In that event, they might be inclined to form different hypotheses on the basis of the data. However, the same process would then apply to these hypotheses. That is, they could arrive at an ultimate agreement on the meaning of the available evidence and on the likelihood of one hypothesis over the other.

Interviewer: Is there an increasing use of the public education system to further the political goals of various groups, as is evidenced, for example, in the busing of schoolchildren?

AR: Of course. And it supports what I said earlier about the problem of public education. A school ruled by the state will be influenced by the politics of the state. The use of busing is proof of that. And there is a further source of the government's influence: its financial support for the schools. If someone, whether a private individual or a government official, provides money for a school, he has to judge whether that money is being spent properly. This is a value judgment to be pronounced on every investment—in fact, on every action man takes. It would be a dreadful irresponsibility if anyone gave money with no concern about the purpose, or the effectiveness, of the spending. The government cannot avoid interfering in the content of public education. And since government is a political institution, political considerations would have to come first when officials were deciding how to use the money.

Today, people go through the embarrassingly superficial pretense that the government will provide only the buildings and other material tools of education, but will not meddle in the intellectual content. It should be obvious to anyone that you cannot draw a division of that kind. Education requires material means. By refusing to subsidize the strictly material needs of some school that does not offer what a government official believes is a proper education, the state is pressuring the school to change its curriculum. There is no way to separate the material from the intellectual. The power to dispense material means of support is the power to determine the use to which those means are put. With respect to schools, this translates into control over the content of education.

Public education is one of the most disastrous and far-reaching steps toward statism. Because of it, the youth of this country have to enter life under a severe handicap. The honest and intelligent ones will have to spend a long time fighting against and discarding all the wrong ideas they have been taught.

Interviewer: Do you agree with many civil rights leaders who argue that integrated schools are an essential ingredient of any educational system?

AR: No, I do not. Civil rights are a political issue, and should not be settled in the schools. You do not make children the pawns of a political game. The cause of civil rights has to start at the level of defining, protecting and fighting for the individual rights of *all* men, which of course includes minorities. As I have said many times, the smallest minority on earth is the individual.

Today's civil rights leaders are undercutting the justice of their cause when they claim that in order to assert their own rights, they have to violate the rights of others. Not only will they lose any moral grounds for their own battle, but it won't be long before they lose their own rights. When you violate anybody's rights, you violate the rights of all. A society cannot respect the principle of individual rights part-time.

Certainly, racial segregation by the government is unconstitutional. It contradicts all American principles and is morally evil. Individual rights apply equally to every human being, regardless of his color. However, forcing children from various neighborhoods to sit in the same classroom to achieve integration is racism. It doesn't matter whether you make children race-conscious for the purpose of integration or for the purpose of segregation—the principle is the same. You should not assign children to schools on the grounds of race.

In addition, the practice is totally futile. Merely having a racially mixed school is not going to make the children respect each other's rights. It is not going to teach them the principle of individualism. It will only create more racial friction and resentment because the children are being forced to integrate. Nothing that is involuntary is going to solve a moral problem. I agree with the civil rights movement in its opposition to any form of segregation enforced by law. A government has no right to discriminate against any citizen. But for all the same reasons, I am against the enforcement of anti-segregation laws against private citizens—as is proposed in a bill now before Congress, which would forbid discrimination in private establishments. You cannot legislate morality. If you try, you are infringing the rights of some men for the benefit of others. When you do that, you are abrogating the principle of rights.

Racial prejudice is certainly evil, but like any moral issue it has to be fought by moral means—by private, voluntary action. One should fight against segregation by means of economic boycott and social ostracism. Let those white people who oppose racism boycott all segregated establishments. This would destroy segregation much more quickly than any other method.

Above all, let me stress that any attempt to solve a moral issue by force of law is a denial of legality and morality. Freedom means not only the freedom to do right, but also the freedom to be wrong, provided you don't force your errors on anyone. We understand why we have to defend a Communist's freedom of speech, even though his ideas are evil. We don't have to agree with him, we don't have to listen to him, we don't have to give him the means of spreading his ideas. But we have to leave him free to express them. In the same way, we have to allow a racist to express his ideas on his own property. If he wants to be a segregationist, he is evil and we have to fight him, but we have to do so by moral means. We cannot violate his rights. We don't have to deal with him, but we have to protect his right to be wrong on his own property.

Interviewer: *Would you comment on the case in New Jersey of the professor who stated that he would welcome a victory of the Vietcong in Vietnam? One of the issues in the recent gubernatorial campaign was whether this professor ought to be fired since he was teaching at a state university.*

AR: I have not followed the case in great detail, but judging only from some newspaper reports, I think the professor was enormously wrong—and so were his opponents. When his country is at war, a man has no moral right to speak in favor of the enemy. People may criticize the government's policy, and may even criticize the conduct of the war. But when the country is under threat of physical force, one may not express sympathy for a military enemy who is killing Americans. This principle applies not only to teachers, but to everybody.

The disgusting hypocrisy and confusion around this issue lies in the fact that we are at war, yet we do not call it war. It is typical of modern epistemology that something is supposed to be both A and non-A—that if we don't identify it by its proper name, somehow it is not what it is. Although the war in Vietnam is not officially called a war, so long as there is physical fighting and American soldiers are being killed there, it *is* a war. The professor's remarks were totally immoral, and politically would have been classified as treason if the country acknowledged the fact of the war. It is the charade of the "cold war" that permits people to pretend there is some kind of doubt here on the question of treason.

Further, there was the false implication that somehow a teacher has a different standard of freedom than other citizens. But being a teacher does not give someone any special privileges, nor special handicaps. The problem here is created by the existence of state universities. A state university is supposedly owned by the people of the state and, if so, they have the right to demand that no traitors to the country be employed there. After all, the first duty of any government is to protect its own citizens. Therefore, the citizens can legitimately object to employing someone who expresses sympathy for the nation's armed enemy at a time of war.

But when you have such confusion on this issue, raising it in a gubernatorial campaign is irrational. This professor's remarks could not possibly harm this country as much as our own government's foreign policy does. Our government openly adopts a friendly attitude toward the enemy—Soviet Russia—and is now considering official dealings with Red China. If this is America's policy, how can some inconsequential little assistant professor create any serious threat to the people of New Jersey? This was a moral issue, on which the professor was wrong. But to make it into a political issue is ridiculous, in the context of the disastrous trend of our foreign policy. One must never fight an issue out of context. The professor's remarks were of no significance to anyone, except perhaps his students, and they had the option of withdrawing from his classes. I think the state had the legal right to keep him or to fire him. Morally, of course, he should have been fired.

Interviewer: What do you think about certain groups that want their children to be educated in their own culture or language or religion? Are they robbing the child of something?

AR: Nobody has the right to dictate how a child should be educated. The premise that government, or public opinion, should prescribe by law what is right for a child is enormously improper. It is a parent's responsibility and privilege to decide how a child should be educated. Of course, it is everyone's privilege to express ideas on education, and you could explain to a parent why the particular viewpoint in which he wants to educate his child is wrong. But that is a different issue. It does not mean that you would forbid the parents from educating the child in their own beliefs. You would have to fight the battle on a philosophical level. If, for example, you consider the Catholic viewpoint wrong, you can try to persuade people about the nature of Catholicism, or religion. But you cannot fight by keeping someone's child from attending Catholic school. If a Catholic parent wants to educate his children there, you cannot forbid that choice. If it's a private school, that is the parent's privilege.

Interviewer: In an Objectivist society, how would the socialization of children take place? How would a child acquire his values?

AR: By "socialization," I assume you refer to the somewhat Freudian idea that a child simply absorbs society's values from his parents and teachers— that a child by nature is a kind of amoral savage who must be "socialized." I disagree with that emphatically. That is not how a child acquires values. As Aristotle identified, a human being is born *tabula rasa*—that is, he has cognitive apparatus, but it is empty of content. A child's ideas, values and character develop as he gains knowledge; there is nothing pre-set in his mind. He is not a savage at birth, nor is he a moral ideal. A child is born blank, cognitively and morally. He acquires his values by thinking, or by evasion. The kind of child who will become a mentally healthy, rational human being acquires his values by his own thinking on every level of his development. Such a child does not accept on blind faith anything that adults tell him. He accepts nothing except that which he understands, and as his knowledge grows, his values take form. He critically weighs what he is told, from the first time that he is able to face the issue of choice and values.

A child who does not care to undertake the responsibility of thinking will engage in mental evasion. And then he *does* accept by osmosis and by imitation the values imposed on him by his parents, teachers or neighbors. But that is already a neurotic child. That is a child who has defaulted on the proper function of developing his mind, and he has done so by his own volition. The people in a child's environment can help him become a rational human being, or they can hinder him. Most philosophies lead parents to do their utmost to discourage rationality and independent thinking in children, so that most grow up under a heavy handicap. However, no child can be turned away from reason for life. He cannot be marred forever by something he might have accepted at the age of five. No parent and no social background can determine a child's future rationality or lack of it. That is entirely up to the child.

In an Objectivist society, children will probably be the greatest beneficiaries. If a rational philosophy is dominant, it will be the responsibility of the parents—and they will know how to fulfill it—to teach their children a rational approach to values. And that consists of one simple principle: never deliver moral ultimatums to a child. Never tell a child: "This is good because I say so." Instead, always say: "This is good because . . ." Give the child a reason that he can understand. To train a child to be a rational valuer means always to give him explanations for anything you ask of him, or anything you advocate. That is the way to raise a rational child in a rational society.

Interviewer: *At what stage, then, should a parent, who is trying to educate his child properly, stop saying "Do this," and start saying, "Do this, because . . ."?*

AR: From the very beginning—from the time that the child learns to speak. To be more precise, it would be from the time the child can conceive of an alternative. At first—although I don't think a general rule can be made about this—a child may obey because he does not know any difference. But by the time he learns to speak, I believe that he already has some capacity to recognize alternatives. If a parent has to tell a child to do something, it means that the child has the comprehension of an alternative, of performing or not performing a certain action. If he has that much understanding, it is at that very stage that the parent must always be sure to explain, in terms of the child's knowledge, why a certain action should be performed. Let me stress that a parent must keep track of what is or is not understandable to the child—a task at which most parents fail, or never even give any thought to. One cannot lecture a child on philosophy, if it is totally outside his understanding. But within the confines of the child's knowledge, if he can understand the reason for a certain action, that reason should always be given to him. In specific cases of parents who follow this policy, I have observed—and most people would be surprised to learn—to what extent it works. The child does cooperate, and he thereby learns two things: responsibility for his own actions and the workings of cause-and-effect. He understands that certain actions lead to certain desirable or undesirable consequences. In this way, the child takes the first steps in acquiring the proper attitude toward action, reasons and knowledge.

Interviewer: *How can parents guard a child against improper influences, like salacious literature or bad playmates?*

AR: Regarding salacious literature, nothing a child reads will ever corrupt him unless his premises have already been corrupted by himself, his parents or others. A parent does not control every garbage can in town for fear that a child might start eating tainted food, and the same principle applies to intellectual food.

The parent should see that the child does not read books the parent considers wrong for him—remembering always that even if the child does read them, either he will not understand them or they will not affect him. What a parent has no right to do, though, is to attempt to reduce the whole country to the level of his ten-year-old, so that for fear that a child will read an inappropriate book, all of us are allowed to read only the literature suitable for ten-year-olds. The same goes for movies, television and every other activity. After all, a society is not geared to the requirements of any particular group of citizens, of any age, and certainly not to the requirements of children. It is the job of parents to provide the proper environment for their children and bring them up to be adults. It is not their right to demand that adults remain in a state of arrested development in order to protect their little children—who will not be protected by such a policy anyway. In other words, the desire to censor adult material for fear that it might adversely influence children is merely a parent's attempt to escape from his own intellectual responsibility—to escape by the fashionable means of declaring: "There ought to be a law." The advocates of this approach are saying: "If you do not know how to raise your children, just use force against others, including book publishers and booksellers, and you might solve your problem that way"—which, of course, you won't. I am against censorship of any kind, even of pornography, which I loathe; but I would fight to the death for the pornographer's right to publish whatever he wishes. If there are people who want to buy pornography, or people who don't know how to protect their children from it, let the responsibility be on their heads, not on ours.

As to association with bad children, this is a wider problem, which really involves the question of how to inculcate the right values in your child. If you are educating your child properly, he will not be subject to the influence of so-called bad playmates. In fact, he will not even select them.

Interviewer: At what point does the parent's right to choose the child's method of education end? At what point should the child be able to choose for himself?

AR: Legally, at twenty-one or eighteen, or whatever the official age of adulthood is. But if you are speaking morally, the parents don't have that power even when the child is five. In other words, even though the child is obviously not free to escape and to go to another school, if his teachers give him only limited, slanted information—as would be the case in a religious school—that education will not take. No education can condition a child's mind to such an extent that he is unable to think for himself. Even the worst education in the world cannot cripple a child's mind entirely—just as the best education will not force a child to think if he doesn't want to. An inferior education will only bore him and delay his progress. But he can overcome this obstacle if he chooses to use his mind at all.

On this point, let me address college students directly. Aren't all of you victims of our educational system, to a certain extent? I sympathize with you enormously. If you learn anything at all, if you come out of college today with something more than what you went in with, it is only because you exercise critical judgment. It is only because you do not blindly accept whatever your professors say. All of you are handicapped, because college education is in a state of chaos. The worst aspect of it is that in every classroom you enter, you confront a different epistemology. There is no one, basic epistemology accepted as proper within any university, and therefore the fundamental *method* of thinking differs from professor to professor. In the formative, college years, when a man establishes his thinking, you should be learning a proper, orderly epistemology. Instead, you are constantly subjected to chaos. Just as you begin to hope to understand one professor, you enter the next classroom, where the professor is on totally different premises. None of the professors has a clear-cut system, and they all contradict one another.

There are exceptions, of course, but there isn't a university today that is exempt from this kind of trouble. All that any student can do is what I said before: exercise critical judgment. Do not think that you are in a religious school, where you must accept as dogma anything your professors say. Above all, do not blame yourself if you do not understand your professors. This is the one piece of advice I am very eager to give to all college students. The modern Kantian epistemology is devised to give you an inferiority complex. It is so deliberately irrational and unclear that a conscientious student often reproaches himself for not grasping it. You sit in class and you do not comprehend what the professor is saying, but you look around and everybody else seems to understand. So you think the fault is yours. But everybody else is looking around with the same thought in mind. And that is what I want to warn you against. If I can help you at all, this is probably the most important advice I can give: do not assume that others understand when you don't; do not even assume that the professor understands—or intends to—since understanding is not one of the objectives of education today. Use your mind fully. Try to understand. But when you begin to be convinced that your professor is guilty of contradictions, note that fact very carefully and do not start to doubt the efficacy of your own mind.

Romantic Literature

The role of a fiction writer is to present things, not as they are, but as they might be and ought to be.

Interviewer*: What is the Objectivist definition of art?*

AR: Art is a selective re-creation of reality according to an artist's metaphysical values. By "metaphysical values," I mean those that deal with man's fundamental relationship to existence—those pertaining to the nature of man, the nature of the universe in which he lives, the foundation of his proper values. Fundamental questions of that kind belong to the science of metaphysics, and it is with metaphysical values that art is primarily concerned.

Interviewer: *And how would you define Romantic literature?*

AR: Romantic literature accepts a formulation by Aristotle as its basic principle: the role of a fiction writer is to present things, not as they are, but as they might be and ought to be. It is literature based on the idea that man has volition, and is able to direct the course of his life and achieve his values. It concerns itself primarily with the role of values. Romantic literature presents life in terms of man's pursuit of values and his dealing with value-conflicts—not conflicts between a helpless creature, which is man, and some sorts of external forces. The formal expression of such an approach is a plot. The defining characteristic of Romantic literature is a basic plot structure.

Interviewer: *If art re-creates reality, would you then say that fantasy is not art?*

95

AR: No, not necessarily. Fantasy is merely a selective, exaggerated way of expressing some view about man's position in the universe. Fantasy is a proper form of art, provided it has some intelligible meaning. A fantasy that you can translate into broad fundamentals is a legitimate form of art. But a fantasy for fantasy's sake, which does not apply to man in any way and is not translatable into human concerns, is bad art.

Interviewer: Do you consider Atlas Shrugged *to be a Romantic novel?*

AR: Yes. I call myself a Romantic Realist. Like the Romantics, I am concerned with the role of values in human life. But the traditional Romantics of the nineteenth century accepted a code of values—altruism—that was inapplicable to man's existence, and therefore very few of them dealt with actual problems of their time. A signal exception is Victor Hugo's *Les Miserables.* Predominantly, though, serious Romantic literature has been escapist, in the sense that it deals either with distant historical periods or with issues irrelevant to man's actual existence. And that is why I also call myself a Realist. I am concerned with human values applicable to man's existence on earth today. I deal with real, contemporary problems, but in terms of a rational, Objectivist code of values.

Interviewer: In Les Miserables, *as I understand it, reason was one of the least important values for Victor Hugo. In the way he organized his plot and in the way he motivated his characters, his driving interest seemed to be passion and emotional imagery. Do you think this is a general Romantic trend?*

AR: Certainly not. When I refer to the school of Romanticism, I am speaking regardless of the particular values or the particular morality a Romantic writer might select. For instance, I disagree with Hugo's philosophy almost from beginning to end, and yet his sense of life—his emotional, subconscious view of man and of existence—is closer to Objectivism than that of any other writer. Hugo has a great conflict between his conscious, alleged convictions and his subconscious, true ones—true in the artistic sense, because every man writes from his subconscious sense of life. In some cases, a man's subconscious values correspond to his conscious, rationally validated values, and he has no conflict. There are such writers, though not many. In most cases, though, a writer's sense of life and his conscious convictions clash badly. In Hugo's case, he was not a thinker at all, and his philosophy is full of contradictions. But what directs his writing is his sense of life, which saw man as heroic, as possessing free will, as capable of controlling his destiny and therefore motivated by his chosen values. Philosophically, this view is incompatible with some of his professed beliefs, but it is the dominant element in his writing—which is why I admire him.

Interviewer: You defined Romantic literature as re-creating reality as it might be and ought to be. In an ideal, Objectivist society, where that which might and ought to be, actually is, would there still be a place for literature, or for art itself?

AR: That is a very mistaken question, on several counts. To begin with, the most that an "Objectivist society" could mean is one in which the dominant trend, philosophically, is Objectivist. But you surely cannot mean that the establishment of such a society will automatically make everybody in it rational and moral. This is almost a Marxist viewpoint—the notion that a social system determines the intellectual convictions and moral character of its members. It does not.

Furthermore, an ideal Objectivist society would demand of its members much more independent thinking and rational consistency than any other type of society. It would impose a much heavier burden—if you want to call it a "burden"—of thinking. When you live in a free society, you have to stand fully on your own. You have to know exactly why you agree with the dominant philosophy, if you do. And you have to carry the thinking further. You need to understand what has been demonstrated as true so far, and then proceed as an innovator to expand human knowledge, not to contradict it—because now it does not grow by contradiction. The formation of your character will not be guaranteed at all by the ideal society. It is still entirely up to you to grasp moral values and to apply them. And this is where you would need art, perhaps more than in any other society—if there are degrees of such need—because the function of Romantic art is to concretize and to project for you the values that are essential to the proper life of a human being.

Incidentally, I do not mean that in such a society there would be nothing but Romantic art. There might be many schools of art, but the dominant trend would favor Romanticism. People would enjoy it much more than Naturalistic studies, and certainly more than studies of human depravity. But there would be no laws prescribing what art or literature should be. It would be up to each individual to decide for himself, and you would have a wider variety of viewpoints in such a society than in any other.

Interviewer: But if people are already living by the proper principles, do they still need art to convey what might be and what ought to be?

AR: There are two aspects to the function of art, and your question focuses on the lesser one—on the didactic aspect, on the role of art in teaching man what an ideal way of life is. That is really art's minor role. Its major role is to project the ideal as an end in itself, to provide man with the sheer pleasure of contemplating that ideal. Whatever any individual may learn from art is fine, but it is a secondary consequence. The primary purpose of art is contemplation for contemplation's sake, and the better the man, the more he needs it. Man needs to contemplate the concretized ideal as an inspiration, as a value in itself—and that is the function of art in an ideal society.

Interviewer: To amplify your definition of Romantic literature, would Shakespeare, Kafka or Huxley be considered a Romantic author?

AR: No. Kafka's writings are morbid examples of fantasy symbolism. They are not Romantic literature. Shakespeare's work is more Classical-Naturalistic drama. He is Naturalistic in the sense that he simply takes man as he is, rather than as he might be. Shakespeare sees man as a deterministic being, as the helpless pawn of destiny. He sees man as destined by his nature to be ruled by tragic flaws, which will ultimately defeat him. In Shakespearean tragedies, man is not in control of his life. He is moved, not by values, but by circumstances and by that inner fatality.

Huxley is a very bad writer and perhaps as bad a thinker. Or rather, he is not a thinker, but a mystic. What he writes is a mixture of unintelligible symbolism and the lowest type of Naturalism. He also treats man as a deterministic entity. He copies man's ugliest aspects, exaggerates this hideous view and then adds symbolic horrors. This approach is true of all modern literature, and observe how Naturalism, with its denial of values, leads to it. The process begins with presenting men "as they are"—which means: as any writer happens to have observed some men in real life—and then replacing values with wild, incomprehensible, mystical symbolism of a very malevolent kind. Huxley is a good example of this transition.

Interviewer: In your interview for Playboy *magazine, you said that one of the worst things about contemporary literature was its indulgence in the study of depravity. But couldn't one learn a great deal from a study of depravity, by critically evaluating it?*

AR: One might, but the purpose of art is not to educate you. You may learn something from an art form, but its main function is to portray man's nature and his relationship to existence. Further, you can learn something from the study of depravity only if you have some idea of the *positive* standard—the standard by which you are able to evaluate certain actions as depraved. You cannot grasp a negative without first upholding some kind of positive. In this respect, we can learn a lot from Dostoevsky, whom I would classify as a Romantic. He presents the negative, but from a strongly moralistic standpoint. Dostoevsky presents man as he might be and ought *not* to be, and he makes very clear that man ought not to be the type of character his novels depict.

But the modern school of depravity presents evil sympathetically. Its basic principle is that man cannot help it—that no matter how depraved man gets, fate, usually in the form of "society," makes him so. That is, people who are not depraved somehow make the depraved person what he is. In any case, modern literature is full of compassion for the depraved on the grounds that the poor little so-and-so couldn't help it. That is not a moral viewpoint, nor is it even one from which you could learn anything.

Interviewer: Could you give some specific examples of authors of this kind of writing?

AR: I read so very few of them, but Nabokov would be an example. Faulkner would be another example. And there are many lesser ones, including the authors of practically any modern novels.

Interviewer: You described yourself as a Romantic Realist. Are there any serious Romantic writers today whom you would not consider escapist?

AR: No, not yet—but there will be.

Romanticism versus Naturalism

Philosophically, *Anna Karenina* is the most evil novel in world literature, at least among the major works that I have read.

Interviewer: Our topic is Romanticism versus Naturalism in literature, which will be explored in part by contrasting the novels of Victor Hugo with those of Leo Tolstoy. Miss Rand, how would you define the terms "Romanticism" and "Naturalism"?

AR: Romanticism represents the school whose basic principle is that the purpose of literature is to present things as they might be and ought to be. Romanticism is concerned primarily with man's value choices. It is based on the premise that man has free will—that he has the power to choose his values and to achieve them, and that his life is shaped by his own choices. Therefore, Romanticism deals with universal principles of morality and of human psychology, which apply to man as such—to a metaphysical concept of man in any era and in any circumstances.

Naturalism is the school based on the premise of determinism. This is the idea that man's life is determined by forces beyond his control. Predominantly, though not exclusively, Naturalistic novels see man as the passive product of his social environment. Thus, value choices are excluded from Naturalism's metaphysical view of man. The purpose of Naturalistic literature is, in effect, merely to record whatever the author has observed in any given period or any given circumstance. The author is actually supposed to be a reporter or a photographer. By the way, the term Realism is sometimes used interchangeably with Naturalism. But that creates a confusion. I prefer to draw the division between Romanticism and Naturalism.

Interviewer: Isn't the character of Levin in Leo Tolstoy's Anna Karenina *an example of Romanticism more than of Naturalism, since he makes choices affecting his future?*

AR: Not really. You could say more accurately that Levin is somewhat of a satire on a Romantic character. In other words, this is Tolstoy's view of what a volitional man would be like, and it's not a very impressive or flattering portrait. Levin is not a very convincing idealist, nor does he amount to very much. He is a rather futile character who is not really in control.

Interviewer: In Victor Hugo's Les Miserables, *police inspector Javert holds the value of the law very highly and he sticks by it consistently throughout his life. Would you say that he is a character one can respect because of that?*

AR: This is more a moral than a literary question. As he is portrayed, Javert is too petty a man, in a way, for the grandeur of the concept Hugo wanted to present through him. Javert pursues Jean Valjean, the hero, across a whole lifetime. The reason for the pursuit is a minor, almost technical infringement of the law. Javert, who is supposed to represent the grandeur of the law, sacrifices his life ultimately over a trivial issue.

Now, in part, this may be Hugo's precise intention, since he wants Javert to symbolize the idea that when the pursuit of justice, with its ruthless single-mindedness of purpose, becomes the pursuit of legalistic technicalities, it defeats itself. It becomes a contradiction of justice. Therefore, for Hugo's thematic purposes, the character is presented brilliantly. But if you ask, "Can one respect such a character?"—I would say yes and no. Given the pettiness of the particular events that prompt the pursuit of Valjean, Javert's motivation is not the kind for which you would really respect a man.

But Javert does rise to the stature of a giant at the end, when he commits suicide because he sees himself caught in the conflict between his concept of legalistic justice and a higher, moral justice. When he discovers that Valjean has performed a heroic action, Javert is torn between the necessity to arrest him and the admiration he feels for Valjean. Javert lets him escape, and then commits suicide—which is one of the most dramatic scenes in the novel and a magnificent illustration of how a great Romantic writer dramatizes a moral abstraction in terms of a single event. But whether Javert makes an appealing character is a somewhat different question, to which I would answer: not very—not until that climactic scene, when he achieves a spiritual grandeur that he has not exhibited in the rest of the novel.

Interviewer: Javert chose the law as a value at a very early age and never re-examined his choice. Do you think that when he found out he had to question it, he couldn't go on existing?

AR: That is true. He took the law as an absolute, and never gave any thought to its moral base. And that is the conflict that destroyed him.

Interviewer: When the title character in Anna Karenina *pursues what she feels will be her ultimate happiness, doesn't she go through the kind of existence that could be portrayed only by a Romantic writer—one of striving for, and often attaining, a better life?*

AR: No. Philosophically, *Anna Karenina* is the most evil novel in world literature, at least among the major works that I have read. There may be a lot of modern junk that is much worse philosophically, but one couldn't consider such books seriously. But among grand-scale novels—that is, among classics with serious themes—this is the most morally evil. Now, this fact does not necessarily detract from the book's literary quality. But you are raising the issue of the theme, and the essence of *Anna Karenina* is that it is the most profoundly anti-Romantic novel ever written. When you say that the book has a Romantic theme because Anna is seeking personal happiness, you are focused on one aspect in isolation. The pursuit of happiness itself does not yet constitute a theme. The theme has to say something *about* the issue of happiness—and what this novel is saying is that it is futile to be motivated by happiness.

I want to stress this, and I am glad for the chance to express my view publicly. I have been frustrated over this issue since the age of sixteen, when I first read *Anna Karenina*. It ruined my reading habits, if you want a slight biographical aside. It took me longer to read that thing than *War and Peace*, a much bigger book and one that I do not particularly admire but that I find more value in. *Anna Karenina* took me six months to get through. While I was reading it, I forbade myself to read anything else, because I knew that otherwise I would never finish the book.

The thing that antagonized me so profoundly is that practically every line, every characterization, everything—and there is a unity in this book, which does constitute a great work of art—is consistently employed for a very evil purpose. Every element of the book is united to show that it is futile to look for happiness. Anna is presented, not as a villainess, not as a woman who is just looking for some cheap adventures, but as a serious woman who is deeply in love. Her husband and her social life are portrayed as being extremely unsatisfying for a woman of that type. We are clearly shown that Anna is someone who is better than her circumstances, and that she is therefore miserable. Yet the author's message is as follows: "Right or wrong, you have to obey the social standards of your surroundings, even if they are irrational—even if you are miserable. Accept, submit and conform. If you attempt to rebel against social convention, you will be punished."

The most offensive element in the novel is the description of how the romance between Anna and Vronsky deteriorates, of how aimless they both become when they feel they have nothing to live for once they have been ostracized by society. In other words, they have no personal, creative aims of their own. Now, naturally, romantic love alone would not fill anybody's life. But what is appalling in this novel is the absence of any concept of an independent, creative existence. Tolstoy presents these two rebels as better than average types, and yet they have no goals in life. They have nothing with which to occupy their time once they are rejected by society. If you are acquainted with the Objectivist concept of "social metaphysics," this is the perfect novel to illustrate it—but from an *approving* perspective. Social metaphysics is a psychological neurosis, from which a majority of people today suffer, that places the opinions of others above the facts of reality. Tolstoy comes across as an arch-social metaphysician, because the sole meaning of *Anna Karenina* is: "Conform—right or wrong, you cannot exist without society." That, in brief, is my view of the novel.

Interviewer: Doesn't the character of Levin defy society and attain his happiness through his own work and his own mind? Isn't he portrayed positively, as achieving his purpose in life, while Anna doesn't because of the failing within her?

AR: Only on a minor, insignificant scale. In other words, his goal is modest. He is a kind of safe, average mediocrity, and as such he succeeds in his humble, little, plodding way. But what do you take as the flaw in Anna's character? I am asking, because I don't quite agree with you. Where is the flaw?

Interviewer: I think it's in her inability to do anything. She has no purpose in life, other than this affair with Vronsky. Eventually, her aimlessness turns into jealousy and causes the relationship between her and Vronsky to disintegrate.

AR: But if Tolstoy's purpose was to criticize Anna for this, she would be presented entirely differently. Tolstoy would have indicated that the trouble is not a woman who defies convention, but a woman who is non-productive. That is not the way he presents her. Incidentally, in that period of Russian history, the idea of a career woman would be practically inconceivable, certainly to a Naturalist like Tolstoy. There wouldn't be very much that she could have done in Russia, although she might have been able to do more abroad. Nevertheless, she could at least have had some intellectual interests, which in that period were beginning to appear even in old Russia. But Tolstoy does not present any critical analysis of her from that aspect. He does not present a lightweight woman who just isn't good enough to have any goals in life. Instead, he shows a passionate, serious, courageous woman who is looking for meaning in life and thinks she has found it in love. And the punishment she receives is not for loving a man, but for defying society. From the way the disintegration of the affair is written, Tolstoy shows very clearly that there could be no other end to that affair. He doesn't offer any indication that the trouble with these two is that they are just empty social parasites. No, the trouble is that they are social rebels. The novel's message is that there is no such thing as a world of independent goals. Someone like Levin is merely a safely conforming mediocrity; he is not a man of great stature; he is not a rebel. The rebels here are Anna and Vronsky, particularly Anna. And that is what Tolstoy is denouncing.

Interviewer: *In several of Tolstoy's novels, especially* War and Peace, *one encounters philosophical discussions that are not directly relevant to the plot. And in Hugo one finds a filling-in of historical details, which are also unrelated to the plot. Why does this occur in nineteenth-century novels?*

AR: The phenomenon in Tolstoy—where characters engage in lengthy, abstract discussions that have no relation to their own lives or to the progression of the plot—is a failing of Naturalism. Expressing the meaning of events in terms of action is contrary to Naturalism's basic premises. Naturalism holds that man cannot choose his own goals, and that events in a man's life do not have a purposeful progression, such as is required by a plot. Naturalism is opposed to a plot structure. If a Naturalist wants to express ideas in a novel, he has to present them in the form of irrelevant conversations. By the nature of his premise, ideas cannot be integrated into human actions and cannot direct the course of a human life.

On the other hand, Hugo's asides were more a convention of the nineteenth century. A great many writers felt it necessary to insert nonfiction dissertations on whatever subject they were dealing with in the story. This technique is a bad error. Literarily, it is unjustifiable and unnecessary. It is not a flaw in Hugo's novels, because if those discourses are omitted, the structure of the novel is perfect. They are merely elaborations by the narrator; they are not discussions by the characters. They are simply nonfiction essays by Hugo, brilliantly written, on various historical aspects of the period with which the story deals.

Why was this done? Since Hugo, Walter Scott and a great many of the Romantics in the nineteenth century were engaging in a totally new literary form—the Romantic plot novel—and were departing from reportorial writing, it is my hypothesis that this technique was an attempt to give reality to their invented stories. By showing a great attention to historical detail, by writing well-researched treatises in the middle of a novel, they were trying to anchor the story to reality. They were trying to convince the reader that even though the story was an abstraction, it was intended to apply to reality—that the author was not merely engaging in fantasy. These novelists were attempting to make their stories realistic, in a way that was really not necessary.

Interviewer: Is there a parallel between Anna Karenina *and* The Fountainhead, *in that both novels portray rebels against society?*

AR: You are right in only a very broad sense. In *The Fountainhead*, I take exactly the opposite moral viewpoint from Tolstoy's. Roark and Dominique are shown not only as being right morally, but as winning in practice. They are not punished for their rebellion. They actually triumph.

Interviewer: In Anna Karenina, *don't both Oblonsky and Levin show that Tolstoy was able to interweave a philosophy stemming from the hope of achieving something better in life?*

AR: I've already discussed Levin. As to Oblonsky, he is the worst representative of the conforming mediocrity. Here is this superficial, woman-chasing husband, whom his wife is supposed to forgive. Tolstoy's point is that if Oblonsky's wife is upset by her husband's infidelity, she is guilty of romanticism, because she shouldn't expect so much from a man. She shouldn't expect fidelity, and should simply put up with his cheating. Isn't that what Oblonsky represents? Why would you take him as representing a better type of person?

Interviewer: Because in his work, he was a very good official. And in his discussions with Levin about various social changes, they decide on improvements that might be achievable.

AR: But I would interpret it the other way. Oblonsky could be a totally immoral man in his private life, but might be a good administrator. To put it colloquially, this is the idea that there is some good in the worst of us, and some bad in the best of us—so let's not aspire to perfection.

Interviewer: *Why do intellectuals generally regard Romantic novels as "escapist," and Naturalistic novels as "realistic"?*

AR: The fundamental reason lies in modern philosophy, which has to influence esthetics—one of the branches of philosophy. The dominant schools of philosophy today are engaged in a war against the conceptual level of man's consciousness. Since they all repudiate reason, the Naturalists consider any abstraction—any projection of a broad, universal meaning—an escape. They are concrete-bound. Reality, to them, is only whatever you are able, by chance, to observe in your own backyard.

Abstraction—the projection of human potential, the projection from a small concrete to the wider implications embracing all of mankind—is contrary to modern philosophy and, consequently, to the trend of modern literature. What do today's thinkers believe Romanticism is an escape from? Well, it *is* an escape—an escape from being concrete-bound, although that is not what they mean. They think Romanticism is simply an escape from sordidness, because they see Naturalism as presenting the seamiest and lowest part of life, as if nothing better ever existed. If one writes—even in a Naturalist novel, though that is rare—about something good or valuable in human life, a true Naturalist will regard that as fantasy. Since he judges life statistically, reality to him is whatever is the numerically dominant type of man. Anything higher than the average is thus an escape. From what? From the gutter, from the mean, from the low. In fact, it is Naturalism that is an escape—an escape from abstractions, an escape from the necessity of seeing life from a broader perspective than the range of the immediate moment.

The Visual Arts

My favorite painting is Salvador Dali's *The Crucifixion*. . . . It expresses a glorified view of man, and of his relationship to existence.

Interviewer: Do you believe there is an objective standard for measuring esthetic quality in art?

AR: Every human activity can, and must, be judged by an objective, rational standard. So long as men are doing something, an objective criterion of judgment has to be involved. It is only a question of whether men care to discover it or not. But if their activity has any validity at all, it must be subject to rational judgment.

What is the criterion for judging art? My answer will have to be very condensed, because the subject cannot be covered in detail in a single lecture, let alone a single broadcast. The Objectivist definition of art is as follows: Art is a selective re-creation of reality according to an artist's metaphysical values. Observe that I am saying "re-creation," which does not mean a creation out of a vacuum, but a selective rearrangement of the elements of reality to convey an artist's metaphysical—that is, fundamental—view of man and of existence. This is the general criterion, applicable to all the arts.

Since art is a re-creation of reality, the individual branches of art have to be defined by the medium of expression each uses. Literature is a conceptual art, which re-creates reality by means of concepts, that is, words. Painting, a visual art, re-creates reality by means of color applied to a two-dimensional surface. Sculpture is a visual art that re-creates reality by means of a three-dimensional form made of a solid material. Music is an audible art, and its medium is the re-creation of metaphysical, or sense-of-life, emotions by means of sound produced by periodic vibrations of sonorous bodies. Architecture is in a class by itself because, although it is a visual art in one respect, it is part esthetic and part utilitarian. It creates an object, a building, for human use, but according to certain esthetic values. And then there are the interpretive arts—singing, dancing, acting, et cetera—in which the medium is the person of the performer.

These are the basic definitions of the branches of art. How then do we judge a particular work of art? The standard of judgment is implicit in the definition: we judge it by the correlation of ends and means. We judge a work of art, not by the philosophy it expresses, but by how well the artist has expressed a certain view, whatever it might be, through the means of his particular art. For example, when we judge a painting, we do not say that a painting with the right philosophy is superior to a painting with whose philosophy we may not agree. In judging art, we are talking about the *expression* of a philosophy, not the philosophy itself. We judge a painting by identifying how well the painter has conveyed his sense of life by the means applicable to his art—that is, in terms of paint applied to a two-dimensional surface. Has he projected a distinguishable, consistent sense of life, and how well has he done so? How appropriate are his means to his end?

This is still a very generalized description. To be more exact, one would have to define the standards by which to judge whether the painting is well-executed and well-integrated. Here, again, objective standards are definable, and they have been defined, but I won't go into that at present. It is sufficient to indicate the general rule: look for such things as consistency, harmony (in the sense of integration), purposefulness—all to achieve a non-contradictory effect.

Interviewer: Do you think an artist can judge can his own work objectively?

AR: If he cannot, nobody can. An artist *must* judge his own work objectively, and of course he can. Whether or not an artist does so, is a different issue—and, unfortunately, most do not. There is more mysticism in the field of art than in any other human activity. Most artists are trained to work by so-called instinct or inspiration. They are taught to create by indefinable emotions. That is a psychological flaw in most artists. To ensure a proper, conscious approach to art, it is mandatory that an artist be able to identify what he has done and to judge it objectively.

Interviewer: The Impressionists were the first painters who believed in what we might call "art for art's sake." They were motivated by a "sense of art"—that is, they were concerned with the materials they dealt with more than with their subject matter. What do you think of that approach?

AR: You mean a purposeless concern with means divorced from ends? Does that make sense? Can one arrive at anything by that method? You are saying that painters are concerned with "a sense of paint," rather than with what that paint is to be used for. If you talk about "a sense of art" in that way, you see that it amounts to nonsense, which, incidentally, is exactly what modern art has become. The Impressionists, though, were still tied to reality somewhat, but they were busy dissolving reality into pure sensations.

The excuse given by many modern artists is precisely that they care only about the process of art and not the object of art. Well, that would be like a worker who is concerned with his movements in digging a ditch, but not with the actual ditch. The actions of such a worker would be meaningless and purposeless. Art is not the activity of putting paint on a canvas, and paint itself does not constitute art. The putting of paint on canvas is not an end in itself, but a means to an end—the end being what that paint re-creates on that canvas. Therefore, you cannot be concerned with "a sense of art" while ignoring what art *is.* You cannot have a "sense" of an activity while denying the nature of that activity.

Interviewer: Is it valid for a painter simply to deal with the phenomenon of light?

AR: It's valid within certain limits. An artist deals with the whole sphere of visual perception, and re-creates that perception for a certain purpose, which he wants to express. Therefore, light is certainly one of the important elements in painting. But what is improper is context-dropping, where the artist, in effect, declares: "I will be concerned only with light." That would be like a writer who is concerned only with grammar and not what his sentences add up to.

Interviewer: One of the prevalent views among advocates of modern art is that art cannot be defined. Since Objectivism holds that all concepts are to be derived from facts of reality, what observed facts relevant to the artists and the person viewing art would give rise to your definition of art?

AR: The definition comes from observations of what kind of objects and what kind of activities constitute art. These observations have to begin with the first objects of art ever produced. This does not mean that you have to take into consideration everything that anybody might ever decide to call art. Rather, it means that you have to identify the essential characteristics of all art, as it has existed from the earliest time and regardless of the particular school of art to which the objects belong. You have to ask yourself: If this kind of object and this kind of human production have any meaning, what is it? This is the opposite of the modern approach, which takes the activity first and totally ignores the result of the activity. Today's attempt at a definition is to say, "Art is that which artists do." This of course leaves wide open the question of just who is an artist. Well, today an artist is anyone who is in with the ruling cliques that define him as an artist. That is the present situation with respect to the definition of art—but it certainly cannot be taken seriously in terms of esthetics.

Whenever you ask where the definition of any concept comes from, you have to look at the facts of reality which that definition is intended to identify. Here, you define your view of art and validate it according to the facts—the artworks and the activity that went into them—you observe in reality. Today's artists are departing from any reference to objective reality, as is made clear when they say that art is something that cannot be defined. I would say, in the widest sense, that what cannot be defined, cannot be done and should not be attempted. (Of course, one *can* define the work of non-objective artists—only, not in terms of art.)

Interviewer: If we had looked back in history and had found non-objective paintings among the ancient artworks, would that have given us reason to include non-objective art in the concept of art?

AR: No. If the early artists did nothing but non-objective art, their work would not give rise to the concept of *art*. It would simply be covered by such concepts as "dirt" or "junk" or "dabs of paint." Such activity would be categorized as making pointless objects or using paint without purpose—examples of which could be found on the floor of any paint shop, from the time that men began to manufacture paint. There would be no validation for calling such things art.

To arrive at the concept of art, you have to consider only those works that cannot be covered by any other concept—that is, by any other facts of reality. If you find a phenomenon, such as art, that is not covered by any concepts of utilitarian objects, and that serves a new kind of psychological purpose, then you can form a new concept. But if you had begun with nothing but non-objective stuff—which, incidentally, is how any child begins if he is given a box of paint—you would not identify it as art.

Interviewer: What is the psychological purpose of art that you just referred to?

AR: The purpose is implicit in my definition: the re-creation of reality according to an artist's metaphysical values. And by "metaphysical," I mean pertaining to the basic nature of existence or, more precisely, to man's relationship to existence. The psychological purpose of art is to concretize man's widest, philosophical abstractions—to represent to man, in the form of a particular object that can be grasped perceptually, a complex sum of conceptual abstractions. That is what an artist expresses when he creates a work of art. And that is what a viewer, or reader, derives from a work of art; that is the source of his pleasure.

Interviewer: If artists are supposed to represent their own values in their paintings, isn't it true that modern artists are in a sense representing their own lack of values in their paintings?

AR: Yes. You cannot usurp a legitimate human activity without being bound by its laws. When non-objective artists try to present meaningless chaos as if it were art, what they are actually presenting, and reflecting, is the chaos of today's philosophy of irrationalism. Only, since the irrational is the impossible, they are not creating a view of an irrational universe; they are destroying the very concept of a view of the universe. They are the product and the parallel of modern philosophy.

Interviewer: Then they do perform a useful function, in that they reflect the intellectual chaos of the modern world?

AR: Yes, you could put it that way. Only that's a pretty expensive way of performing a useful function. It's being useful by means of destruction.

Interviewer: Can a painter be justified in being an advanced photographer, simply recording in detail what he sees around him, with no higher purpose?

AR: The Naturalistic school of art comes nearest to that approach. And the error of that school is twofold. First, it is physically impossible to record every single little detail. Even a camera does not fully do it. The most Naturalistic painter still has to exercise a certain kind of selectivity. But second, an attempt at photographic representation conveys the view that man cannot select his values and can only observe and record indiscriminately. This approach projects determinism, which is at the base of all Naturalistic art.

Interviewer: Film has been defined as the combination of sight and sound to create an image. Is film a visual art? And if not, what category would you put it in?

AR: Film is a composite art, made up of an integration of other arts. But yours is an inexact definition, which doesn't lead us anywhere. For example, an audible art does not create an image. There is an obvious equivocation here. If film is only a matter of combining sight and sound in some unspecified way, you could have a magic lantern and play a recorder on the side, and call it all a film.

Film combines all other human arts that the medium can employ. Primarily, of course, it is a dramatic medium; therefore, it involves literature. It is presented visually; therefore, it involves painting. It involves sculpture and architecture, in the sense of the three-dimensional projection of sets. It involves acting, which is an interpretive art. It involves music, singing, dancing—any art form can be used in film. A similar art is opera, which combines drama and music, along with acting and singing. But film is a much wider composite; it is a sum of all the other arts. Therefore, potentially, film is probably the greatest of the composite arts. But I don't mean that any particular film has actually reached that level. No existing film has even approached the potential of this art.

Interviewer: Don't some of the possibilities of film—such as two apposed shots, cut next to each other to create something that does not exist in reality—necessitate a redefinition of art?

AR: I don't see how. Let's say the scene alternates between what goes on inside and outside a house. This technique does not change anything. It is still a re-creation of the elements of reality according to the artist's values. It is still a way of rearranging elements in order to convey a total. It is not unrealistic, because in reality we are able to see both aspects of the scene, only not in such quick alternation as we do in films. But that is the advantage of the art.

Interviewer: Many works of art done on a religious theme are very appealing. But isn't there a contradiction between mysticism and rational values?

AR: The contradiction is only apparent. I prefaced my remarks by saying that when you judge a work of art, your primary concern is not with the kind of philosophy it expresses. If you look at an object esthetically, you are not concerned with whether its philosophy is true or false, but with what the artist is projecting and how well he is doing so. Now, a religious philosophy may be irrational—and it is. But that is not our main concern when we consider a religious work of art, nor is it the artist's.

Religion was the primitive form of philosophy. Observe that most of the early artworks expressed religious themes. They had to, because art expresses a view of man's metaphysical relationship to existence—and that view was given to the artists by religion. Once they accepted it, that is the philosophy their artworks expressed—and with great power and talent.

Remember also that art deals with abstractions, and that a religious painting may therefore have a meaning much wider than that of a particular religious philosophy. For instance, my favorite painting is Salvador Dali's *The Crucifixion*, the one that hangs in the Metropolitan Museum. It definitely has a religious theme, but what the painting expresses is wider. It expresses man's triumph over pain. It expresses a glorified view of man, and of his relationship to existence. One can admire and appreciate the painting, whether one agrees with the particular religious theme or not. One can take in the wider abstraction, which every philosophical theme necessarily contains.

Interviewer: Can you give other examples of works in the visual arts that project an Objectivist sense of life?

AR: I wouldn't go so far as to say that *The Crucifixion* projects an Objectivist sense of life. That would be unfair to Objectivism and to Mr. Dali, who, if I can understand him at all, is very far from Objectivism. This painting does not have an Objectivist sense of life, but it has one that is compatible with certain aspects of Objectivism, namely, the glorification of man. If you want me to mention other paintings, it's very hard offhand. I can give you the names of some other good painters, though. Of today's artists, I would name Capuletti, a young, rising artist who is a student of Dali's and is very much in the same school. Of the classical artists, I would name Vermeer, not for his subject matter, but for his technique—for his epistemological sense of life, which projects the kind of rational clarity that is compatible with Objectivism.

· *16* ·

Cyrano de Bergerac

[*Cyrano*] is the greatest play in the history of Romantic literature. . . . The greatness of the play lies precisely in the fact that
the theme transcends the morality that is used to illustrate it.

Interviewer: In your writings, you have named Cyrano de Bergerac *as an
extraordinary example of Romantic art. But it seems to me that* Cyrano *bears
a strong relationship to non-Romantic art—for example, to Shakespeare's plays,
many of which feature a hero who possesses some fatal flaw that in the end destroys
him. In Cyrano's case, we have a man who was born with a physical defect. He is
influenced psychologically by it, and is unable to achieve his highest value, the love
of the heroine Roxanne. Is* Cyrano de Bergerac *really a Romantic play?*

AR: Not only is it a Romantic play, but it is the greatest play in the history of
Romantic literature. First of all, you are making a mistake when you compare
it to the tragedies of Shakespeare. The tragic flaw in Shakespeare is always
intellectual or psychological. The point of Shakespearean tragedies is that
man is defeated by a tragic flaw inside himself, which he cannot help having
and which destroys all his achievements. Man, according to the philosophy
explicit in Shakespeare, is not in control of his life. This is the premise of
psychological determinism.

A *physical* flaw, however, is not in the same category. The point of
Cyrano de Bergerac is to show a man's triumph over a physical defect, not his
defeat by it. Cyrano's failure to gain love does not contradict the Romantic
spirit. The fundamental principle of Romanticism is that a man has free
will. He has the power, as Cyrano certainly does, to choose his values and to

achieve them. The question is, however: what *kind* of values? No philosophy could claim that if a man realizes he has free will, he is guaranteed any value he wishes. There is no guarantee that even a man with a perfectly rational philosophy will automatically achieve everything he sets out to. There is no guarantee that a man, with or without a physical handicap, will attain happiness in romantic love.

But more than that, love is not the theme of the play. To judge the philosophy of a play, ask yourself what its theme is. And the theme of *Cyrano de Bergerac* is the greatest one in world literature: man's integrity. The play presents a man of perfect integrity, who preserves it to the end, in spite of the most dreadful challenges to his spirit.

Once you realize that this is the theme, ask yourself how the author would present it in the form of a play. How would he put it into action—which means: how would he dramatize it? If a Cyrano in real life never faced any obstacles, he would still be a man of integrity. Obstacles are not what create integrity; one does not have to be subject to tragedies in order to demonstrate one's integrity. But on the stage, you could not possibly present a man of integrity if there were no events that tested him. In order to isolate the abstraction that represents the theme, Rostand had to present his hero in the worst conceivable situations. He had to confront Cyrano with every kind of defeat, existentially, in order to show that the hero preserves his integrity.

This point is conveyed eloquently in the last speech of the play, when Cyrano knows that he is dying. He is fighting imaginary enemies—imaginary at this moment, but they are the enemies he had fought all his life: prejudice, compromise, stupidity. He declares that in spite of the fact that these enemies have robbed him of all rewards, both professionally and personally—despite the fact that they robbed him of fame and of love—there is something that he carries to heaven, untouched and unsullied. In the play, the expression is translated, unfortunately, as "my white plume." It is more eloquent in the French original, when he says "mon panache," which means a knight's Plume of Honor—a symbol of integrity. Cyrano is saying, "In spite of the worst that life could do to me, I have preserved, unbreached, my integrity." And he dies with full pride and self-esteem. That is the theme of the play. For a dramatization of human integrity, I would challenge anyone to imagine—let alone to execute—anything better.

Interviewer: *In the play the hero is physically ugly, and yet, in terms of his soul, is beautiful. Why did Rostand bring these elements into his play, and how do they relate to the theme of integrity?*

AR: In relation to the theme, this is another instance of Rostand's having to give his hero a handicap. If a man were rich, handsome and intelligent, and had all the advantages in life, there would be no way to dramatize any difficulties. Rostand had to show a man rising above his handicaps. He had to show how the worst that nature and society could do to him does not destroy his freedom of spirit, his moral capacity and his integrity.

But if the question is why Rostand chose to present such an issue in the specific form of a conflict between a man's physical appearance and his spiritual values—that decision was a result of Rostand's own philosophy. And I must say that the philosophy of *Cyrano de Bergerac* is disastrously wrong. It has two fundamentally false premises (which run through most of Rostand's works). The first is the Christian dichotomy of soul and body. Rostand, as evidenced in this play, strongly believed in this dichotomy, and presented a man of great soul who was handicapped by a somewhat deformed body. The second is the altruist morality. Observe that Cyrano acts throughout the play as an altruist of the worst kind. He sacrifices himself to the woman he loves, and even when he could have had her, after Christian's death, he lets her suffer and mourn her husband for ten years, without telling her that he is the man she actually loved.

It is interesting to note that one cannot dramatize a wrong morality convincingly. One cannot apply it to life and put it into action. Philosophically, this play is an enormous *negation* of altruism. It could almost have been written, though in different terms, by an enemy of altruism, because it demonstrates the futility and absurdity of an altruist morality. By his sacrifice, Cyrano achieved nothing but unnecessary suffering for himself, Roxanne and Christian.

All this is relevant, though, only if you are examining the validity of the play's moral premises. But it is not important when you consider the play as drama. The truth or falsehood of an author's philosophy is not an esthetic matter. You can take it up with the author in a philosophical discussion. And in any such discussion, Objectivists would have to disagree with Rostand's views, because integrity is hampered, and leads to tragedy, when it is placed in the service of an altruist morality. But for the purposes of a play, you must accept the author's theme as the criterion, and judge only his esthetic means. You must judge only how well or how badly he carries out his theme.

Here, Rostand's theme is one with which we can all agree: the importance of human integrity. The philosophical terms in which he chooses to present it, as well as the values he regards as being involved in a man's integrity, are secondary matters. The fundamental issue being portrayed is not the particular content of a morality, but man's relationship to morality as such. Even if the specific ideas on which he acts are wrong, Cyrano exhibits fidelity to his values better than any figure in dramatic literature. The greatness of the play lies precisely in the fact that the theme transcends the morality that is used to illustrate it. The theme does not belong exclusively to the morality of altruism—in fact, altruism makes it almost impossible to practice integrity in real life. Integrity is loyalty to one's values; esthetically, the specific values a man chooses are irrelevant. What *is* relevant is that Rostand's theme can be appreciated by any man of integrity, regardless of his particular morality—and that Rostand's theme is superlatively dramatized.

Interviewer: Is there a limit, however, beyond which certain philosophical assumptions in a work of art may be so odious to a reader that the work simply cannot be appreciated even esthetically?

AR: Yes. That point would come when the values involved are so contradictory that no dramatization is possible. They would not integrate into any kind of story and would lead to nothing but contradictions, so that the audience would not be able to accept any part of it.

The best illustration of this is today's cult of depravity in literature, with its demand for sympathy for the villains—that is, sympathy for human evil. Nobody could dramatize this view convincingly, neither in novels nor in plays. The demand for sympathy is a moral issue. Therefore, the author is using some element of morality. He is telling you that you ought to have good will, that you ought to feel kindness toward some creature. Simultaneously, though, he is showing you the creature as a moral monster. When he asks you to sympathize with cold-blooded murderers, he is asking you to sympathize with the destruction of morality. He is asking you to have moral consideration for evil. There is such a contradiction here that no rational person could regard it as good art. And the contradiction would infuse every part of such a work, and would forbid any sort of integration. Consequently, the artwork would never be convincing, even if one tries to grant the author's premises, because one cannot grant a contradiction. It is the author's premises, in such cases, that would destroy the work. They would take it out of the realm of all values, including esthetic values.

Interviewer: I'd like to explore the nature of Cyrano's altruism. Roxanne says she would die if anything were to happen to Christian, so Cyrano protects him and represents him by writing his letters. But why does Cyrano continue the deception once Christian dies?

AR: Actually, Roxanne said she would die, not if anything happened to Christian, but if she found that he was not the spiritual giant she hoped he was. She had fallen in love with his appearance and, not yet knowing him, had doubts about his soul. It is this love of hers, and her declaration that she would die if she were disappointed by Christian, that motivated Cyrano to try to fake reality by posing as Christian's soul.

His purpose in keeping up the deception even after Christian dies, is not made clear in the play, except in one beautiful line. And that gives you a clue as to what Rostand intended. When Roxanne finally discovers the truth, she says about Christian's last letter, which had been written by Cyrano: "The tears on this letter are yours." Cyrano answers: "Yes, but the blood is his." That, apparently, is what Rostand meant to give Cyrano as a motive. It was an issue of loyalty to one's promise. Remember, Christian was shot when he stepped out of the besieged camp in order to let Cyrano tell Roxanne the truth. Cyrano apparently felt that since Christian had died for his love, he, Cyrano, did not want to break his word to a dead man. It was a matter of honor to him that he not destroy the image of Christian in Roxanne's mind.

When Christian is dying, Cyrano is guilty of another white lie. He tells him that Roxanne had chosen Christian once she had been told the truth about their deception. Cyrano then continues living by that white lie. Morally, if you go outside the confines of the play, Cyrano's action is certainly as wrong as one could imagine, and it had tragic consequences. But his action is in the spirit of the play, and it fits the characters. Observe that all three characters involved are of enormous stature. They take intellectual, spiritual values very seriously. It was in service to one such value--protecting Christian's memory in Roxanne's mind—that Cyrano maintained the pretense.

Interviewer: Although Cyrano's defect was physical, it seemed to have led to a defect in his mental processes. He was preoccupied with the size of his nose, but it could not have been nearly as bad as he thought it was.

AR: You are taking a somewhat superficial approach. He did *not* make a significant issue of it, and it never influenced the crucial decisions of his life. He did not try to hide or apologize for his nose. In fact, he flaunted it. He was a realist about it. He made it a principle that he would not fake reality, so he admitted openly that he had a defect and refused to let people insult him because of it. He was brave and candid about it. This is not a man affected by a physical defect, in the modern psychological sense. A man who *was* affected would form psychological defenses, evasions, compensations, et cetera. Cyrano's physical infirmity did not affect his mind. He fully accepted his flaw as a fact of reality. And it did not, of course, motivate him in any major decision. The fact that he thought he could not have Roxanne's love would not change if, let us say, he did not have his long nose. If he were a man of normal appearance, but still the woman he loved was in love with someone else, he would be in the same position. The nose, in this case, is only a symbol; it does not affect the character's psychology.

Interviewer: But isn't Cyrano afraid of ridicule, which cripples his relationships with women? He says that there is no swordsman he fears, but that when he encounters a woman, he is helpless. Doesn't this stop him from expressing his true feelings for Roxanne, and then impel him to represent Christian, as the next best thing?

AR: He isn't afraid, in the sense of cowardice. Here, again, he is merely being a realist. As he states in one of the speeches, he has suffered ridicule all his life. He observes that in fact people do hold his appearance against him, and he acts accordingly. But he never feels hopeless. When Roxanne first sends her duenna to make a date with him, Cyrano is quite hopeful. He thinks that perhaps he has a chance. He never gives up hope, but he knows that he has a severe handicap, and he is a realist about it.

Interviewer: Broadly speaking, this play is a tragedy, and yet Rostand chose an almost comic framework for a great deal of it. Why did he do this? Does it help his theme in any way?

AR: No. The play, of course, is a tragedy, and the comedy in it is marginal. Ninety percent of the events are serious. The comedy is not an inherent part of the story, but it plays a significant role in the characterization. When you judge humor, you must always identify what is being laughed at. In *Cyrano* all the humor is directed at evils. To laugh at something is to deny its importance and to refuse to take it seriously. Cyrano laughs at stupidity, at compromise, at the conventional standards of morality of those around him—and his stature is thereby elevated. He rises above evil, and above misfortune, with a laugh. Rostand uses humor as a means of lifting his hero above the circumstances and the premises of those around him. It is a heroic type of humor, and Rostand even subtitled *Cyrano de Bergerac* "a heroic comedy." He did not mean "comedy" in the literal sense of the word; he really meant more to say "a heroic play."

· 17 ·

Favorites in Art

Siegfried, an old, silent German movie, directed by Fritz Lang
. . . is as near to a perfect movie as anyone has yet produced.

Interviewer: Miss Rand, we will be questioning you today about your tastes in the arts. But first, do you think that anything meaningful can be discovered about a person from his artistic tastes?

AR: Yes. In fact, I want you to attempt to derive my basic premises, or sense of life, from my literary and esthetic preferences. My own books here are omitted from discussion, because they are a different issue. Of course they would reflect the same sense of life, but try not to judge from what you know about my writing. Judge me only by the tastes that I have in the arts.

Interviewer: Do you like mystery fiction, and if so, what kind of heroes do you admire?

AR: I like mystery fiction very much. I would not, however, select it as my favorite type of fiction. It is not the type with which I most identify myself, or in which I feel most at home. But there are definite personal preferences I have in that area. My favorite author in the field at present, considering his entire body of work, is Donald Hamilton. His hero, Matt Helm, is my favorite "mystery" or "adventure" or "secret agent" type. I like the early work of Mickey Spillane—the Mike Hammer stories; I do not care for his newer series about the secret agent Tiger Mann. And I like Ian Fleming, who writes the James Bond books. I like the three of them in that order.

123

Interviewer: Is there a difference between these three heroes and the ones I like, such as Nero Wolfe and Hercule Poirot?

AR: Heroes such as Nero Wolfe or Hercule Poirot are not Romantic figures. By "Romantic" I mean: embodying certain values. Wolfe and Poirot embody only one value, which is the intellect or the deductive mind. Their personal characteristics are not very appealing. Whereas the three I like have heroic personalities. All three, in different degrees, certainly have ingenuity or mental resourcefulness, but that is not their exclusive characteristic. They are heroes in a wider, more complete sense.

Interviewer: Is that as a result of their philosophical premises? Or would you say that the difference is more that your three, by being involved in action, are more attractive as human beings than the strictly cerebral characters?

AR: The latter. They are more complete personalities. Each one's interests involve his entire personality, and he fights for the values he believes in. The rest of his life—granted, as presented in very primitive form in a detective story—feeds his main goals. Whereas Hercule Poirot, for instance, apart from his role as a detective, is a typical, little next-door Babbitt. He leads a very conventional life. Nothing distinguishes him from other human beings, except when he functions as a detective, in which role he has a brilliant mind. The same is true of Nero Wolfe, who spends his time growing orchids and being a gourmet who indulges in pleasures of the senses. Those activities constitute his life, when he is not being a detective. These two men are not very inspiring qua personalities. That is why they do not come across as heroic. With the three characters I like, however, such characterization as they are given shows that they live for their profession. All their other interests are subordinated to the one central goal, which is fighting for certain values in which they believe. And the fight personally *matters* to them—it is not merely a process of impersonal, mental deduction.

Interviewer: Then you would tend to identify more with the "whole man," rather than with someone who has one well-developed facet and leaves others undeveloped.

AR: That's right, except that the term "whole man" has dangerous connotations. I don't like the term. Let's call it the "consistent man." I do not consider valuable or attractive the development of any one aspect of a man at the expense of inconsistency in his other aspects. I think that a rational man has to be consistent, and therefore his leading values, whatever they are, have to be reflected in every facet of his life.

Interviewer: Do you like westerns or science-fiction at all?

AR: I don't particularly like westerns. I don't object to them, but such westerns as I have read have been extremely unintellectual. They depict men engaged in plain physical action and facing simple physical danger. There are no moral values or moral conflicts involved, except of the most primitive kind—the honest cowboy against the cattle rustlers. And the rest is just a physical struggle, with the two sides being established in very crude terms. Therefore, westerns bore me.

As to science-fiction, or any form of fantasy, I am interested only in the projection of something applicable to actual existence. I would like intelligent science-fiction very much, but I can't think of any that I have actually found. That is the hardest field of all to execute successfully. The science-fiction that consists in creating the impossible for the sake of the impossible—the kind in which men are put into fantastic situations which are contrary to reality or which cannot be translated into any abstraction applicable to reality—is the type I don't like. It also bores me, for the following reason: I am much too committed to this earth. I love this earth as it is, and as it might be and ought to be. Therefore, a radical departure into what might *not* be, doesn't interest me.

Interviewer: Most people classify westerns, science-fiction and mysteries together as escapist literature. Since you like mysteries and dislike science-fiction and westerns, do you think the classification is wrong? Or what do you think is the difference?

AR: I do think the classification is wrong generally. A much more exact classification in literature would be: Romantic versus Naturalistic. Romantic literature deals with man as he is, metaphysically, and as he ought to be. It deals with universals, with fundamental aspects of man's life. In that sense, it is only Romantic literature, on various levels of detail and depth, that is applicable to life. Whereas, Naturalism, which merely records what has happened or what choices some men have made, is a form of escape. It is an escape from the real metaphysical issues of life—into statistics and purposeless, non-valuing observations. It is Naturalism that I regard as "escapism."

Within the realm of Romantic literature, whether you prefer detective fiction, westerns or science-fiction—or you like them all equally—depends on what you get out of the basic premises of each type. But none of them is "escapist," unless what you seek in them is the unreal. If you specifically enjoy that which is not applicable to man, then your pleasure *is* a form of escape. But that is not true of these three categories of writing as such. It may be true of certain individual writers—but that is also the case with writers in any category of literature.

Interviewer: Which of the comedians of the last twenty or thirty years do you like best?

AR: To begin with, I don't like comedy very much. This doesn't mean that I am opposed to humor, but it is a secondary issue in my preferences. I am a very, very earnest person. I take things so seriously that humor is a marginal issue to me. I can tell you the type of comedy I like very much, though it wouldn't be of personal importance to me. It's the Ernst Lubitsch-type—the sophisticated, Romantic-plot comedy. But as to a particular comedian, I can't think offhand of any I like, neither male nor female. I can tell you the negatives, though. I can't stand Jerry Lewis. I can't stand Phyllis Diller, although she's quite clever. I can't stand any comedian whose style consists in making man look ridiculous, in appearing grotesque or in satirizing the essence of man—not any particular aspect of man, but man as such. That's the predominant kind of comedian today, at least to my knowledge.

Interviewer: Wouldn't humorists who makes fun of pompous figures in social and political fields appeal to you?

AR: I might find them amusing, but this is such an unimportant type of amusement that I wouldn't say I enjoy it. I might laugh, but I would forget the humor in the next moment and it would leave me empty. It is not representative of my sense of life.

Interviewer: Do you like satire at all?

AR: Moderately. I like certain types. But as a field, no, not particularly.

Interviewer: What about the theater? What preferences do you have? I take it you don't like comedies that much, and probably not musicals. Do you like only drama?

AR: I like certain types of comedies. And I like operettas, which are somewhat different from musicals. I like operettas by Kalman and Lehar. These are quite distinct from today's musicals, which are more satirical than Romantic. I like Romantic comedies, such as those by Noel Coward and Oscar Wilde. But I would never say that any of this—except for the operetta music—reflects my sense of life.

Interviewer: What do you think of the operettas of Gilbert and Sullivan?

AR: I can't stand them. That's a very good question, if you want to find out something about my premises. I am positively allergic to their operettas, both to the content and to the music, but particularly the music. The content is often very clever and witty, but the sense of life projected is so satirically anti-man, that there isn't a redeeming feature anywhere. It is as if Gilbert and Sullivan were laughing at everything about man. And therefore, the sound of their music makes me uncomfortable.

Interviewer: Would you say that underlying comedy in general is a premise that de-glorifies man, and that therefore there is no comedy with which you can identify?

AR: No, that isn't true at all. Comedy depends on what it is that you are laughing at. For instance, the Lubitsch comedies project an enormous benevolence. They laugh at human weaknesses or troubles, and the net effect they present is that man triumphs and that life is worth living. Humor as such is not destructive. But there is no comedy with which I would identify personally. There is no comedy I would hold as enormously important to me as an object of enjoyment. I take life much, much too seriously to enjoy a comedy that may achieve a proper end, and may present a proper message, but does so by light means. I am not interested in it; I think life is much more serious.

Interviewer: To switch the discussion to music, would you give a brief description of your preferences with regard to three composers: Beethoven, Wagner and Rachmaninoff?

AR: I couldn't give you a musical description, because I am not an expert on that, and because it's not fully relevant to what we are discussing. A musical description would be plain esthetics, and you are asking me here about my personal preferences. But I'll tell you what I hear in their music as their philosophy of life.

With regard to Beethoven, I am profoundly opposed to his music, specifically from the sense-of-life aspect. Esthetically, I can hear that he is a great musician. I have to acknowledge the skill with which he is presenting what he is presenting. But his music has what I call a malevolent universe. It is in essence the view that man is doomed, that he has no chance, that he cannot achieve his goals, that he cannot triumph on earth—but must struggle just the same. It is the view that has been called Byronic, because Byron is the arch-exponent of it. It's the belief that man must struggle even though he has no chance of winning, and that he must perish heroically. That is a malevolent view of man and of the universe, and that is what I hear in practically everything Beethoven has written.

I think Wagner, unfortunately, is enormously vulgar, so that a sense-of-life appraisal is almost irrelevant. There is a certain musical value in some of his compositions. I would not classify him as particularly great. His melodies, which are the element by which I principally judge a composer, are enormously lacking in originality or inventiveness. If you strip them of all their trimmings, his melodies are, with rare exceptions, street-organ or circus music. What Wagner makes his reputation on is precisely the trimmings—the technical, alleged virtuosity of his orchestrations, with a dozen leitmotifs all mixed together, amounting to nothing. What I hear in his sense of life is malevolent pretentiousness. It is not a profound view of life. It is the view of a manipulator, of somebody who is playing on the fringes, but does not really have much to say.

Of all the serious composers, Rachmaninoff is my favorite. There, I hear an enormous, heroic sense of life. Rachmaninoff projects that life is a difficult struggle, but that man will ultimately win. There is an almost tragic benevolence in him—tragic in the sense that there is always a massive struggle and sometimes a great deal of pain in his music. But he always projects the victory. Man is not defeated, as he is in Beethoven's music. Man triumphs—but at an enormous price. So Rachmaninoff does not represent my exact sense of life, but in the field of serious music, he comes nearest.

Interviewer: Of the three Greek playwrights, Aeschylus, Sophocles and Euripides, which one comes closest to your view of life?

AR: None. All of them are on such a malevolent and deterministic premise that what I have read of theirs, I have done only as a matter of literary duty. They bore me, quite frankly; I do not see great literary value in them. It is certainly necessary to evaluate them historically, for their time and place, but I have never liked them. Their basic sense of life is that man is a helpless pawn of fate. Some of their characters may be of great stature, even heroic, but their deterministic philosophy is antagonistic to my view of life.

Interviewer: You've said that you don't like Naturalistic literature. Would you have the same view toward the writing of history?

AR: Certainly not. History is a valuable science. The writing of history, qua science, is enormously important, as is any legitimate inquiry into any subject that has a rational value to man. It is precisely because history is important that Naturalistic fiction is not. The recording of what has actually happened, for whatever values we may derive from it, is the job of science. It is not the job of a novelist. And incidentally, it is Aristotle who made that point. He said that fiction is more important than history, because history presents things as they are, while fiction presents them as they might be and ought to be. There is certainly a scientific value in learning about things as they are. But it is on the basis of things as they are that we can go further—to things as they might be and ought to be, i.e., to things as we will make them. That is what I consider the most important function of a novelist. The job of a historian can be done very well by the historian—is not the province of fiction.

Interviewer: *Which are your favorite motion pictures?*

AR: My favorite is *Siegfried,* an old, silent German movie, directed by Fritz Lang. Although I dislike that particular legend (and it is quite a malevolent-universe one), this is as near to a perfect movie as anyone has yet produced. It is a perfect exercise in total stylization. There is not one frame of film that is accidental. The whole production is stylized to the director's central theme. Every movement is calculated. It is so beautifully produced that it is the only movie that shows the full potential of film as an art medium. It shows perfect integration of several different arts: literature, acting, dancing—even painting, because every frame of that movie, if you stopped it, is a perfect composition visually. Therefore, as an integration of all the potential possessed by movies, *Siegfried* is the highest example I have seen so far. The story itself does not represent my sense of life. But the perfection with which it is done does represent what I expect of art.

Interviewer: *Is this not a purely esthetic judgment of the kind that you did not want to make about Beethoven?*

AR: Yes and no. That's a good question. Yes, if it were only the technique of *Siegfried* that I admire. But this movie is more than technique. It is integration—the integration of purpose—which in itself is an enormous value. It is the view the director projects of man's complete control over life. It is the perfection with which he is able to take a medium and put every aspect of it under his control. That is a different issue from mere technical proficiency. It is the perfect integration of the various aspects of life in one medium, and that is what appeals to me personally.

Interviewer: *It's the fact that the movie was made in this way, rather than the movie itself, then?*

AR: In a way, yes. That's a very good way of putting it. I like the fact that this was made, rather than the particular story content.

· 18 ·

The Nature of Humor

You cannot laugh at the universe as a whole, because if *everything* is incongruous, there can be no such thing as incongruity—and there is no ground at all for humor. Everything cannot be absurd.

Interviewer: What do you think is the essence of humor?

AR: Let me take a little time to explain my theory of humor. Actually, it is not a theory that I originated; I have to give credit for it to an acquaintance of mine. Humor is an attribute pertaining exclusively to human beings. An animal's consciousness is not capable of such a thing as a sense of humor. What, then, is the root of humor? What does it express, fundamentally?

Humor rests on the fact that human consciousness is volitional. Man has to grasp reality according to certain rules, and he may be right or wrong. His consciousness is fallible. Yet it is vital for him to grasp reality correctly. To laugh at something is to deny its importance and to refuse to take it seriously. We laugh when two elements are present. One is the denial of the metaphysical validity of the object of laughter; the other—crucially important—is the denial of the efficacy of the consciousness involved. To put it more simply, every instance of humor involves some element of incongruity, of contradiction. Now, for something to strike us as incongruous, we have to know what is congruous, i.e., what is non-contradictory and real.

In most types of humor, the joke involves the denial of the validity of someone's consciousness. For instance, take the simplest, oldest kind of joke: Someone asks: "What does the buffalo stand for on the nickel?" And he answers: "Because it can't sit down." Here, the joke is at the expense of the

131

listener, who assumed that the question referred to some special purpose of the buffalo, which in normal conversation would be the implied meaning. And the answer comes by switching contexts and by telling the victim, in effect, that the answer was obvious, only he missed it. Therefore, it is the listener's consciousness that is out of control, or not efficacious.

Every pun you make involves the same procedure. You switch contexts— you switch the meaning on somebody's consciousness—and what then appears humorous to you is the inefficacy of that consciousness.

The same principle applies to comedy situations. Consider the basic farce set-up. You see a pompous dowager walking down the street, and she slips on a banana peel. This arouses laughter. Why? Because there is a switch. There is a contradiction between her pretensions—or the image she attempts to convey—and reality, which is, in effect, undercutting her pretensions and creating a breach of her dignity. In that case, you laugh at the victim—the dowager—who deserves to be cut down, and at her inefficacy in dealing with reality. She pretended something, and reality undercut her.

This is the essential nature of humor. It is obvious why it doesn't apply to animals. They have no such category as the efficacy or inefficacy of their consciousness. The question "Am I perceiving reality correctly or incorrectly?" does not apply to an animal, which has no self-consciousness; an animal has no awareness of the operations of its own consciousness. The question does apply, exclusively, to man.

From this psycho-epistemological basis, humor can take an infinite number of forms. Of course, its moral character depends upon what you are laughing *at*. To give the briefest summary of the basic categories, without going into the many subcategories and applications, I will quote a passage from *Atlas Shrugged*. Dagny Taggart wonders about the nature of humor as manifested in her brother Jim and in Francisco D'Anconia, and she observes the following: "Francisco seemed to laugh at things because he saw something much greater. Jim laughed as if he wanted to let nothing remain great." This represents the broad division between different types of humor. I regard as moral the kind of humor that laughs at something worthy of being laughed at—namely, something evil or vicious, which does not deserve serious consideration. The immoral type of humor is the kind that laughs at the good—that laughs at values in order to undercut their metaphysical significance and to undercut the consciousness of those who take them seriously.

This, in broadest essence, is my theory of humor.

Interviewer: I'm not quite sure I understand your reference to laughing at, or tearing down, something that is good. What type of good things might be attacked by humor that is not moral?

AR: Let me give you the broadest example: the phenomenon of today's theater of the absurd. What does it laugh at? At the nature of the universe, and particularly at man's consciousness. The purpose is to express the idea that man is incapable of grasping anything, that the universe is unintelligible to him and that man is ridiculous because he attempts to understand and fails. This is a case of laughing at something good. This is laughing at the essence, and at the most serious aspect, of man's nature.

Interviewer: I assume you're talking also about sick humor. You mentioned the example of the dowager slipping on the banana peel. But laughing, let's say, at a cripple who slips on a banana peel is another thing altogether.

AR: You are quite right. The sick jokes, which are always at the expense of some dreadful illness or suffering or death, are sick because they attempt to undercut the significance of things that are in fact very serious, and are not to be laughed at. If one laughs at a cripple falling, to what is one denying reality? The fact that he is a cripple? But that *is* a fact; if he falls, he is helpless and he suffers. That is not an object of humor.

Interviewer: In terms of immoral humor, the movement seems to have gone from questioning man's ability to cope with reality to questioning reality itself. Do you think this trend is coming more to the fore, and is a dangerous sign?

AR: I don't think it's dangerous per se; it's a consequence, not a cause. I think it's a revolting sign. I am not prepared to say whether this tendency is growing or not. But as I mentioned, every instance of humor involves the denial of a certain view of reality, and implies that there is a correct view. You laugh at a certain man or event, because it represents something contradictory and therefore incorrect. But when the moderns begin to laugh at the universe as such, the absurdity in their position is that they are laughing without any point of reference. You can laugh at certain things within the universe, which you assume is intelligible. You cannot laugh at the universe as a whole, because if *everything* is incongruous, there can be no such thing as incongruity—and there is no ground at all for humor. Everything cannot be absurd. It is only by reference to something non-absurd that we can judge certain actions, people or events as absurd. Just as the moderns have non-novels and non-heroes, which are called "anti-novels" and "anti-heroes," this sort of trend really represents *anti*-humor.

Interviewer: Is there any reason for the specific means we have of expressing humor? For example, why do we laugh, instead of having some other reaction?

AR: You are really asking why we are built in a certain way and not any other. That is like asking why we cry when we are sad. The answer is: because we are so constituted. According to our physiology, that is the expression appropriate to a certain kind of emotion. The means of expression are something within our nature; we cannot choose them. The physical sound of laughter is something determined by our physiology. What we are concerned with here, though, is the *psychological* meaning of that laughter. We're concerned with the nature of human consciousness, which expresses itself by laughing.

Interviewer: Well psychologically, then, why do we, for example, go "ugh" at a pun? I assume that's not an inbred reaction at all.

AR: No. If we say "ugh," that is just a conventional part of sub-language. What does it express? Disgust, or indignation or reproach toward the punster. It is simply a conventional sound, which is not quite a word, but implies what a word would have named.

Interviewer: Do you believe that much of today's humor, by such comedians as Bob Hope or Woody Allen, depends upon identification with a bumbling type of underdog?

AR: Not necessarily. Since I am not greatly addicted to humor, I'm not well-acquainted with modern comedians. I've seen Bob Hope on television, but that's about all, and I don't believe I've ever seen Woody Allen. So I couldn't answer with assurance. But as a general proposition, I don't think one has to identify oneself with the underdog in order to be humorous. Some humorists, however, may adopt that approach. Take Charlie Chaplin, the most famous one. He specifically identifies himself with the bumbling underdog. But observe the wider meaning. He presents his helpless little bum as a symbol of mankind. One's identification with a figure of helplessness implies that this is one's view of man and of man's destiny. And in laughing at the bum, or in putting yourself in his position, you project the bum's view of life and therefore pass a very negative judgment on the nature of man and of his place in existence.

Interviewer: Within the field of literature, where would you place humorous writing, compared with, say, Romantic literature?

AR: To begin with, there are Romantic types of humor. Romantic comedy is a very broad category, in which some very good works have been written. Take Oscar Wilde and my favorite, Noel Coward, as examples. They write

Romantic humor. It is benevolent humor. It laughs at problems that in fact are not serious, and it shows the triumph of the good characters and their values. But it laughs at the unpleasantness of life. It laughs at negatives. Therefore, Romantic humor is a perfectly appropriate part of literature.

There is a great school of literature in satire. Some of the best works in that field have been written under great difficulties, such as the threat of censorship in dictatorships or monarchies. When men are not able to offer open criticism, sometimes they get away with a great deal by means of satire, by presenting the evils of the time in a humorous form. And in that way, without having to be explicit about it, they deny the metaphysical significance of those evils. That is also a legitimate part of literature.

On the other hand, professional humorists are, almost without exception, unhappy people. Humor is a dangerous tool, particularly when it becomes one's basic tool. Since it consists in essence of negation, a humorist who spends his life looking at the metaphysically wrong side of things, at the inefficacy or errors of human consciousness, has a view of the universe that could make him nothing but unhappy. Or rather, I would put this in reverse: he starts with a bitter view of life, which leads him to express himself predominantly by the negative means of humor.

Interviewer: *Would you call this escapism?*

AR: That word is so dubious that I don't know whether I would use it. But from a certain aspect, yes. It is escapism from the responsibility of a serious and explicit expression of his criticisms.

Interviewer: *What do you think about the proposition that people who have endured suffering have to develop a sense of humor about things?*

AR: I don't agree with that at all. It is an unwarranted generalization. I don't think suffering leads to humor. Frustrated indignation—psychological or political—or the desire to engage in moral protest does lead men to the profession of a humorist, particularly a satirist. But a benevolent humorist, one like Noel Coward or Oscar Wilde, will have a different motivation.

But observe an interesting fact in this connection: the institution of the court jester during the Middle Ages. The only criticism permitted in that type of society had to come in the form of a joke. The jester was the only one who could insult the king, or disagree with him, and get away with it, because, by the nature of his profession, he was doing so as humor. Implicit was the statement: "Don't take me seriously." If he is not taken seriously, he can permit himself a great many comments that he could not make otherwise. He can permit himself things for which he probably would be executed if he didn't hide them under a cloak of humor. This is another indication of the unhappy or dangerous aspect of humor. It sometimes serves as a weapon for people who, because of outside circumstances or because of psychological factors, do not dare express their ideas except under cover of a joke.

Interviewer: Do you think one can tell something about the state of a society by the kind of humor that is prevalent?

AR: I would not take it as the main indication, but it certainly would be one eloquent piece of evidence about the general state of a given culture, at least of its mainstream. There are as many different types of humor as there are different expressions of serious art. But the type of humor that is characteristic of a particular time and did not exist in other times—yes, that would be a strong indication of the nature of the culture, which means, of course, the nature of its dominant philosophy.

Interviewer: You used the phrase "serious art," as distinguished from humor. Does that mean humor is an "unserious" art?

AR: No, and I'm glad you picked up on that. As I uttered it, I wondered whether I should qualify it. I simply meant to put "serious art" in quotes. But to be exact, I would have to say: "art dealing with serious subjects directly, without the method of humor"—which does not mean that intelligent humor cannot be part of serious art. I meant to refer more to the attitude taken toward the subject, rather than to the quality of the art.

Interviewer: Can humor really be benevolent? Isn't humor actually a way by which one avoids dealing with something, by engaging in the physiological response of laughter rather than choosing to deal effectively with whatever is being laughed about?

AR: No, not necessarily. To begin with, we're speaking about more than merely a physiological reaction. You can laugh aloud at certain things, but humor is wider than that. There are many humorous things at which one merely smiles. This is not a physiological issue; it's an intellectual-psychological issue. The use of humor is not necessarily a way to avoid dealing with a subject seriously, particularly not when it comes to satirical humor, which makes its point very explicitly.

Benevolent humor is like dessert at the end of a meal. If you feel happy, or you want to express a cheerful outlook, and you laugh at the appropriate subjects, you are merely expressing your fundamental attitude toward life. Laughter can become wrong only if you make it your *exclusive* expression.

Humor is such a broad subject and such a broad tool that you cannot make general rules like the one you suggest. It is true that humor *can* serve as an escape. But you have to examine individual categories of humor in order to make a judgment. The worst type of humor, psychologically and morally, is the type that hides malevolent, antagonistic statements—ones that a man does not have the courage to convey openly—under a laugh. You see that very often today. Let us say someone has no good reason to insult another person, and is properly afraid to do so, but he nonetheless wants to. He'll do it under cover of a joke, and then if caught at it or reproached, he will say, "Oh, don't take me seriously." That is the usual method of moral cowards, and that type of humor is enormously evil.

Interviewer: *In looking at real-life situations in our culture, does a serious person find much to laugh at today?*

AR: Only in a bitter or sarcastic way. There is nothing wrong in laughing, but nobody would laugh very cheerfully today. There is a great deal of the ludicrous going on, because there is a great deal of irrationality. People are guilty of a great many contradictions, and a great many of their actions are funny. Therefore, there is room for humor today, but it wouldn't be cheerful humor; it would be sarcastic or satirical.

· 19 ·

The Foundations of Morality

Mankind has always treated morality as if it were a mystical or religious subject. I claim that morality has to be a rational science.

*Interviewer: Most systems of morality rely for their validity on the concept of
God, of a transcendent author of morality. Without God, who or what determines
morality?*

AR: This is really an epistemological question. What you are asking in effect
is: "Without some mystical authority, where does man get his knowledge?"
Morality, along with the rest of the sciences we call the humanities, is not different in this respect from the physical sciences. You do not rely on revelation
in the physical sciences. One of the most important points in *Atlas Shrugged*
is that the trouble with the world is that men employ a completely different
approach for moral issues than for scientific issues. Morality, which is a code
of values and actions, has to be as rational as any other scientific discipline.
But mankind has always treated morality as if it were a mystical or religious
subject. I claim that morality has to be a rational science.

*Interviewer: If it is up to man to identify an objective moral code, what protects a
finite being from making an error in this process?*

AR: Nothing but his own intelligence and integrity. The issue here is the same
as in science, where man is also not guaranteed against error. Man has to arrive
at knowledge by a rational process. And that process is not infallible. Man can
make errors, and so he has rules by which he can trace his errors. The science

that provides these rules is logic, which is the art of non-contradictory identification. If a man makes an error in his reasoning, sooner or later it will lead him to a contradiction. By that means, he can know that he has made a mistake, can retrace the steps of his reasoning process and can unearth his error.

But logic is only a method. What do we apply that method to? To the material that comes from our senses. Reason is the faculty that identifies and integrates the material provided by man's senses. And the purpose of the most important branch of philosophy—the science of epistemology—is to provide us with the principles that lead to correct reasoning and enable us to arrive at correct conclusions.

Interviewer: Is there anything that provides us with scientific evidence for a system of morality?

AR: Yes, of course—that very reality which science studies and within which you have to act. Morality is a code of right and wrong choices. How will a man decide what is right or wrong? By judging the universe in which he lives. What are the facts? What choices are open to him? What kind of goals should he have and what should he do about them? How should he achieve them? All this material comes from the very same world that science studies. The purpose of morality is to provide you with a code of action—and you act in the physical world.

Interviewer: Is the recognition of an objective reality a prerequisite to a correct system of logic?

AR: Not only to a correct system of logic. For there to be *any* knowledge or consciousness, there has to something you are conscious *of.* That is the prerequisite—the inescapable axiom at the beginning of any science or of any question you may ask.

Interviewer: In your view, then, we must have a rational and objective set of first premises from which to work. How do you propose that all men learn to begin from an identical set of first premises?

AR: There are two very simple answers to that. First, as far as metaphysics is concerned, all men live in the same universe, they face the same reality and they perceive the same things. Second, as far as epistemology is concerned, all men are of the same species. We all have the same form of consciousness, the same method by which we are aware of reality, the same kind of cognitive apparatus. Therefore, since we have the same means of knowledge and we are observing the same reality, we can arrive at the same conclusions. Objectivity consists in arriving at conclusions that cannot be refuted by any rational means. "Objective" means that which corresponds to reality in man's mind. It means the human grasp of that which exists outside his consciousness, in the objective world. The same knowledge is available to all of us.

This does not mean, however, that all men will *want* to know. Therefore, it doesn't mean that we have to wait for all of mankind to accept the right morality before we are convinced that it is right. But it does mean that all men should be able to grasp the right morality, provided they are willing to make the mental effort. It should be, in principle, demonstrable to all men—which is different from saying that all men will be interested in the demonstration.

Interviewer: Even though we all perceive the same reality, men still approach reality in antithetical ways—altruistically versus egoistically, as one example. This indicates that all men do not proceed from that initial perception of reality to the same conclusions. Yet you say that men must grasp the first principles of reality, proceed through an objective system of logic and arrive at the same conclusions.

AR: Again, compare this to the situation in science. Observe that different people—certainly in different countries or in different periods of time—act differently in matters relating to physical science. They have different diets, they have different methods of production, et cetera. And in the life of each individual, you observe that he learns different things with each passing year. Now what does that mean? The widest abstraction pertaining to the issue of human differences is the fact that men are not omniscient or infallible. Men do not know everything, and the content of their consciousness is not always correct. In fact, particularly in today's world, it is predominantly as incorrect, and as evil, as it could be. All we can learn from the fact that human beings differ is what we can learn about ourselves introspectively—namely, that men do not know things automatically and they do not know them infallibly. Every human being has to acquire his knowledge by a volitional process of observing, thinking, reasoning, learning.

Very few men conscientiously go through that process. Most men act mainly according to their emotions, or they simply accept by osmosis whatever ideas are floating around in their culture. So there will be differences among men—but this fact has no relevance to the issue of what is true. Man has to pursue knowledge throughout his life if he wants to survive. The purpose of knowledge is to define, on a wider and wider scale, what is true about the world in which we live and how we should act in relation to it. Therefore, you do not start any inquiry by asking yourself: "How many errors have people made?" or: "How many people disagree?" You look at the facts and you ask yourself: "What is true?" Once you have discovered the truth, you may then be concerned with communicating it to others. But to arrive at the truth you have to use a process of reason—a process that will be available, and communicable, to other men. That is all that should concern you—not the fact that many of them may disagree.

Interviewer: You say that man's perception of what is true will lead him to a correct way of life. But how is it that man can perceive egoism as true and can also perceive altruism as true?

AR: You are forgetting the crucial importance of whether men arrive at their conclusions by means of reason or by means of non-reason—by feelings, intuitions, revelations or whatever other alleged sources of knowledge they may claim to have. The real issue here is that reason is a volitional faculty. Your senses function automatically in perceiving reality. We all see the same thing, with differences only in the efficiency of our senses. That is, we might have better or weaker eyesight, but we all see automatically. But we don't *think* automatically. In order to deal with reality above a baby's level, man needs a rational process, which he has to be willing to initiate. Most men are not.

More than that, most systems of philosophy, particularly in ethics, are deliberately irrational, on principle. They are *anti*-rational. With very rare exceptions, they denounce reason as limited, misleading or false. They advocate some form of revelation, which simply means the formation of ideas by means of emotions. If men do not function by means of reason, their only alternative—the only other psychological faculty they possess—is their feelings. But emotions are not tools of cognition. Therefore, men may evade facts. They all face the same reality but some may choose to fake reality, to lie about it, to perpetrate a fraud on themselves and others. That is possible to men. You have to consider only men's *rational* claims to knowledge, and then you have to judge whether they are true or false. But the mere fact that men make claims proves nothing. Claims based on emotions are of no importance whatever.

· 20 ·

Altruism

Altruists offer you a choice between sadism and masochism: either you torture others or you torture yourself.

Interviewer: *To begin with, how would you define altruism?*

AR: Altruism is an ethical system which claims that man has no right to exist for his own sake; that the sole justification of his existence is the service he renders to others; and that self-sacrifice is his cardinal virtue, value and duty. Altruism regards man as a sacrificial animal. The word "altruism" was coined by Auguste Comte in the nineteenth century to mean the placing of the interests of others above one's own.

Interviewer: *Many people interpret altruism to mean benevolence. Why do you think that altruism and benevolence are not the same?*

AR: This is a package-deal fostered by the altruists. It furthers their purposes to suggest that altruism merely means kindness, or benevolence or respect for the rights of others. I would venture to say that an overwhelming majority of people believe that this is what altruism means. They believe that if you give a dime to a beggar, you are an altruist. Nothing could be further from the truth. Altruism does not claim that you should help others when and if you can. It claims that you should subordinate your own interests to the interests of others and that others should take first place in your life as a moral duty. In that case, kindness is impossible. If it is your duty to give away your last penny to anyone who might need it, you are simply giving him his due. In

143

fact, altruists say that it is his right to *demand* your penny. Therefore, it is not an act of kindness or generosity or charity on your part; it is a moral duty. In reality, altruism makes benevolence among men impossible. If you have to regard others as mortgage-holders on your life—if their claims have to supersede any interest of your own—then you can feel nothing but fear and hatred toward other men, since they are a threat to your own existence. And if you do not satisfy their claims, you have to consider yourself morally guilty. That makes any authentic benevolence among men impossible.

Altruism entails other contradictions. There is no reason you should consider the benefit of others a value, if you do not consider your own benefit a value. Altruism demands that you regard everybody as a value except yourself. According to an altruist, no human being has any right to any happiness or any existence of his own; he has only the duty to serve others. Altruism regards men as objects of sacrifice for others. That is *not* a theory of benevolence. There can be no benevolence among men unless we recognize man's basic moral and political right to exist for his own sake, neither sacrificing himself to others nor others to himself—which is precisely what altruism denies.

Interviewer: Why would anyone accept altruism, under your definition of it?

AR: Very few people really do, but the theoreticians of altruism certainly accept it. Most people ignore the question and simply try to get by with a kind of amoral attitude. Most people do not have a consistent moral theory to guide them—that is, a theory they understand, accept and fully practice. To the extent that they do accept altruism, the reasons are many. The main one is that men realize that, so long as they have to make choices, they need some kind of moral code—a code to define the values and goals they will pursue. They realize the need, yet they have not been offered any code other than the altruist one. In one form or another, altruism has been the dominant moral theory of most societies in history. Such attempts as have been made by philosophers to devise a different moral code have been so impracticable that they could not offer any competition to altruism. Also, most people are afraid to be left on their own in moral issues—more so than in any other area of life. Men are not afraid to be scientists. In cognitive issues, involving the discovery of new knowledge, men are not afraid to stand alone in the face of nature. But in issues of values, they are terrified to have to stand alone and define what is objectively right or wrong. These are the most general reasons that men accept altruism, or at least pay lip service to it, but there are many others.

Interviewer: One common variant of altruism is the belief that you should help only those who are worse off than yourself. Is that at the core of altruism?

AR: I'll refer you to *Atlas Shrugged*, because I presented the issues there much better than I could here, impromptu. But to restate just the essence of my view—yes, that is what altruists hold. And the result is that need, pain, failure and disaster are made into the leading purpose and value in life. In other words, altruism amounts to the following principle, which you can see being adopted in politics today: If a man fails for any reason, whether through his own fault or through accident, that failure gives him a mortgage on the lives, the earnings, the property and the services of those who have not failed. The result is a hierarchy of values in which the zero is the dominant standard. To the extent to which a man lacks any values at all—material, spiritual or intellectual—he has a claim on his betters. To the extent to which a man *has* achieved any values, he is the sacrificial animal for any zero-holder who can present his lack as a claim against achievement.

Interviewer: Wouldn't a consistent altruist have to give up his possessions even to someone who is better off than himself?

AR: Altruism cannot be practiced consistently. A man who is a full altruist would have to find a cannibal village and offer himself as a meal, because that would be the only way he could make a total sacrifice for the sake of others while deriving nothing in return. A complete altruist is guilty of a contradiction every time he eats, because his morsel of food may be needed by someone else. The altruists try to get out of this by saying that you should reserve for yourself only the minimum necessary for you to go on serving others. But that in itself is a contradiction. What is the minimum necessary? But the main question is why life should be that way. Why should the needs of others have primacy over your own? This question, incidentally, has never been answered by any philosopher of ethics. The sole base of altruism has always been mystical. The alleged virtue of sacrificing to others has to be taken on faith, because a rational justification for it has never been, nor can be, offered.

Interviewer: Is it fair to say that an altruist would have to replace his own evaluations with those held by other people and that, consequently, nobody would be able to hold an independent value?

AR: Yes, of course. It has been claimed many times—and this is the base of any collectivist dictatorship—that just as you must sacrifice your material possessions for the sake of others, you must also sacrifice your intellectual integrity. Holding on to your own idea of what is true is attacked as a selfish action; you are urged instead to sacrifice your views to what others believe, or wish, is true. According to altruism, you must always agree with the majority, because it is selfish to hold out on the grounds of loyalty to your own convictions. That, of course, is the basic evil of altruism: the demand that you sacrifice your mind.

Interviewer: What estimate of oneself is implicit in the morality of altruism? And what are the psychological consequences of trying to accept such an impractical morality as altruism?

AR: The basic consequence is a total lack of self-esteem—or as near to total as a man can come and still remain sane and alive. A man who accepts the theory of altruism has to regard himself as being of no value. It is his self-esteem that he has to renounce on every issue, intellectually and spiritually. He must give up the desire to make something of his own life and to achieve happiness. The very idea of looking at oneself as merely a means to the ends of somebody else, whether it's one other person or the total of mankind, implies a lack of self-esteem. That is what happens at the start. And to the extent that someone attempts to practice altruism, he diminishes his self-esteem more and more. Now, what most people do is abandon morality. They decide that nobody can be perfect, and that they are pursuing their ideal "as best they can." They tell themselves that that they will not attempt to be consistent altruists, but will feel guilty and will sacrifice to others once in a while. This amoral kind of existence means the destruction of any firm principles of morality and of any firm base of self-esteem.

Interviewer: Isn't the sheer holding of an altruistic value a selfish action, since one is holding a conviction of one's own?

AR: No. You are mixing two categories, by equivocating about "selfishness." You are implying what is known as psychological egoism, which is the theory that anything you do is necessarily selfish because you choose to do it. That is *not* the standard of selfishness. Yes, your actions must be motivated—but a motivated action is not necessarily a selfish one. A selfish action, in the proper sense of the word, is an action consciously aimed at your rational self-interest. In order to take a selfish action, you have to be able to demonstrate logically why that action suits your own purposes. You have to demonstrate what it accomplishes for you. But the mere fact that you want to take a certain action does not yet make it selfish. Most people, in fact, spend their lives engaged in self-*destructive* action, which they nonetheless choose to take. Observe any neurotic, who is bound for self-destruction, yet is acting on his own emotions, on his own subconscious, irrational urges. That is not the definition of a selfish action. Emotions are not tools of cognition, nor are they moral criteria.

The fact that a man wants to do something does not tell us whether or not it is for his own, proper benefit.

Interviewer: The choice that an altruist offers is either being selfless and sacrificing yourself to others, or being selfish and sacrificing others to yourself. Is there a third choice?

AR: Yes, because that's a false dichotomy. The assumption behind it is that men's interests clash, so that the good of one man must be achieved at the price of the suffering of another—and therefore the issue is only whom to sacrifice. This means that altruists offer you a choice between sadism and masochism: either you torture others or you torture yourself. But it is their metaphysical view of man's position in the world that has to be challenged here. At the base of altruism is the view that man exists in a malevolent universe, where he is constantly threatened with destruction and disaster. Man is thus a doomed being, and his main concern has to be the avoidance of disaster, not the achievement of values. On this premise, one has to live—I was going to say, "like an animal," but that would be an insult to animals, because they do not live that way—by eating others or by turning oneself over to cannibals to be eaten.

One's self-interest cannot be achieved by the sacrifice of others. The idea that selfishness consists in sacrificing others is only a psychological confession by the altruists. The rational interests of men do not clash. They cannot be achieved by infringing the rights or sacrificing the interests of anyone. But I underscore *rational* self-interest, which is not determined by emotions, wishes or whims.

Interviewer: What consequences are there to a man's conceptual abilities if he tries to practice the morality of altruism? Is his ability to think warped in any way?

AR: Yes, of course. Altruism robs him of incentive, and places him in a contradiction. Man cannot do any kind of intellectual work if his basic standard is: "What do others want of me, and in what way can I serve them?" In the broadest sense, if that premise were accepted, there could not be any progress in a human society. The moment a man saved a bushel of potatoes from his harvest, instead of investing it in a larger harvest next year, he would have to give it away to those incompetent neighbors who were unable to grow their own potatoes—or, more often, *unwilling* to grow their own. The unable are a marginal issue in human life, and consist of a very small number of people. Predominantly, the issue of need is an issue of unwillingness to carry one's own weight and the desire to get an unearned share of somebody else's effort.

A man who accepted the altruist premise would never be able to rise above the lowest elements, morally and intellectually, in the population. He would constantly have to be concerned with sacrificing himself to them. It would be disastrous not only existentially, in the sense of stagnation, but also psychologically. A man could not function on that premise for very long. He would destroy his psychological efficacy, for lack of incentive and for being caught in an impossible contradiction.

Interviewer: Many people, after years of living by altruism, find that they are most comfortable when they are with people who are generally nice to them, who approve of what they are doing and so on. The altruist steps in and says, "Follow that up by making others your primary concern, and that's the way you'll achieve happiness." Will you comment on that?

AR: To begin with, whether or not people feel comfortable in a certain situation is not a moral criterion. I'm sure that cannibals feel very comfortable after eating a meal, but that would not be grounds to say: "You see, this is how happiness is achieved, so follow their example." Feeling a state of comfort is irrelevant to the question of whether that state is moral or immoral. That question must be answered cognitively, not emotionally.

But more than that, the fact that man wants the company of others is not a proof that man is fundamentally a social animal. It is not a proof that the primary in your existence is your relationship with others, which should then determine your view of yourself and of morality. Social relationships are a consequence of your own premises and values—they are not a primary. Who is society? It is only a number of individual men. And you will discover, theoretically and historically, that only to the extent to which men accept the premise of individual, selfish rights, and of each man's pursuit of his own happiness, are they fit to live in society. Only on that basis can they have benevolent, cooperative relationships with one another. But on the collectivist-altruist premise of placing the interests of the group first, you achieve only the destruction of yourself and of the group.

There is a journalistic issue I want to mention. Just recently *The New York Times* published a survey of the prevalence of drugs among teenagers, predominantly children of well-to-do families. This was not an issue of the evil influence of the slums, as the humanitarians always claim about such problems. This was happening among affluent youngsters, college students included. What the survey found was that in a shockingly overwhelming number of cases, young people start taking dope for social reasons. They take it because that is the fashionable thing to do and they want to be "in." They want to belong to the group. They are considered outsiders if they do not join. The desire to conform, in all the cases cited, was the dominant reason that teenagers acquired the dope habit. I think this is an extreme, but very eloquent, illustration of the results of placing the group first. I wonder how many people realized, in reading that story, that the education given to young people today—with the stress on belonging, on getting along with others—is responsible for this problem. If someone places the group first, he is going to accept as good anything the group does. And the leaders of such groups will not be able to arrive at any rational standards, either. The result will be some irrational, group standard of the good, such as taking dope—the most eloquent example of self-destruction.

Interviewer: *There are people who find that they can't get pleasure out of the productive activities in their lives. Could this be due to their having accepted altruism in any way?*

AR: Yes, on two counts. First, the idea of independent achievement is so frowned upon by the altruist morality that a man could be discouraged from seeking a career, particularly if his own ideas are not too firmly formed. More than that, the knowledge that he will be denounced if he succeeds will also discourage him.

But second, and more important, is the fact that altruism makes him feel that somebody will take care of him. He feels that it is not necessary for him to be productive or to take an interest in his own career. To the extent that he fails, he will become a first mortgage on the life of everybody else, which gives him an incentive not to succeed. Without altruism, many more people would realize that there is no escape from the responsibility of carrying one's own weight, of providing for one's own survival and of being productive.

Let me raise another aspect to this question. It is not true that everyone who is intent on a productive career is anti-altruistic. You will find that there are very productive people who function properly in their own fields, yet accept the morality of altruism. They are eager to give away a large part, sometimes all, of the results of their productivity. They are glad to have dependents, worthless relatives and dubious charity causes to support. Yet in their careers, they are acting on the proper principle of self-responsibility. Ask yourself why people like that support altruism.

There is a very important issue here. There are two types of unearned values someone can seek. One is the unearned in matter, the pursuit of which creates a simple financial parasite, who is supported by somebody else's effort. The other, which is much more complex, and more important here, is the unearned in spirit. After all, productive work is not the only aspect of one's life. A man may be very productive, but may be neurotic, confused or evasive in other aspects of his life. He may lack authentic self-esteem and he may try to buy it by means of altruistic actions. A self-made rich man who is anxious to be an altruist by giving away his wealth is seeking unearned admiration from others. He is a man who lacks self-esteem and believes, consciously or subconsciously, that he can derive a sense of his personal value from the gratitude or praise of others. In fact, nobody feels genuine respect for an altruist of that type, but it helps him maintain the illusion of a self-esteem that he lacks.

Psychologically, this type of man is more evil than the crude, material parasite. The men who are after the unearned materially are much less of a threat to mankind than the men who are after the unearned spiritually. The latter are parasites who want either political power over others by means of force, or social power by means of the alleged respect of others.

Interviewer: What is your view of sacrificing for "greater goals," such as dying when fighting for virtue, honor, morality—or for a country that one believes embodies these ideals, such as the United States?

AR: The answer lies in a careful understanding of what sacrifice is. Keep the definition clearly in mind. A sacrifice is the surrender of a greater value to a lesser one, or to a non-value. In other words, you perform a sacrifice when you give up something of great value to you for the sake of something less. The typical example is giving up some value of your own to somebody else who may want it. That is the altruistic form of sacrifice. Now, you want to know what is the motivation of men who die for a great cause. The first question to ask yourself is whether men have a self-interest in great causes, such as patriotism. And the answer is obviously yes. If you have a free country like the United States—and even though it's not fully free now, it was and can be again—isn't it to your most personal, selfish interest to protect and maintain that free system? It is not a matter of indifference to you whether you live in America or under some monstrous dictatorship. The United States, then, is conducive to your own selfish interest, and if it is being threatened, you have to protect your values. It is to your interest to fight for a free country, because the alternative will affect you personally in a dreadful way. And, in reason and morality, you cannot expect someone else to fight for a value that you need. You have to fight for it yourself. Therefore, when a man dies for what you call a great cause, he is fighting for his own values and ideals, and is in fact is performing, properly, a very selfish action. He is declaring, in effect, that he is unwilling to live on any terms other than those he considers right. He is unwilling to live as a slave.

Interviewer: Let us enlarge the analogy from dying for one's country to dying for an even greater cause: mankind.

AR: "Mankind" is not a cause.

Interviewer: If we sacrifice for our country, you say we are sacrificing for our own betterment.

AR: I say that it is not a sacrifice.

Interviewer: But if one sacrifices for mankind, is that not also for his own betterment?

AR: What do you mean by "sacrificing for mankind"? Let's make it more specific, because I believe you misunderstood a certain point. When you risk your life for your country, it's not for the geography that you die, nor for the other citizens in that country. You are dying for your own personal way of life, since you know that the alternative would be expropriation, enslavement and murder. Therefore, you are literally fighting for your life, since you have to live somewhere. Now, what specifically do you mean by "dying for mankind"?

Interviewer: I don't mean dying for mankind, but rather sacrificing for mankind, because when you raise the level of mankind, you raise your own level.

AR: That is where your fallacy is. The opposite is true. When you raise your own level, in the sense of any rational achievement, a secondary consequence is that all mankind profits, each person to the extent of his own rationality. When you attain any rational goal, it is of benefit to other men because they too gain a value from it—new knowledge or a new product. Every discovery you make as an individual is a benefit to others. But you cannot reverse that process. How would you go about improving all mankind first, and only then profiting by that improvement? If you are able to improve mankind, it means that you already are in an advanced position—that you are a leader who can convey something of value to others. But you cannot say, "I am not able to improve mankind, but I will die in the attempt to make that improvement and I will learn something from it." It is an impossible process.

Interviewer: If someone who has great potential as a leader in the field of business instead enters the field of teaching and raises the level of mankind through the sacrifice of his own material wealth or comfort, is this not a good thing?

AR: No, it would be the most evil thing he could do. The rule you should use is this: the profession that feeds your own interest is the one you would be best at. The sacrifice of the businessman who becomes a teacher would be senseless.

What advantage is there in educating a lot of people if nobody can profit by it? You are projecting a situation in which we would all be educated—but would be starving, in rags and in the gutter, because nobody would be in industry. In other words, there is no such thing as benefiting other men at the expense of a leader. If a leader is a man of value, then what he chooses to do in pursuit of his *own* interests will be of greatest benefit to everybody. There is no moral justification for his choosing to do something else, nor would he achieve any good result by doing so. Sacrifice is *neither practical nor moral*. What kind of cannibalism would make you assume that a great man is not entitled to the profession he prefers, just because others need his services more elsewhere—even granting your premise that they do? Their need is not a mortgage on his life.

· 21 ·

Individual Rights

The alleged right to a minimum sustenance means that a man, with no effort on his part, is entitled to sustain his life . . . [i.e.,] that some men are to be enslaved to the minimum—or maximum—needs of others.

Interviewer: You have spoken favorably about the right to freedom of speech and other human rights, but I take it you would not agree with the usual list of rights so much publicized these days, such as the right to a minimum standard of living, the right to a free education, et cetera. What's the basis of the distinction? Can you define the term "right" in such a way as to make the distinction clear?

AR: A right is a moral concept, applicable only in a social context. On a desert island the question of rights would not arise, even though the question of morality certainly would. On a desert island a man needs a moral code, a knowledge of what is right or wrong for him to do, as much as he does in society. But the concept of rights pertains strictly to relationships among men. It is a social application of morality.

Rights are conditions of existence required by man's nature for his proper survival. By "proper survival" I mean the survival of man qua man—survival in that form which his nature as a certain kind of living entity requires. The question of what conditions of existence are necessary for man's survival is a metaphysical one, which rests on the nature of reality and the nature of man. Just as man cannot properly survive on the desert island by random means, so there is only one proper way for him to survive in society: by means of rights. The principles naming what he may or may not do in relation to other men

153

have to be derived by the same standard and from the same definitions as the principles of ethics. When he deals with others, the conditions required for the proper survival of man—not "mankind," but every *individual* man—constitute his rights.

What does man's nature require for his proper survival? Above all, that he use reason. It requires that he make his perception of reality his first concern and his basic virtue, and that he act on the rational judgment of his own mind. There is no way for him to provide for even his simplest needs without a process of thought. By his nature, man has to support his own life by his own effort. Since survival is not automatically provided to him by inanimate matter, nor is it granted to him as manna from heaven by some superior power, man must work for his own survival. His life depends on his own actions. In order to survive in a social setting, therefore, he has to have the *right* to his own life. If man's survival qua man is our standard, then it is right for man to support his own life. In order to do that, he has to be free to act on his own judgment. Therefore, he has the right to freedom. In order to decide what goals to pursue, he has to be free to choose his own values and then achieve them if he can. Therefore, he has the right to the pursuit of happiness. And since man is not a ghost, but an integrated entity of consciousness and matter, he needs material goods in order to survive. He has to sustain his life by the product of his own effort. Therefore, he has the right to property—the right to work for his own values and to keep the result of his work.

This is the basis of individual rights, as I define them. I reject the two current fallacies on this issue. I reject the idea that man is endowed with rights as a gift from God. The supernatural notion of rights has undercut and invalidated the very concept of rights. And simultaneously I reject the modern substitute for the mystical view of rights—namely, that the source of rights is social, and that rights are privileges bestowed by society. To claim that rights inhere in society is a contradiction in terms: if an individual doesn't possess any rights, then there is no way for society to possess them, since society is only a number of individuals. But more than that, if rights inhere in society, then an individual man exists not by right, but by permission. And society may revoke that permission any time it chooses. The social theory of rights is thus a total *denial* of rights.

Let me return to the original question about why I would not recognize the "right" to a minimum standard of living and so on. That idea of rights is a contradiction. It demands, as a right, values that in fact do not belong to man in nature. The alleged right to a minimum sustenance means that a man, with no effort on his part, is entitled to sustain his life. Since nature does not provide man automatically with this sustenance, the only way to implement such a right is to deny the rights of other men—to charge some men with the unchosen responsibility of supporting the one who is to be guaranteed a sustenance. This means that some men are to be enslaved to the minimum—or maximum—needs of others. Not only is this a vicious concept, but whatever you might wish to call it, it cannot possibly be a right. Nobody can have a right to the unearned. Nobody has the right to claim any minimum guarantee, because it can come only from other men—and nobody may claim the right to enslave others.

Interviewer: *Would you say that government has any rights?*

AR: Government as such, none. Government officials are men, and they cannot have any rights different from those of every other individual. All rights have to be universal, pertaining equally to all men. There is no other way to make the concept of rights tenable or even intelligible. Rights belong to an individual and, since they are derived from his nature, the same rights belong to *all* individuals.

Yes, in his official capacity, a member of government does have certain obligations, but so has every man. For instance, a businessman does not have a different right to life than does, say, an artist; only the forms in which they implement their rights differ. In the same way, a government official does not acquire any new rights when he undertakes his job. So the government, as an institution, has no rights. But in a free society, the government is the agent of the citizens, and it has the delegated right to act for them—in very specific issues. I won't go into a discussion of the proper functions of government, except to say that its basic task is to protect individual citizens from those who initiate physical force. Therefore, the government possesses delegated rights. But in and of itself, it can have no rights.

Interviewer: *Your ethics is based on the requirements of man's survival as a rational, productive being. Some would argue that since sheer physical survival is a precondition of everything else, people should be provided with a minimum standard of living. That is, if you let people starve and die, no other, more worthwhile form of survival is possible to them.*

AR: This argument is a blatant case of context-dropping. I have gone to great lengths, in both "The Objectivist Ethics" [in *The Virtue of Selfishness*] and in *Atlas Shrugged*, to demonstrate the meaning of man's survival. The sense in which I use this term applies not to the range of the immediate moment, but to the whole span of a human life. A life based on a standard of brute survival of the moment usually ends with that moment. Living that way is one of the most disastrous policies that man can adopt. When I speak of survival, I speak of the long-term, lifespan survival of a man in every aspect that is open to his choice. This means that at no time can man hold some immediate benefit above his knowledge of the long-range cost. A rational being does not live like an animal, on the range of the moment. This is precisely what man's proper survival forbids.

You say that if we do not support certain people, they will die and nothing else will be possible to them. But this is not an issue open to our choice. Man's position on earth is such that if he does not provide for his survival, nature will not take care of him. Therefore, the universal, rational law of morality applicable here is that every man is responsible for his own survival and that he cannot become a mortgage on the life of another man. For you to have the right to life does not mean that someone else has to lose *his* right and spend his existence supporting you. The confusion here is between the right itself and the *result* of that right. If you have the right to live, it means you have the right to work and to produce the material goods required for your survival. It does not mean that somebody else must produce those goods for you just because you need them.

Interviewer: What about people who are handicapped and cannot provide at all for themselves?

AR: Since by definition, they can survive only through the assistance of others, they cannot make their need a mortgage on the men without whom their own survival is not possible. If anyone were sincerely concerned over the plight of the handicapped—who, incidentally, are a small minority of mankind—then for their sake, if for no better reason, he should leave the productive and able men free, since they are the only ones who can provide for the handicapped. Any such provision can be nothing more than an act of charity. It can come only from voluntary gifts—from the surplus of the productive man, when and if he wishes to help. If he has reason to wish it, his assistance may be a very fine act. But it is not a *duty* on his part, and is not a *right* of the handicapped. A right has to be based on nature. The handicapped are handicapped. They can count only on the kindness of the non-handicapped to help them. They cannot demand it as a right.

Interviewer: That leads me to an economic question. What would happen if we had a system of laissez-faire capitalism, with only one exception: a law providing relief for the poor?

AR: Exactly what is happening today. The answer does not need to be too theoretical; you can see the consequences in practice. But let me make the theoretical point briefly. Allowing this exception amounts to establishing the principle of collectivism and altruism. Such a law would be based on the idea that some men have the right to claim an unearned, involuntary support from others. This is the principle that makes a man's life, liberty and property subject to the will of society. There is no other basis on which one could justify such a law. The process could then not be stopped until the whole of society collapsed into totalitarian collectivism.

We have already seen a small example of this in a foreshortened, accelerated form. The idea of supporting the needy at public expense was started in 1933 by the Roosevelt Administration. At that time, the claim of those who advocated it was that we have to help—temporarily and under emergency conditions—just the one-third of our own nation that was, according to Mr. Roosevelt, ill-fed, ill-clothed and "underprivileged." This was certainly an improper, altruist-collectivist premise, but people consented to it mainly because they thought that we are a wealthy nation and these are our own citizens. Out of kindness, most people accepted this type of superficial reasoning.

It did not take even a whole generation before we were made responsible for every famine or emergency anywhere on earth. And now we are no longer asked just to help the needy of our own country in an emergency. Instead, we are told to assume permanent responsibility for the welfare of all mankind. We are told that we have no right to our own standard of living until we industrialize, at our expense, every backward nation in the world. If we discover Martians who, instead of being more advanced, are more backward than we are, we would have to support them also. But by that time nothing much would be left of a free society. This is why a principle is an absolute, permitting no exceptions. You cannot, out of charity, sympathy or any other reason, introduce an evil principle into society and impose it on people by governmental force.

Interviewer: *Often people ask whether you would have let all those people starve in 1933. I take it that your view is that, had there not been all the governmental meddling in the economy in the first place, no such crisis would have occurred.*

AR: Exactly. All depressions are the result of government interference in the economy. The depression of 1929 in particular was due to the credit policies of the Federal Reserve Bank. The solution was to decontrol as rapidly as possible. Only there weren't enough thinkers and statesmen at that time to propose such a course.

Interviewer: *So government is called upon to cure the disease that government itself has caused. Would that be a good way to put it?*

AR: Yes, and you see the same thing going on to this day.

Interviewer: Nevertheless, the disease is there. Doesn't it then require government action to cure it?

AR: This is like asking, with deadly germs in your system, whether you shouldn't take a dose of even more virulent germs as the cure. Obviously not. It is not government action that is required, but the *repeal* of government powers. The approach to social or economic troubles should be the same as in medicine, or any other field: before you attempt a cure, you must discover the cause. And if you discover that the cause is a long series of government controls, then the only cure possible is to start decontrolling and removing those causes, one by one.

Interviewer: During this process of decontrol, which would have lasted several years, do you think thousands of people in the United States might have starved?

AR: No, certainly not. To begin with, they were not starving. The United States has never known what starvation really is, in comparison with what has happened in Europe and the rest of the world. Private charity would have taken care of any actual acute need. But above all, what was needed was more opportunity for employment. For that, you must set free the men who are able to create jobs—the businessmen, the industrialists, the financiers. You certainly do not chain them at the time you need them most. Of course, morally, you should never chain them.

Interviewer: It is sometimes asked whether all men should have bread before any men have caviar. I think your answer would be: "In order for all men to have bread, some men must have caviar." Would you agree?

AR: Emphatically. That is what I would answer if I could think of such a good remark so quickly. Yes, that sums up my view perfectly.

· 22 ·

The Ethics of Objectivism

> You cannot claim values if you do not value the *valuer*. . . . To value anything other than your own life *as a primary* is a contradiction in terms.

Interviewer: You uphold an ethics of egoism. The term "selfishness" creates a mental block and evokes feelings of guilt in most people. They can't understand, for example, how personal relationships could exist under your ethics. Do you think that love or friendship should be unselfish?

AR: Friendship and love, particularly romantic love, are the most selfish relationships possible. But I have to elaborate. People do get blinded with guilt when they hear the word "selfishness." This is one of the cultural charges that I bring against the doctrine of altruism. It has convinced men that if they do not want to sacrifice themselves to others, the only alternative is to be some kind of Attila and to sacrifice others to themselves.

The first thing a man would have to do in considering the Objectivist ethics is to define his terms fully and precisely, and to put aside any emotions, particularly guilt, until he understands what he is dealing with. Then he may examine his feelings, but his feelings are not tools of cognition. He will certainly never understand the Objectivist ethics, or any ethics, by means of guilt. An emotion of guilt is the most destructive to a man's mind. A guilty man is barely capable of thinking. Guilt is certainly one emotion that should be put aside when one wants to consider an ethical system. Any guilt he may feel is the product of altruism and of the doctrine of original sin—the view that man is depraved by nature, and so should embrace the role of sacrificial animal.

Since no man with any remnant of self-esteem would welcome the role of sacrificial animal, guilt is perpetuated in him. He knows very well that he does not, and should not, want to be a victim, and therefore he is blinded with guilt over his selfishness, which is in fact the best part of him: his self-esteem.

Now let me define "selfishness" as Objectivism sees it. After establishing man's life as the standard of morality, the Objectivist ethics begins by saying that since man can survive only by his own efforts and since his capacity to value is a condition of his nature as a living being, he can live only for his own sake. He can live only by taking himself as his highest value, as the goal of all his efforts. Why? Because that is where his valuing capacity comes from. To claim that you value service to others as a primary, above your own interests, is a logical contradiction. You cannot claim values if you do not value the *valuer*. If you attach no importance to yourself and your own judgment, you have denied the base from which your capacity to value comes. To value anything other than your own life *as a primary* is a contradiction in terms.

The next step is to determine what is to be done with that primary. How do you implement it? What does it mean to live only for your own sake? The basic choice you need to make is to live by means of your own rational judgment and to be guided by nothing but reason. But above that basic level, the next choice you have to make is a choice of values. What kind of things do you consider valuable by a rational standard, and how do you want to pursue them?

One of the highest values to a man of reason and self-esteem is other human beings. Of any category in the universe, human beings are of greatest interest to him. It is only a man with an inferiority complex who despises mankind. Someone of self-esteem certainly values man, since he values himself. I don't mean that he loves his neighbor as himself, but that he attaches enormous value to man as a phenomenon. And the kind of man he deals with makes a great difference to his life. If he deals with nothing but morons, scoundrels, cowards and fools, there can be no pleasure and no advantage in it. Such men are only dangers or burdens to him, providing him with nothing but cause for contempt and boredom. On the other hand, if he can deal with men of ability, of moral character, of stature—if he can see in other men that which he values, if he can see in them the virtues he creates in himself—then there is a selfish gain to him, on several counts. On the practical level, it is to his advantage to deal with other independent, productive, intelligent men. On the so-called personal level, it is to his advantage to deal with men he can respect and admire.

If you believe that friendship or love has to be unselfish, it simply means that you do not care about people at all. It means that it makes no difference to you whether your friend is good or bad, whether he has virtues or nothing but flaws—that you are his friend only for what *he* can derive from the relationship, while you derive nothing, neither material nor spiritual. This is the most man-hating, most un-humanitarian view of human relationships possible. No one would care to be your friend if you literally told him, "I don't give a damn about you. It gives me no personal happiness to know that you are good or bad, happy or miserable, but I am very concerned only for your own sake."

It is in this sense that friendship, and particularly love, must be the expression of your most profoundly selfish values. It has to be the expression of the following premise: Men of virtue, men who represent your own standards, are valuable to you, and you enjoy them in the form of *personal*, not merely functional, relationships. By "functional," I mean involving a business exchange, as is the case with, say, your grocery clerk. All you expect from him is that he do his job honestly. You are not concerned about his person, beyond a general respect you grant to any human being—unless he has proved himself to be too evil to deserve even that. You do not expect a personal relationship; you merely have a functional relationship involving a certain exchange of services or goods. In personal relationships, however, it is the value of the person as such that is of selfish interest to you. If you don't value the person in this way, you cannot be a friend, nor can you be in love.

Interviewer: What would you say to the so-called egoists who equate selfishness with cheating and lying to get whatever they desire?

AR: Egoism does not mean subjectivism, or what I call whim-worship. It does not mean that man has the right to take his whims as his standard of value. It does not mean that anything he desires to do is right just because he desires it. The subjectivist, or hedonist, approach to morality is precisely what Objectivism rejects. A man has the right to live for his own sake, but since a certain kind of policy is required for him to live, he must hold the right values. He cannot choose his values at whim—or rather, he can, but he will perish for doing so. Whim-worship is evil morally and impractical in action. A man has to choose his values by reason. When a man decides that a certain course of action is right, he has to be able to justify such action rationally—not simply by declaring, "Well, it's I who have chosen it."

Interviewer: Perhaps the word "egoism" itself is an unfortunate one, and should be abandoned, because of its historical associations.

AR: No, I want to redeem that word from the improper package-deal to which it's been subjected. If egoism means "acting for your own interest,"

I challenge the idea that following blind whims and emotional, causeless preferences is to your self-interest. No one could ever validate that as a moral principle.

Interviewer: In your book For the New Intellectual, *you speak of a rapprochement between the new intellectuals and the businessmen. What practical steps can the two take?*

AR: The intellectuals have to reject all the epistemological agnosticism so fashionable today. We have to reject neo-mysticism—the idea that our mind is impotent and that we act by means of subjective values, approximations, arbitrary postulates, et cetera. We have to adopt a rational epistemology, and then approach the practical issues of existence—the issues of morality and politics, of what actions are right for man and what is the proper social system—by means of reason. We need to follow logic, in the Aristotelian sense and as its meaning has been expanded by Objectivism. The content of such an epistemology has not yet been published in book form. However, those who are interested can get my fundamental epistemology—including its base in Aristotle and, at the same time, its differences in certain respects with Aristotle—from *Atlas Shrugged.*

Once we have this rational base, intellectuals should assume the responsibility of giving philosophical guidance to society. They should take the responsibility of translating their theories into reality and of never advocating contradictions or the kind of theoretical constructs that are inapplicable to reality. In a colloquial sense, I would say that Objectivism is a philosophy for living on earth—a purpose that should define the role of an intellectual. An intellectual should be the integrator of ideas and the formulator of principles for men in all other professions. He should be the leader, who shows them what to do.

On the other hand, businessmen should realize that they cannot function on the range-of-the-moment, merely dealing with material production and never caring about philosophy. They need to become philosophical. And the intellectuals need to discover practical reality. It is out of this trade that the integrative man of the future—or of the present, if any one of us wants to adopt that role—would come: namely, a philosopher who is also a man of action.

Interviewer: You criticize in some detail the philosophy, particularly the ethics, of Immanuel Kant. Don't you agree with Kant on at least two points? First, do you agree that morality is objective, and not—as contemporary philosophers believe—a matter of subjective taste?

AR: Yes. Only I do not agree with Kant's view of what constitutes objectivity. He is an arch-subjectivist epistemologically, even though he claims to be the opposite. But as to the basic principle that morality has to be objective—yes, I certainly agree with that. It's not a crucial point of Kant's system, nor is he the originator of that idea. I wouldn't call it agreement with him if I say that in this respect he was right in principle. But I would add that he was never able to implement the idea. He was never able to stick to the idea of an objective ethics, precisely because his view of what constitutes objectivity was so wrong.

Interviewer: Let me turn to the second point. A central principle of Kant's ethics is the categorical imperative, or the principle of "universalizability"—that is, you should act in such a way that you could wish your actions to become a universal law of human conduct. It seems to me that you too use this concept in discussing moral behavior. For example, you believe it is wrong for a person to live as a parasite. I assume you would argue that if everyone lived that way, there would be no producers left for the parasites to keep draining. So you do seem to appeal to "universalizability," and to have some common bond with Kant.

AR: No, I don't agree with that concept as Kant stated it, nor would I argue against a parasite in the terms you just outlined. In other words, I would not argue that if everybody was parasitic, then everybody would have to die, and so it's wrong. That would be the Kantian method. I say that the parasite exists only to the extent to which he takes advantage of men who are moral and productive, and that left to his own devices, without their support, the parasite would not be able to survive. That is what's wrong with his behavior. He is contradicting the requirements of his nature as a man. He is not supporting himself and, by my ethics, he is therefore immoral. This is not the same as saying that the proof of parasitism's evil is that all mankind would perish if all mankind were parasites.

I certainly subscribe to universality as a principle, in the sense that any moral law has to apply to all men equally. But I wouldn't derive it in the same manner as Kant. I wouldn't say that the test of morality is its universal application. I would simply say that morality, if it is to be a code applicable to a certain kind of living species, namely, man, has to apply to all members of that species. If it is not applicable to all men, it is debatable whether it could even be classified as a code of morality.

But now to criticize Kant himself—his law of "universalizability" consists of form without specific content. Two opposite actions could both claim justification by the categorical imperative, under Kant's approach to morality (and I give credit to one of the questioners here for having given me this illustration). If I say I do not want to assume the responsibility for anyone else's life, and do not expect others to help me if I am in trouble, I would be in accord with Kant's imperative. On the other hand, another man could say he is willing to accept a duty to help others when they are in trouble, in order to have the right to count on their helping him when he is in trouble. That also would be consistent with Kant's imperative. Here are two opposite choices that fit into the same Kantian formula. The real problem with his formula is that it introduces an element of the subjective—the element of a wish—into the basic imperative, as Kant calls it, of a morality he claims is objective. He says you must act as you would want all men to act. But what I or anyone else might *want* does not make it objectively right. A desire or a wish is not a proof of morality.

Interviewer: One form in which Kant presented his "universalizability" principle was: "Don't do what you could not wish everybody else would do."

AR: Again, that ultimately means subjectivism as the standard.

Interviewer: Kant qualifies this somewhat by adding that the principle refers to what a moral man could wish. But still, there are no criteria set forth by Kant to deduce, for example, whether one should choose to give help to others and expect it in return, or not to give help and not expect it.

AR: Exactly. Just as an aside, isn't it circular to say "what a moral man could wish," when you are dealing with the basic principle of a moral system? How are you going to be a moral man before you know what system of morality you should follow? This method assumes that you are moral before you have even learned what Kant offers as his basic moral premise.

Interviewer: One application of the "universalizability" principle is the golden rule—do unto others as you would have them do unto you. And I take it that you would similarly say about the golden rule that it might be applied in this way: "I will help you commit your crimes, because I would want you to help me in committing my crimes."

AR: Yes, and it is applied that way quite often today. The golden rule, incidentally, is older than Kant, so he is not original even in his categorical imperative. But the golden rule is simply a colloquial, non-exact, non-philosophical formulation of what I would call objectivity. That is, if you claim something is morally good, you must grant to other people the same status and the same rights you expect for yourself. In effect, the results of moral objectivity could be interpreted as conforming to the golden rule. But the golden rule would not be the premise directing your conclusions, because it also consists of form without specific content.

Interviewer: Bernard Shaw once said, "Don't do unto others as you would have them do unto you. Their tastes might be different."

AR: I quite agree with him. An exchange of undesired Christmas presents is the best colloquial example of that.

Interviewer: As a final question, what can each individual do to help achieve a more rational society?

AR: The answer is implied right in your question. He should first of all make himself as rational a human being as possible. He should clarify his own ideas; he should organize his own thinking into a coherent frame of reference; he should eliminate contradictions. He should convince himself of his own basic premises, and then proceed to enlarge his knowledge and share it with others to the extent he can.

Objectivism can be a great help to him. But I've always prefaced such a statement with the admonition that nobody should or can accept Objectivism on blind faith. I suggest to anyone interested in Objectivism that he study it, weigh its basic premises and convince himself by his own critical judgment that it is true. Then he can proceed to spread these ideas further by every means open to him—by private discussions, by sending letters to editors, by writing articles and books, by making speeches and giving lectures, by any means consonant with his own profession.

It is actions of this kind that constitute a culture. And if you want to change the culture, it is precisely by individual enlightenment and individual action that you can do so. And I will certainly wish you success.

3

ON TELEVISION AND RADIO: AYN RAND IN AMERICA'S LIVING ROOMS (1959–1981)

· 23 ·

"The Mike Wallace Interview," ABC-TV, 1959

You have no right to tell the man who produced the wealth how you want him to spend it. If you need his money, you can obtain it only by his voluntary consent.

Mike Wallace: Throughout the United States, small pockets of intellectuals have become involved in a challenging and unusual new philosophy that seems to strike at the very roots of our society. The fountainhead of this philosophy is novelist Ayn Rand, whose two major works, The Fountainhead *and* Atlas Shrugged, *have been bestsellers. Her point of view is still comparatively unknown in America, but if it ever did take hold, it would revolutionize our lives. To begin with, Miss Rand, can I ask you to capsulize your philosophy? What is Randism?*

AR: First of all, I do not call it "Randism." I don't like that name. I call it Objectivism, meaning a philosophy based on objective reality. Now let me explain it as briefly as I can. My philosophy is based on the idea that reality exists as an objective absolute, that reason is man's means of perceiving it and that man needs a rational morality. I am primarily the creator of a new code of morality that has so far been believed impossible, i.e., a morality based not on faith, not on emotion, not on arbitrary mystical or social edict—but on reason. It is a morality that can be proved by means of logic.

This is merely an introduction. Let me now define what my morality is. My morality is based on man's life as the standard of value. Since man's mind is his basic means of survival, I hold that if man wants to live on earth, he has to hold reason as an absolute. He has to hold reason as his only guide to action and he must live by the independent judgment of his own mind.

169

His highest moral purpose is the achievement of his own happiness. He must neither force other people nor accept their right to force him. Each man must live as an end in himself and follow his own rational self-interest.

Wallace: You put this philosophy to work in your novel Atlas Shrugged. *Let me start by quoting from a review that appeared in* Newsweek. *It said that you are out to destroy almost every edifice in the contemporary American way of life: our Judeo-Christian religion; our modified, government-regulated capitalism; our rule by majority will. Other reviews have said that you scorn churches and the concept of God. Are these accurate criticisms?*

AR: I agree with the facts but not the evaluations. I am challenging the base of all these institutions. I am challenging the prevailing moral code of altruism—the precept that man has a duty to live for others and to sacrifice himself for their sake. The institutions you name are a result of that morality.

Wallace: What do you mean by "sacrifice"? You say that you do not like the altruism by which we live; you like a certain kind of Ayn Rand-ist selfishness.

AR: To say that I "don't like" altruism is too weak. I consider it evil. Self-sacrifice is the precept that man needs to serve others as a moral duty, in order to justify his existence. That is what most people believe in today.

Wallace: Well yes, we're taught to feel concern for our fellow man, to feel responsible for his welfare, to feel that we are, as religious people might put it, children under God and responsible one for the other. What's wrong with this philosophy?

AR: You've named what turns man into a sacrificial animal—the idea that man must work for others, concern himself with them or be responsible for them. That is the role of a sacrificial object. I say that man is entitled to his own happiness and that he must achieve it himself. He cannot demand that others give up their lives to make him happy. Nor should he wish to sacrifice himself for the happiness of others. I hold that man should have self-esteem.

Wallace: Can't man have self-esteem if he loves his fellow man? What's wrong with loving your fellow man? Christ and every important moral leader in man's history have taught us that we should love one another. Why then is this kind of love, in your mind, immoral?

AR: It is immoral if it is a love placed above oneself. It is more than immoral; it is impossible. When you are asked to love everybody indiscriminately—to love people without any standard, to love them regardless of whether they have any value or virtue—you are asked to love nobody.

Wallace: But in your book you talk about love as if it were a business deal of some kind. Isn't the essence of love that it is above self-interest?

AR: Let me make it concrete. What would it mean to have love above self-interest? It would mean that a husband, if he accepted the conventional morality, would tell his wife: "I am marrying you just for your own sake. I have no personal interest in you, but I am so unselfish that I am marrying you only for your own good." Would any woman like that?

Wallace: Should husbands and wives tally up at the end of the day and say, "I love her if she's done enough for me today," or "She loves me if I have properly performed my functions"?

AR: No, you misunderstood me. That is not how love should be treated. It should not be treated like a business deal, but every arrangement has to have its own terms and its own kind of currency. And in love the currency is virtue. You love people not for what you do for them or what they do for you; you love them for their values and their virtues, which they have achieved in their own character. You don't love causelessly. You don't love everybody indiscriminately. You love *only* those who deserve it.

Wallace: And if a man is weak, is he beyond love?

AR: He certainly does not deserve it. But he has free will. If a man wants love, he should correct his flaws, and then he may deserve it. But he cannot expect the unearned—neither in love nor in money, neither in spirit nor in matter.

Wallace: You have lived in our world and you recognize the fallibility of human beings. There are very few of us in this world who are worthy of love, by your standards.

AR: Unfortunately, yes, very few. But it is open to all to make themselves worthy of it. And that is what my morality offers them: a way to make themselves worthy of love, although that's not the primary goal.

Wallace: How does your philosophy translate into the world of politics? I think most people agree that one of the principal achievements of this country, particularly in the past twenty years, is the gradual growth of social, protective legislation based on the principle that we are our brothers' keepers. How do you feel about the political trend of the United States and the Western world?

AR: The same way everybody feels—except more consciously. I think that the trend is terrible, that we see destruction all around us and that we will continue to move toward disaster until and unless all those welfare-state conceptions are rejected. It is precisely these trends that are bringing the world to disaster. We are now moving toward complete collectivism, a system under which everybody is enslaved to everybody. And we are moving that way only because of our altruist morality.

Wallace: *You say "everybody is enslaved to everybody." Yet this came about democratically. Free people in a free country voted for this kind of government. Do you object to the democratic process?*

AR: I object to the idea that people have the right to vote on everything. The traditional American system was based on the idea that the majority would prevail only in narrow political affairs and that the majority's power was limited by inalienable individual rights. Therefore, I do not believe that a majority can vote away a man's life or property or freedom. I do not believe that a majority vote makes the decision right.

Wallace: *Then how do we arrive at action? How do we arrive at our leadership? Who elects? Who appoints?*

AR: We arrive at decisions by the Constitutional process, as we once had it. People elect officials, but the powers of those officials are strictly limited. They have no right to use force against any citizen, except a criminal. Those who have initiated force are punished by force. That is the only proper function of government. We should not permit the government to initiate force against people who have not themselves used force against anyone. We should not give the government, or the majority, or any minority, the right to take the life or the property of others. The original American system was based on that principle.

Wallace: *When you say "take the property of others," I imagine that you are talking about taxes. You believe that there should be no right by the government to tax. You believe that there should be no such thing as welfare legislation, unemployment compensation, rent controls and things like that.*

AR: That's right. I am opposed to all forms of controls. I am for an absolute, laissez-faire economy. I am for the separation of state and economics. We have *for the United States, as described in* Atlas Shrugged, *if we continue on sent course?*

f the present trend of collectivism and anti-reason continues, yes. That direction in which the country is headed. But I do not believe in his- al determinism and I do not believe that people have to keep going in direction. Men have free will. If they choose to change their thinking, erica will not become a dictatorship.

allace: How can you expect to reverse this trend when, as we've said, the country run by majority rule, and the majority seems to prefer to vote for this modified elfare state?

AR: I don't believe that. You know as well as I do that the majority today is not given a real choice. The majority has never been offered a choice between controls and freedom.

Wallace: How do you account for the fact that an almost overwhelming majority of the people who are regarded as our leading intellectuals and our leading indus-trialists—the men you seem to admire the most, the men with the muscle and the money—favor the modified capitalism that we have today?

AR: Because it is an intellectual issue. Since they all believe in collectivism, they do favor our mixed system. But most people have never been given a true choice. You know that both parties today are for government controls. There are no voices to offer a view in favor of capitalism, economic freedom, individualism. That is what this country needs today.

Wallace: Isn't it possible that we all believe in our present system because we are all basically lonely people and we all understand that we are our brother's keeper?

AR: You couldn't say you understand it, because there is no way in which you could justify it. Nobody has ever given a *reason* that men should be their brothers' keepers. You have had every example, which you see all around you, of men perishing from the attempt to be their brothers' keepers.

Wallace: You have no faith in anything—only in your mind?

AR: That is not faith. That is a conviction. Yes, I have no faith at all—only convictions.

Wallace: Where did this philosophy of yours come from?

a separation of state and church, which led to peacefu.
ferent religions after a period of religious wars. Simil.
government from economics, by rejecting any regulat.
trade, you will have peaceful cooperation and justice an.

Wallace: You are certainly enough of a political scientist to knov
ments spring up in reaction to other movements. The labor i
welfare legislation did not spring full-blown from somebody's he
It was a reaction to certain abuses that were going on. Isn't that i

AR: Not always. It actually sprang from the same source as the
"abuses" you mean the legislation originally established—in a b.
enterprise—to help industries. If then, in reaction, labor leaders g
to initiate legislation to help labor, they are merely acting on the sa.
ple that it is proper for the state to legislate in favor of one economic
another. I am saying that nobody, neither employers nor employees
have the right to use state compulsion for their own interests.

Wallace: When you advocate completely unregulated economic life, in which
man works for his own profit, you are asking for a devil-take-the-hindmost,
eat-dog society. One of the main reasons for the growth of government contr
was to fight the robber-barons, the very people you admire most—the hard-heade
industrialists, the successful men who perverted their power. Is that not true?

AR: No, it isn't. This country was made not by "robber-barons," but by independent men—by industrialists, who succeeded on sheer ability.

Wallace: Of course they succeeded.

AR: I mean without political force or political help. But at the same time,
there were industrialists who did use government power as a club to help
them against competitors. They were the original collectivists. Today the
liberals believe that that same compulsion should be used against the industrialists, for the sake of workers. But the proper principle is that there should
not be any compulsion at all. The regulations are creating "robber-barons."
They are creating capitalists with government help, which is the worst of all
economic phenomena.

Wallace: Ayn, I think that you will agree with me when I say that you do not have
a great deal of respect for the society in which you and I currently live. You think
that we are going downhill fairly fast. Do you predict dictatorship and economic

AR: Out of my own mind, with the sole acknowledgment of a debt to Aristotle, the only philosopher who ever influenced me. I devised the rest of my philosophy myself.

Wallace: I would like to know a little about you—where you were born, where your family is.

AR: I was born in Russia and came to the United States about thirty years ago. I came here alone and I have no way of finding out what happened to my parents.

Wallace: You are married. Is your husband an industrialist?

AR: No, he is an artist. His name is Frank O'Connor.

Wallace: And does he live from his painting?

AR: He is just beginning to study painting. He was a designer before.

Wallace: Is he supported in his efforts by the state?

AR: Most certainly not.

Wallace: He is supported by you for the time being.

AR: No, by his own work. Actually, in the past by me, when necessary, but now it isn't necessary.

Wallace: And there is no contradiction here, in that you help him?

AR: No, because I am in love with him selfishly. It is to my own interest to help him if he ever needs it. I do not call that a sacrifice, because I take selfish pleasure in it.

Wallace: Let me put one specific case to you. Suppose that under your system of self-sufficiency, one single corporation were to get a stranglehold on a product or a raw material that was vital for the national defense and then refused to sell it to the government. Then what?

AR: Under a free system, no one could acquire a monopoly on anything. If you look at economics, and economic history, you will discover that all monopolies have been established with government help—with franchises, subsidies or other government privileges. Under free competition, no one could corner the market on a needed product. History will support me.

Wallace: Ayn, let's say there is a deposit of uranium in Nevada. It's the only one in the United States, and we need uranium for self-defense. And let's say that in the Soviet Union the state controls uranium. Suppose a strange man got hold of this uranium in Nevada and said, "I will not sell it to my government." According to your philosophy, he should not be forced by the government to sell that uranium.

AR: But you are setting up an impossible fantasy. Any natural resource so scarce that one man could control all of it, could never become so vitally needed. And so long as—I'm using your example—a natural resource exists in more than one place in the world, no one man is going to control it.

Wallace: Let's take another case. How do we build roads, sanitation facilities, hospitals, schools? If the government is not permitted to tax its citizens, we have to depend upon the trickle-down theory, upon noblesse oblige.

AR: I will answer you by asking you a question. Who in fact pays for all those things?

Wallace: We all of us pay for these things.

AR: When you ask how we are going to build hospitals or roads, and admit that you want to take money by force from someone, you acknowledge that someone is producing the wealth that makes those things possible. Now, you have no right to tell the man who produced the wealth how you want him to spend it. If you need his money, you can obtain it only by his voluntary consent.

Wallace: And you believe in the eventual goodwill of all human beings, or at least of that top echelon of human beings who you believe will give willingly?

AR: No goodwill is necessary—only self-interest. I believe in private roads, private post offices, private schools.

Wallace: When industry breaks down and there is mass unemployment, we should not be permitted to get unemployment insurance. We do not need Social Security. We'll depend upon the self-interest of these enlightened industrialists whom you so admire to take care of things when the economy needs a little lubrication and there are millions of people out of work.

AR: Study economics. A free economy will not break down. All depressions are caused by government interference. And the cure that is always offered is to take more of the poison that caused the disease. Depressions are not the result of a free economy.

Wallace: I'm sure that you have stimulated a good many people to read Atlas Shrugged *and* The Fountainhead. *I'm equally sure they will be stimulated by the reading even if they do not agree.*

AR: Thank you.

Wallace: Thank you very much. As we said at the outset, if Ayn Rand's ideas were ever to take hold, they would revolutionize the world. And to those who would reject her philosophy, Miss Rand hurls this challenge: "For the past two thousand years, the world has been dominated by other philosophies. Look around you. Consider the results." We thank Ayn Rand for adding her portrait to our gallery, one of the people other people are interested in.

· 24 ·

For the Intellectual, University of Michigan Television, with Professor James McConnell, 1961

Throughout history, men were ruled by an alliance of the man of faith: the Witch Doctor, and the man of force: the Attila.

EDITOR'S NOTE: This television interview, conducted by Professor James Mc-Connell of the department of psychology at the University of Michigan, took place upon the publication of Ayn Rand's book For the New Intellectual. *It included brief opening and closing statements by her.*

AR: I have held the same philosophy I now hold for as far back as I can remember. I have learned a great deal through the years, and extended my knowledge of details, of specific issues, of definitions, of applications, and I intend to continue expanding it. But I never had to change any of my fundamentals. My philosophy, in essence, is the concept of man as a heroic being, with his own happiness as the moral purpose of his life, with productive activity as his noblest activity and reason as his only absolute.

James McConnell: *I suppose it's true, at least in one sense, that every novelist is a philosopher, but I think very few novelists have devoted the time and the energy that you have to the development of a consistent philosophical system. So let me begin by asking whether you consider yourself primarily a novelist or a philosopher.*

AR: I would say I am primarily both, equally and for the same reason. My main interest and purpose, both in literature and in philosophy, are to define and present an ideal man—the specific, concrete image of what man can be and ought to be. When I first approached the task of literature and began to study philosophy, I discovered that I was in profound disagreement with all the existing philosophies, particularly their codes of morality. Therefore, I had to do my own thinking. I had to define my own philosophical system in order to discover the kind of premises that make an ideal man possible. I had to define the convictions that would result in the character of an ideal man.

McConnell: You've made the point that leadership in a culture—in art, literature, morality, politics—must be provided by what you call the professional intellectuals. What do you mean by "professional intellectuals"?

AR: The professional intellectuals are, in effect, the field agents of the army whose commander-in-chief is the philosopher. The philosopher, the one who defines the fundamental ideas of a culture, is the man who ultimately determines history. The professional intellectuals are all those whose professions deal with the humanities, as against the physical sciences. These individuals carry to the rest of society the ideas that have been defined by the philosophers. They are the transmission belts. They are the ones who directly determine the goals, the values and the direction of a culture.

McConnell: Is this true in any culture? Would it be true no matter where you found them?

AR: It is true in civilized cultures. But remember that the professional intellectual is a very recent phenomenon. He did not exist prior to the Industrial Revolution and the birth of capitalism. Before that, man could not make a profession of intellectual work. The intellect had no tangible value in those earlier cultures. It is only since the advent of capitalism that man acquired the chance to make a living by means of dealing with ideas. Reason became a practical issue for the first time, reaching its height in the nineteenth century. Today, we are losing this value—and it is the intellectuals who are betraying it.

McConnell: You think, then, that American intellectual leadership has collapsed?

AR: Yes, collapsed and abdicated.

McConnell: How have the intellectuals not lived live up to their responsibilities?

AR: By betraying the very premise that made their existence possible: the importance of the intellect. For decades the intellectuals have been progressively advocating the idea that the intellect is impotent, that reason is unreliable, that we can know nothing for certain. These are men who, proclaiming themselves intellectuals, spend their time denying the validity of the intellect. They are engaged in committing suicide. The rise of such openly mystical, unintellectual philosophies today as Zen Buddhism or Existentialism—doctrines that cannot even properly be called philosophies—is an admission of intellectual bankruptcy on the part of those who accept such doctrines. If a theory like Zen Buddhism, which originated around the fifth century B.C., becomes the latest word of the mind among a group of men, it isn't I who am condemning them; they have condemned themselves by their own actions. They have given up. They have gone back to the mysticism of the Dark Ages.

McConnell: Why do you think they've done this?

AR: Because philosophers are the ones who set the basic premises of the whole intellectual profession, and Western philosophies have been increasingly endorsing mysticism ever since the Renaissance. The Renaissance was the intellectual result of Aristotelian philosophy. It was Aristotle who destroyed the Middle Ages and broke the ground for the Renaissance. But ever since then—while men were achieving incredible progress on the basis of Aristotle's influence, culminating in the nineteenth century—the intellectuals, particularly since Immanuel Kant, were moving progressively against reason. The trend started before Kant, of course, but I consider him the crucial destroyer and the crucial turning point. He was the philosopher who tried to undercut the validity of reason. He did not really succeed, but his is the most skillful system of pushing reason off the philosophical scene altogether. To the extent to which other intellectuals accepted his basic premises, they have been moving toward a "noumenal," mystical world ever since.

McConnell: You mentioned Kant, and you mentioned Aristotle. Under whose influence was the world before the Renaissance?

AR: Before the Renaissance, the Middle Ages were ruled by mysticism. In that period, philosophy was considered a handmaiden of theology. The predominant philosophical influence was Plato, through Plotinus and Augustine. Aristotle's triumph began with Thomas Aquinas, who brought Aristotelianism back into the culture, particularly its most important element—its epistemology of logic and reason.

McConnell: What in particular about Kant's philosophy do you think was responsible for the trend we see today in philosophy?

AR: That very cumbersome, very complex and very phony system of divorcing man's mind from reality. Kant declared that what we perceive is only an illusion created by some special categories and forms of perception in our minds. He allegedly proved that we can never perceive things as they are, which means that if an object is perceived, our perception is incorrect. Kantianism was, in effect, an attack on the whole concept of consciousness —not only human consciousness, but *any* consciousness. It was a denial of the reality of our awareness.

McConnell: This brings up another point. In For the New Intellectual, *mysticism is only one part of a trend you trace. You call the mystics the "Witch Doctors." But you also talk about the men of force, the Attilas of the world. How do they fit into your framework?*

AR: Reason is the only means by which man can achieve knowledge of reality. And by reason, I mean the faculty that identifies and integrates the material provided by man's senses. But reason does not work automatically. Man has to *choose* to think. Man can receive sensory data or integrate sensations into percepts automatically, but he cannot form abstractions automatically. Thinking is a volitional function of man's consciousness. But most men, guided by their philosophers, do not wish to think. They consider reason dangerous or impotent or too much of an effort.

Most human cultures, with rare exceptions, have been ruled by what I call Witch Doctors. A Witch Doctor is any man who takes his emotions, rather than his thinking, as his tool of cognition and his guide to reality. He functions by means of faith. He acts on the basis of blind beliefs, which in fact are nothing more than his wishes. On whatever level of the culture you find such a man, he is a Witch Doctor in his psycho-epistemology—that is, in the way in which he uses his mind.

Since no one can deal with reality or with people on the basis of emotions, the natural ally of the Witch Doctor will always be the type I call Attila. He is the fiercest, most savage tribal chief, the man who acts only on the range of the moment, by means of his immediate sensory perceptions. He is contemptuous of, and refuses to consider, ideas, principles or abstractions. He deals with reality and with other men by brute force. Attila is the gangster, or the dictator, or the military conqueror—or any man who believes that force is practical. Attila is any man who refuses to think and who wishes to loot and enslave others.

Throughout history, men were ruled by an alliance of the man of faith: the Witch Doctor, and the man of force: the Attila. The Witch Doctor provided the goals and the values for Attila to enforce upon the world. The

Witch Doctor also provided the moral sanction. Today, we see the same phenomenon in allegedly civilized form, but the essence remains the same—an alliance of a dictator, like Khrushchev, and his political theorists: the modern leftist intellectuals, who are philosophically Attila-ists. They provide an allegedly non-mystical philosophical justification for Attila's rule of brute force. I call them the neo-mystics, because they are as opposed to reason as were the original, jungle witch doctors.

McConnell: I can see what the mystics or the neo-mystics can give to the Attilas, but why do the mystics need the Attilas? What is the relationship the other way?

AR: The mystic's motivating force is dread of physical reality. He is a man who holds his emotions above reality. In any conflict between his feelings and the facts, he will select his feelings and will deny reality. He cannot deal with reality at all. His mysticism is a form of escape from the necessity of dealing with facts. Therefore, he needs Attila as a protector. He needs Attila to provide his material livelihood and to enforce his edicts on the victims.

McConnell: You said that each culture should have its philosophers and then the intellectuals should more or less put the philosophy into action. What about the role of science?

AR: Science on a wide scale is a very recent phenomenon. The broad achievements of science are the product of the Industrial Revolution, of capitalism and of a free society. Here, I must mention the third type of man who has seldom been the leader of any society. He has been the forgotten and exploited man of history. He is the man who lives by means of reason. He is the man who in his psycho-epistemology is guided, not by his immediate perceptions and not by his emotions, but by logic. This is the man I call the Producer. He creates, not only the material values of mankind, but also, and above all, the *intellectual* values. The first Producer in history, in this higher sense of the word, was Aristotle, the first rational philosopher. Scientists certainly should be Producers. They are the men who are supposed to—and by the nature of their profession have to—study reality by means of reason. Unfortunately, outside their laboratories, most of them are now turning more mystical than any other group of men. The fault is partly theirs, but predominantly it is the fault of the philosophers. Since there is no philosophical guidance being offered at all, many scientists are turning today to a Witch Doctor–type of mysticism of their own.

McConnell: What is the businessman's role in all this?

AR: The businessman is as recent a phenomenon as the intellectual. Before the birth of capitalism, there were no professional businessmen, just as there were no professional intellectuals. Both the mind and material production were enslaved by absolutist governments that represented various combinations of Attilas and Witch Doctors. These governments ranged from feudal absolutism to the absolute monarchies of Europe during the post-Renaissance period. The producers of ideas—the teachers, the philosophers, the early scientists—and the producers of material goods were men without official status and without a profession. They were at the total mercy of rule by force. It is only since the Industrial Revolution and the birth of a free society that a new class of individuals arose: the businessmen. They of course are the Producers in the strictest sense of the word—or should be. And they are the greatest victims of today's society. They are the ones who have been betrayed by modern intellectuals. Both businessmen and intellectuals are committing suicide by destroying each other, and the fault belongs with the intellectuals.

The businessman has to use his mind to deal with reality. He has to study facts to produce material goods. He is the man who serves as the transmission belt for the discoveries of science. He takes the innovations of a theoretical scientist or of an inventor, transforms them into useful products and, by putting them into mass production, makes them available to all levels of society. The businessman is the one who achieved an enormous, historically miraculous rise in mankind's standard of living during the nineteenth century. He is the man who has lived up to the role of a Producer—the role of a rational, creative individual. But the intellectuals have never given him credit for doing so. They have regarded him as a mindless brute. And, being afraid of freedom, the intellectuals have been looking, since the start of the Industrial Revolution, for some sort of Attila to protect them against the free market of ideas.

McConnell: You've been talking about the bankruptcy of our modern intellectuals. I know that your most recent book is really a manifesto for those you call the "New Intellectuals." Would you mind telling me who they are and how they differ from the old-style intellectuals?

AR: Since it is the current intellectuals who have declared their own bankruptcy by abandoning the intellect, the New Intellectual we need today is any man or woman who is willing to think. It is any man or woman who knows that man's life must be guided by reason, not by feelings, wishes, whims or mystical revelations. It is any individual who values his life, and who does not want to give in to today's cult of despair, cynicism and impotence. It is any individual who does not intend to give up the world to the Dark Ages and to the rule of the collective.

McConnell: This New Intellectual, then, is a fairly recent phenomenon. Have there been any of this type in the past that you would like to point out?

AR: I can name a few historical examples in the most general way. Aristotle is the man I regard as the first intellectual in history, in the best sense of the word. America's first intellectuals were the Founding Fathers, because they were thinkers who were also men of action. They were the men who knew that reason is man's guide to reality, that man can achieve an ideal way of life on earth by means of his reason and that man requires freedom in order to be guided by the judgment of his mind. They understood that men should deal with one another by trade and persuasion, not by force.

The Founding Fathers established, in the United States of America, the first and only free society in history. The economic system that was the corollary of the American political system was capitalism—total, unregulated, laissez-faire capitalism. However, it has never yet been fully practiced. A total separation of government and economics had not been established from the first. It was implied in principle, but certain loopholes or contradictions were still allowed into the Constitution, which permitted collectivist influences to undermine the American way of life. Today it is practically collapsing. There is nothing left except an undefined tradition. The active, intellectual direction of our society at present is *anti*-American and *anti*-intellectual. We are going back to the primordial mysticism and the coercive rule of dictatorships.

The New Intellectuals are those who will stand up for two fundamental values: the value of man's life, of self-esteem, of independence, of inalienable rights; and the value of a free society in which men do not use force against one another.

McConnell: You mentioned in For the New Intellectual *the right of the pursuit of happiness. Do you think this is very important?*

AR: I don't know what could be any more important, if you attach exact meaning to the concept. The pursuit of happiness means a man's right to set his own goals, to choose his own values and to achieve them. Happiness is the state of consciousness that comes from the achievement of your values. What could be more important? But happiness does not simply mean momentary pleasure or any kind of mindless self-indulgence. Happiness means a profound, guiltless, rational feeling of self-esteem and of pride in one's own achievement. It means the enjoyment of life, which is possible only to a rational man acting on a rational code of morality. I couldn't possibly tell you, in a brief interview, what that code is. But those who are interested will find the explanation in my books, particularly in *Atlas Shrugged*.

McConnell: Do you think it's important, then, that we be guiltless in our feelings about this?

AR: I wouldn't even know how to answer such a question. To put it in my terms, I would say it is important to be moral. I would stress the positive, not the negative.

McConnell: Where do the New Intellectuals start and how do they proceed?

AR: Above all, they need an integrated, consistent philosophy of life. Now, to define or even to agree with a new philosophy is a long process. It requires careful thinking, because an intellectual will not accept a philosophy on faith or on arbitrary say-so. If any man takes this issue seriously and wants to become an intellectual, he has to begin by accepting two premises, which I call the basic minimum of civilization. They are not axioms, but a man first has to prove them to himself, and then his mind will be free to consider other questions of philosophy. They pertain to the relationship of reason to emotion, and to the evil of force.

The first premise is that emotions are not tools of cognition. A man has to learn to differentiate his thinking—i.e., his reasoned judgment—from his feelings. He must learn that emotions are not a form of knowledge and are not a guide to reality. Rather, they are the automatic product of his thinking. Therefore, the first thing any intellectual has to understand is that man must be guided by reason, and that it is only on the basis of reason that he can deal with other men. On the basis of emotion, he would have to resort to blind force, because emotions are unprovable. If two men act on the basis of their emotions, they have no means of communication. When emotions are put in their proper place, though—as the consequence of reason, not as its leader—then men have a common vocabulary. They then have a common means of understanding and a common frame of reference. And they have an ultimate arbiter: reality.

This leads to the second premise an intellectual should accept. And that is the basic social principle that no man has the right to initiate physical force. No one has the right to compel another man to act against his judgment.

McConnell: You have been listening to a discussion of the intellectual crisis in modern American society. Our special guest on today's program has been Miss Ayn

Rand, noted American novelist-philosopher, whose analysis of the role of the intellectual holds this hope for the future:

AR: Those who will accept the basic minimum of civilization will have made the first step toward the building of a new culture in the wide-open spaces of today's intellectual vacuum. There is an ancient slogan that applies to our present position: "The king is dead—long live the king!" We can say, with the same dedication to the future: "The intellectuals are dead—long live the intellectuals!"—and then proceed to fulfill the responsibility which that honorable title had once implied.

• 25 •

The Tonight Show, with Johnny Carson, NBC-TV, August 1967

[The century] between the end of the Napoleonic Wars and the beginning of World War I, was the most peaceful in history. . . . And that period was the closest to capitalism the civilized world has ever come.

Johnny Carson: She is probably one of the most intense, outspoken, intellectual voices in America today. Her books, including The Fountainhead, *which was made into a motion picture, and* Atlas Shrugged, *have sold millions of copies, and some people say that her* Objectivist Newsletter *is one of the more vital publications in the world today. This is her new book, called* Capitalism: The Unknown Ideal. *I think you will find her most unusual and most controversial. Would you welcome please, Miss Ayn Rand. It's indeed a pleasure to have you with us tonight.*

AR: I'm delighted to be here.

Carson: I know that you probably don't appear on many shows of this nature. It's kind of a crazy entertainment show generally, although we do like to sit down occasionally and get some views of people who are important in the world today.

AR: I don't disapprove of entertainment. In fact, I've watched you many times.

Carson: I know it's very difficult to state any philosophical principle like Objectivism in a short period of time, or to condense it. But can you give us some basic idea of Objectivism and the principles of philosophy that you believe in?

AR: I'll make it very brief, with the understanding that anyone who really is interested will refer to my books, particularly *Atlas Shrugged*, because I can't give a long discourse and proof here. So I'll just mention the highlights. The basic principle of Objectivism is that man must be guided exclusively by reason. Reason is the faculty that identifies and integrates the material provided by his senses—that's a formal definition. Reason is man's only tool of knowledge, his only guide to action and his only guide to the choice of values.

As a consequence, man's proper ethics is one of rational self-interest, which means that every man has a right to exist for his own sake and must not sacrifice himself to others or sacrifice others to himself. The achievement of his own rational happiness is the highest moral purpose of his life. The only political system that expresses this morality is laissez-faire capitalism, by which I mean full, unregulated, uncontrolled capitalism—a system based on the recognition of individual rights, including property rights, in which all property is owned by private individuals. The principle tying morality to politics is that no man has the right to initiate physical force against other men. Men certainly have the right of self-defense, but no man or group of men—including the government—has the right to initiate force and to compel a man to act against his own judgment.

This is the essence of Objectivism. But if you want me to illustrate what it means—it means that very beautiful song [*The Impossible Dream*] we just heard sung magnificently. Except that my philosophy means the reverse of the song's title. It means that man, if he chooses his ideals rationally, can and must achieve them here on earth. There are no unreachable heights for men. There are no unrightable wrongs. In other words, I approve enormously of that which makes people like the song, but I don't approve of its literal content. I say that man *can* be happy, and *can* achieve the ideal, here on earth.

Carson: Objectivism is very controversial. It is almost contrary to the cultural beliefs people have been brought up with: self-sacrifice, the good of your fellow men, unselfishness.

AR: Not *almost* contrary—the exact opposite.

Carson: And you're saying that man should first serve his own self-interest and be interested in himself first.

AR: I wouldn't say "first"; I would say "only." But this has to be explained. Other men can be of interest to an individual if they represent values—moral values. One serves one's own interests best by finding and associating with the right kind of people. Others can be a great value to a man, but only when and if they correspond to his moral ideas. In other words, man does not have to serve anyone except himself. But he does, in effect, serve others when their interests and their values agree with his own.

Carson: You discuss values quite frequently—why men need values and how they get their values. You say that man comes into the world without any preset notion of values or concepts and learns them. Why is it that very young children are, by nature, selfish? They are completely self-oriented. Do they learn that or is it something inherent in the very young?

AR: I think it's inherent in any living entity. An entity that was not concerned with itself or, to put it better, an entity that did not value itself would not exist for very long. But young children are not yet capable of understanding the issues and, in effect, do not yet have a choice. It is when children begin to speak, when they begin to acquire ideas, that their choice begins. The idea of self-sacrifice is a totally artificial, evil idea, which children—and adults—learn from others. Now, this doesn't mean that if a child were left alone he would naturally be properly selfish. It is an enormous achievement to discover rational selfishness, which means: not acting on whim or the pleasure of the moment, but rationally knowing why some goal is a value to you and how to achieve it. The idea of being rationally selfish is not available to children; it takes a long period of thought, or the proper teaching, for them to discover it.

Carson: You say that man is an end in himself. Why is it that man, at least throughout recorded history, seems to need something else—a belief in the existence of a God, a creator or whatever you want to label it, which I assume you do not believe in?

AR: No, I do not.

Carson: Why has man seemed to need that belief ever since he has been on earth? Is it to rationalize his existence here?

AR: I wouldn't call it a need. I would say he has resorted to it by default. Man has to acquire all the content of his consciousness. He has to discover it by thought, by pursuing knowledge. By defaulting on a proper philosophy of life, men resort to blind faith. Religion is a phenomenon of default; men have not yet progressed out of it.

Carson: You don't think it serves a need for many people? You say it's a need, but a wrong need.

AR: It's a need that fills a vacuum, in that the actual need is for a conscious philosophy of life. Man is a conceptual being. He can't exist range-of-the-moment. He needs a larger view, a long-range plan. By default of rational principles, he falls on religion, because that is all that is offered to him. I regard religion as representing the infancy—the pre-philosophical stage—of mankind, and a great many people are still in their infancy.

Carson: You have given many lectures at colleges. Are college students moving away from religion and toward completely rational reasoning, without faith?

AR: I've never attempted to take a poll of those issues.

Carson: I'm just wondering what they discussed with you.

AR: Here is what I find. Young people, particularly in colleges, are enormously anxious to find rational answers. This is not to say that all of them will always be rational. But they are on a quest for understanding. They want an integrated, consistent view of life. If you begin to speak to them about religion, or any form of mysticism, most of them will not listen with great interest.

Carson: When you talk about morality and a sense of values, does each individual set his own standard of morality? Because one person's morality affects those around him, does it not?

AR: No.

Carson: It does not?

AR: Oh, it affects them, all right. But to say that each person sets his own standard would simply mean subjectivism. No, what sets the standard is the science of ethics, which is a branch of philosophy. Its particular task is to define moral standards. It is up to each individual to decide what he agrees with—to decide which standards he considers rational. Or an individual may discover a new set of standards. That does not make his morality subjective, as long as he does not create standards that apply just to him. And if he does create a subjective code, it is not really a morality. It is just what I call whim-worship.

Carson: *Do you think it is immoral if somebody is not productive or does not produce up to his capacity?*

AR: I wouldn't say that.

Carson: *Well, suppose somebody doesn't want to work. Maybe his self-interest is served by not producing or working to capacity.*

AR: If you're asking me whether every man should be productive—yes.

Carson: *To the limits of his ability?*

AR: Yes, but that doesn't mean he should work himself to death. He may have other interests in his life, too. If you are asking whether every man's first value or top goal should be productive work, on any level of ability—certainly. And if a man does not want to be productive, he is immoral.

Carson: *I think the term you use is an emotional parasite.*

AR: If he places other people above his own productive career—above his own creative mind—then he is an emotional parasite.

Carson: *Do you get emotionally attached to people, and have close friendships?*

AR: Oh, yes.

Carson: *But you don't place their interest above what you do?*

AR: There's never any clash, because I am friendly only with rational people. Among rational people there's no clash.

Carson: *In our culture, it seems that everything springs from the family relationship—little individual groups of husband, wife, child or whatever. How does that grouping fit in with your philosophy?*

AR: Optionally. I don't think that the family is the necessary unit of society. But I do think it is precisely independent individuals who make the best husbands and wives. If they share the same values and interests, they will form the proper kind of lasting unions. But I would never maintain that a family is an obligation on the individual. If a man or a woman cares to marry, that is fine; if not, it's fine also—provided they have rational reasons for their choices.

Carson: What are the greatest hang-ups you find among young people today? I suppose you find a lot of anxieties. That's a word used very often by psychotherapists today.

AR: Above all, the problem is confusion, which often leads to unearned guilt. Some guilt is earned all right, if people consciously do what they know to be wrong. But the more tragic thing is unearned guilt, which occurs when young people, and older ones too, accept a wrong moral standard. They are really not guilty of anything, but are made to feel so by today's culture.

Carson: People say that churches or parents should set the moral standards. Who do you think should set them?

AR: The philosophers.

Carson: The philosophers set them?

AR: You said, "Who *should* set them?" Historically, the churches have set them, for much too long and with disastrous consequences. But if you ask me who should—philosophers.

Carson: And are they?

AR: No, not as they stand today.

Carson: But not all philosophers have the same judgments, do they?

AR: No. And therefore what is the arbiter? Reason.

Carson: Well, it has to come down to the individual again.

AR: Each individual has to decide what he concludes is right. And who then is objectively right? The one who can *prove* his case—the one who can prove the code of morality he advocates, without any contradictions.

Carson: I read an article of yours recently. You were talking about the draft, freedom and the war—about the country having no right to require an individual to serve in the military. You said that if a country is attacked, people will fight, but you didn't think it was right for a country to demand of its citizens a conscripted army.

AR: No, it is a very immoral idea. And it is unconstitutional.

Carson: Can we explore that a wee bit? Now we got a few boos there, which is to be expected. Any time anybody has any views that don't go according to the norm, you're going to have some antagonism. But that's why we want to talk about these things.

AR: Oh, my views will probably be the norm of the future, but not right now.

Carson: You say an army by conscription is usually not an effective army.

AR: The military authorities have repeatedly testified that it is not effective, and that a volunteer army, consisting of men who know what they're fighting for is—speaking in practical terms—a much better army. But the underlying moral issue comes first. I say that no single individual has the right to demand the life of another individual. Each man is the owner of his life. That is the meaning of the idea that man has the right to his own life, not anybody else's. Well, if no single individual has the right to your life or mine, ten million of them do not acquire that right by ganging up on one man. No man has the right to demand the life of another; therefore, neither does a group nor a nation.

Carson: Now, of course, your opponents will say, "But people are trying to take over the world, and if we do not stand fast now and protect our freedoms, we may be lost." What is your answer to that?

AR: That it is a contradiction. What this argument amounts to is that since people are trying to take away your freedom, you should give it up yourself. That is the sole meaning of this kind of reasoning. Morally speaking, you do not descend to your enemy's level in order to defend yourself. Practically speaking, of course, doing so does not work.

Carson: Well, war first of all is terribly stupid. You're not saying, of course, that if this country was attacked, the people would not fight.

AR: If the country was attacked, people *would* fight, because people have always fought for a free or even semi-free country. If you ask me whether it is proper to fight, in self-defense, when your country is attacked, I would say: certainly. Men should volunteer to fight in such a case—because they would be defending their own rights and their own freedoms. But a country does not have the right to compel them to fight, particularly in a war like Vietnam, in which the U.S. has no interests whatever. We have nothing to gain by that war and it is draining this country. Therefore, I am enormously opposed to the whole Vietnam mess, but for opposite reasons from those that the "Vietniks" are yelping about. I do not agree with them. I am against the war because it is useless and senseless, and it does not serve any national interest.

Carson: There are so many questions about the war. It becomes an emotional tug-of-war with many people, because they hear the words "patriotism," "freedom," "Communist enslavement." Do you think sometimes people get emotionally involved in it, rather than rationally explore it?

AR: Today, yes. But that is the whole trend of today's culture—people act on their emotions rather than think.

Carson: What is your answer to people who say that if we do not stand fast in Vietnam, all of Asia will follow and eventually we'll be fighting a war in the United States?

AR: Asia is not the place to start opposing Communism. We have given up so much in Europe, which, if you want to defend civilization—I say, *if*—is the place to begin. But strictly speaking, if we wanted to save the world from Communism, it's not necessary to go to war. All we would have to do is stop helping the Communists economically. Stop building bridges to them, which have supported them for fifty years now. Soviet Russia would collapse of its own evil if the semi-free world did not constantly help it.

Carson: Now, you were born in Russia. You were born in Leningrad—St. Petersburg at the time. Obviously, your personal background makes you tremendously opposed to Communism and what it stands for.

AR: Not for that reason, but because of the evil of the idea of Communism. I've never been particularly patriotic about Russia. Of course, I was very young at the time of the Communist revolution—I was twelve. I am opposed to the whole Russian culture, which is a mystical one. All that I like about Russia is some of her writers and some of her music, but that's about it. I am much more American, in fundamental principles, than I am Russian.

Carson: Do you think it is possible in the long run to co-exist with Communist China? We have existed fairly well with Yugoslavia and some of the other countries that are Communist, without too much problem. That seems to be the big fight of the Western world—the containment of Communist China.

AR: A free country can co-exist with anyone and, incidentally, free the rest of the world by example, if it has a firm domestic and foreign policy. Remember that the U.S. destroyed tyranny, serfdom and slavery all over the world, not by fighting wars, but by example, by adopting free trade. A free country destroys barriers gradually. But for that to happen, it needs a proper political philosophy.

We had the beginnings of it in the nineteenth century, but not the full case, and we lost. Why did we lose? Because capitalism cannot co-exist with the morality of altruism. If and when we return to a proper political system, it won't be a going back; it will be a going forward, because such a system has never yet fully existed. That system would have to be based on a rational morality of self-interest, and if we had such as system, we would not have to fight wars. The nineteenth century, between the end of the Napoleonic Wars and the beginning of World War I, was the most peaceful period in history—the only significant period without a major world war. And that period was the closest to capitalism the civilized world has ever come. Contrary to all the popular nonsense, capitalism does not lead to wars; it is the system of peace. That has been demonstrated in historical practice. But today, with the kind of mixed economy and mixed philosophies that we stand for, we will, ultimately and unfortunately, probably have to fight. If we had better ideas, a country like Russia or Yugoslavia—or the whole damn world—would not be any problem or threat to the United States.

Carson: *Do you think such a day is going to come? We don't seem to be getting too much smarter.*

AR: Nobody can predict the immediate future. I don't know. Men have free will, so it is possible. I don't see any large-scale sign of hope yet, but on the other hand, America is the one country that could not collapse into statism. Whereas Europe always was statist, such a development in America would be contrary to its whole past and all its basic premises. I don't believe that this country could go statist, although what kind of trouble we would get into on the way to liberation, I don't know.

Carson: *You said that you were an atheist. Why does that word bring up such violent reactions from people?*

AR: I think mainly from surprise. I've never found many people who really do believe in God, but the idea of declaring themselves to be atheists frightens them. That's my impression of people, although I must say I don't associate intimately with religious people. Therefore, I would not know what their ideas are.

Carson: Don't you find some religious people who are intellectual?

AR: Oh, yes.

Carson: It's perfectly compatible to be intellectual and still believe in a Supreme Being, isn't it?

AR: Perfectly compatible? No.

Carson: Now, a lot of people probably do not agree with a lot of your views. When you agreed to appear on this show, you asked only that you not be attacked by me. And I said, "No, I wouldn't do that." I don't think it's a good idea to invite a guest on the show and then take issue with his or her views, or bring somebody else on with opposing views and have them yell at each other for half-an-hour. I'd much rather give you the opportunity to express your philosophy. I think people get more information from it that way.

AR: Oh, of course. I couldn't agree with you more.

Carson: This is your magazine, The Objectivist, *which explains your philosophy. We only briefly touched on your philosophy tonight.*

AR: If anyone wants full proof or greater discussion, they will find it in *The Objectivist.*

The Tonight Show, with Johnny Carson, NBC-TV, October 1967

There should be complete separation of state and economics, in the same way and for the same reason there is a separation of state and church.

Johnny Carson: *We have another discussion with one of the most progressive philosophers in the world, Miss Ayn Rand, who was with us about two months ago. Her appearance at that time aroused great interest among our viewers. She is well known all over the world. Her lectures at universities and colleges throughout the country are always standing-room only. She is one of the most widely discussed and debated philosophers on the intellectual scene today. Miss Rand, it's a pleasure to have you back with us this evening.*

AR: I am delighted. I feel that I'm coming back home.

Carson: *I'm glad you've come. When someone appears on this show, especially someone with very positive and absolute views on things, I'm always interested to know what kind of reaction he or she received from the viewers. Were they vitriolic? Did they agree with you one hundred percent, or were they completely the reverse?*

AR: I think the response is a tribute to you more than to me. I received an incredible amount of mail following the show, more than I've ever gotten from any one appearance. The responses were predominantly supportive and in agreement with me. There were very few nasty ones, and those I usually don't read very carefully—they go into a special file. But mostly they were enthusiastic about the way you handled the interview, and for that I myself am very grateful.

Carson: I don't believe in bringing on people with certain views and then either debating them or trying to bait them into something, because that's pretty easy to do. It's not really important whether I agree with your views or not. What is important is that you have some place at least to express them without arguing back and forth.

AR: I'm always glad to discuss ideas, but not to debate them.

Carson: Let's talk a little bit about some of the subjects in your book Capitalism: The Unknown Ideal. *In the chapter called "The Roots of War," you discuss the causes of war throughout civilization. Why do people resort to killing each other to solve their problems, as they are doing right now and have been since recorded history? Do you think there will come a time in our world when there will not be war?*

AR: I don't know whether it will come in our lifetime, but I know that the necessary precondition of peace is that man renounce the idea that the good—any kind of good—can be achieved by force. So long as men believe that they have the moral right, for an allegedly noble purpose, to force other men in the name of their version of the good, wars will continue. As an illustration of this point, observe the very peculiar, and very ugly, phenomenon of today's so-called peace movement. Its supporters claim to want to abolish war. They oppose a fight between two armed adversaries—but they condone or advocate dictatorship, which means: the use of force against a country's own citizens, i.e., against disarmed victims. They support the use of force against the disarmed, for some social purpose. So long as you have that phenomenon, you will have wars.

Carson: And most wars have been carried on in the name of a good cause, have they not?

AR: Yes. And the aggressor, if you observe history, is always the more controlled economy, as against the freer economies. It is always dictatorships that start wars. Observe the last two major examples in this century: World War I, which was started by czarist Russia and monarchist Germany, and then World War II, which was started by an alliance of Soviet Russia and Nazi Germany, with the attack on Poland. In both cases, it was the dictatorship that started the war.

Carson: You mentioned that the country with the least to gain is usually the capitalist country.

AR: Capitalism has *nothing* to gain by war, because capitalism is the productive economy. Capitalism is the only system that does not permit the use of force in social relationships. It is the system that protects individual rights—which means that the use of force is barred from society. Under capitalism, people have no right to impose their ideas by initiating the use of physical force.

Carson: From what I understand in your book, when you say "capitalism," you mean a completely free society, with the government providing only protection for individual rights. The government should have no interest in business whatsoever, other than protecting the individual citizen through the police and those kinds of services.

AR: That's right. Government's function is protecting the individual from the initiation of force, whether by criminals at home or aggressors abroad. This function includes the settling of disputes among citizens through the law courts.

Carson: Then we do not have a true capitalistic society now, in this country?

AR: No, we don't. We have a mixed economy, which means a mixture of some freedom and a great number of controls.

Carson: Which way do you think we are drifting?

AR: "Drifting" is the right word. We are drifting toward totalitarianism, and specifically, toward fascism. Intellectually, statism and collectivism are dead; philosophically or morally, they lost their power about the time of World War II. Therefore, there is the hope that the philosophical trend, which precedes the political trend, will go in the other direction. If mankind is to survive, that's the only way it can go—toward freedom, individualism and laissez-faire capitalism.

Carson: What exactly do you mean by "statism"?

AR: "Statism" means any system which holds that the individual has no rights, that rights belong to society and that society can dispose of the individual in any way it pleases. Statism includes unlimited majority rule. Statism means collectivism and, in practice, it simply means gang rule. It includes such systems as socialism, Communism, fascism, Nazism and the welfare state. Every dictator, of course, is a statist, because he does not recognize the individual rights of the citizens.

Carson: A lot of people say that the way to get along with the Communist countries is to co-exist. But you would advise that we not have any diplomatic relations whatsoever with Russia, and that we shouldn't even be a member of the United Nations, because it includes dictatorships.

AR: I do not believe that the United Nations should exist at all, because it is an organization based on an impossible contradiction. It is supposed to be dedicated to preserving peace and to protecting rights, and yet Russia, which is the worst offender against peace and individual rights, on the largest scale, is one of the charter members. That really amounts to a town's having gangsters as part of its crime-fighting committee.

Carson: So you would urge us to have no dealings whatsoever with the U.N.? Some people take the other side and say, "Well, the U.N. did go into Korea and stop that conflict. And it has shored up certain trouble spots in other parts of the world. It's not perfect, but it's the best we have."

AR: It isn't the best we have—it's the worst we have. By their discussions, the member-states are sanctioning the kind of aggression that, without the United Nations, might not take place. Just as a current example, look at the Arab-Israeli wars.

Carson: I watched the other night when those conferences went on until two or three in the morning. One country after another would get up and say, "Israel is wrong." One country after another would get up and say, "The Arab countries are wrong." And they didn't seem to resolve anything.

AR: And they won't, because they are not concerned with an issue of principle, such as international legality. There is no such principle in the U.N. The Arabs were blatantly the aggressors, with Soviet Russia's help. They were about to throttle Israel, a small, industrial country—the only civilized nation in that part of the world. Yet when the small country achieved an amazing victory, what did the U.N. do? It asked Israel to give up all that it had won. The U.N. has done this in every major international encounter in which Soviet Russia was involved.

Carson: You say that if we sever all relations with a Communist country, its economy would collapse of its own weight. But wouldn't it trade with other countries?

AR: You mean: with other Communist, or statist, countries, which have nothing to trade and which are perishing themselves? The Soviet-Nazi pact at the start of World War II was just such an arrangement, in which the two thought they could trade with each other. And the pact broke up because they had nothing to offer each other economically.

Carson: If all the free countries in the world just said to the dictatorships, "We will no longer try to co-exist with you; we will not trade with you; we will have nothing to do with you," do you think that would be the answer? Would all the dictatorships collapse?

AR: Within a very short time. But today there are really no free countries in the world, only semi-free ones. To institute a firm policy like that, we would need an entirely different philosophy. The destroyer of the world today is the entrenched philosophy of mysticism-altruism-statism. For a free, or even semi-free, country to take a strong stand against Communism, it would need a philosophy of reason, individual rights and freedom. Without that, you could not have a successful world policy.

Carson: Those are the principles of Objectivism, right?

AR: That's right.

Carson: You say we are not a true capitalistic society, because you don't believe the government should control business in any way whatsoever. True?

AR: True. I believe there should be complete separation of state and economics, in the same way and for the same reason there is a separation of state and church. So long as various churches had the political power of the state behind them, we had centuries of religious wars. When that connection was broken—and it was broken really in America—different religions were able to live in peace with one another. We no longer have such phenomena as thirty-year religious wars, which destroy millions of people. If no particular religion has the power to force its views on others, all can co-exist peacefully.

Carson: How do you respond to people who say that without government regulation, businesses would become so large that they would drive out competitors and would control the economy?

AR: You mean it's freedom that leads to monopolies?

Carson: This is what people say.

AR: That is one of the worst fallacies, which originated with Karl Marx. A free, unregulated economy does not lead to monopolies. In fact it makes coercive monopolies impossible. Behind every monopoly, there is always an act of government. Monopolies are created by government interference in the economy, in the form of special privileges, franchises or licenses, which give a power to one company that no competitor can enjoy. Under capitalism no field of production can be closed to competition. It is government intervention that creates monopolies and maintains their power, as it is doing today.

Carson: You recently undertook a task that most people would shy away from. You took Pope Paul to task for his recent encyclical, "On the Development of Peoples." To what did you object?

AR: It's a large subject and I would strongly suggest that those interested read my statements on it in ["Of Living Death," in *The Voice of Reason*]. I am prefacing my answer because this is a serious subject, and I don't want to treat it too briefly. I can give you here only the essentials. You will find the details, the documentation and the quotes in my article.

To begin with, this encyclical is a complete condemnation of capitalism. A great many commentators try to evade the fact that the Pope unequivocally denounces capitalism as an evil system, and that he does so on the grounds of its essential principles: the profit motive, private ownership and competition. These are the elements of capitalism that the Pope regards as vicious, and which are *not* the essential elements of any other system. The encyclical does not condemn any system other than capitalism.

Carson: Is capitalism necessarily bad because there is competition and profit?

AR: That's what makes it *good*. Capitalism is a system based on the right of the individual to pursue and achieve his values, and to keep them. And that is what the encyclical profoundly opposes. It speaks in the name of the morality of altruism. It announces, in effect, that man has no right to exist for himself. It demands that the civilized world assume the burden of the entire globe, and give up all its wealth to the undeveloped countries. The encyclical regards the desire for any wealth above the barest minimum required for survival as "selfish greed." Anything above this minimum is allegedly superfluous. The encyclical never tells us what *is* the barest minimum for survival, and for how long a survival and for what kind of survival. The Pope merely declares that man has no right to the product of his own work if anybody around him is in need—which means: if anybody around him *wants* the product of his work.

We must all sacrifice ourselves to others. The happier, the more successful, the more productive we are, the more we should sacrifice.

The encyclical is a call to destroy Western civilization and sacrifice it to the rest of the world. It is ridiculous to talk as if the Pope merely opposes the rich. He calls for higher taxes in the civilized countries, to help the rest of world. We know very well that it isn't just the rich who pay taxes. We know that the burden of taxation in this country falls predominantly on the middle-class and the poor, and that these are the people the Pope wants to sacrifice. To whom? To anyone and everyone in the world. This means the sacrifice of the American standard of living, which is the miracle of the ages. This means the sacrifice of the kind of abundance that the world had never seen before and, if the encyclical has its way, will never see again. Sacrificed to what? To irrationality, to helplessness, to incompetence, to willful stagnation.

Carson: Many people are brought up to believe that charity is the greatest virtue. You take issue with that, do you not?

AR: I certainly do. I think charity is a marginal issue. There are circumstances under which one would properly want to help others, but not at the price of self-sacrifice. But I do *not* believe that charity is a moral virtue or a moral duty. I regard it as not merely neutral, but as positively evil if a man sacrifices his major values for the sake of another person, or for *any* reason.

Carson: What does one do with the less fortunate people of the world, who cannot produce, whatever the reason?

AR: One leaves them free. If it is true, as you say, that they cannot produce, all the more reason to allow freedom to those who *can* produce. Don't tie up the producers. Those who cannot produce will have to count on voluntary charity—and the richer the country, the more generous it is, as you can see is the case in this country.

Carson: When do you think this ideology of yours might take hold?

AR: When man returns to a philosophy of reason—which, incidentally, the papal encyclical opposes most profoundly. It is really directed against the freedom of man's mind.

Carson: Some people hold that your views on reason are rather selfish—that they are not based on any emotional relationships between people and don't leave any room for emotional involvement.

AR: It depends on the kind of emotion. Do you believe that emotions are necessarily irrational? I don't. Man has to be guided by reason, and if he chooses only rational values, he will not experience irrational emotions. His emotions and his mind will be unified. I believe it is only a fully rational man who can feel profoundly, because he has no inner conflicts.

Carson: Would you ever run for political office?

AR: Certainly not!

Carson: Why not?

AR: Because I think that would be the most self-sacrificial action anyone could undertake, particularly today.

Carson: You might have a point there. Well, Miss Rand, it's always most interesting having you on this program. Whether people agree or not, at least we're discussing issues.

AR: I have enjoyed it enormously.

· 27 ·

Speaking Freely, with Edwin Newman, NBC-TV, 1972

I regard the conservatives as infinitely worse and more dangerous [than the liberals]. I am not a conservative—I am a radical
for capitalism.

Edwin Newman: *Miss Rand, you have described the time in which we are living as "an age of envy." Why do you call it that?*

AR: An age is usually classified by the dominant emotional atmosphere, which is always the result of the dominant philosophical ideas, such as the Age of Reason or the Age of Enlightenment. Today, due to the modern philosophical trend—specifically, due to the real destroyer of the modern world: Immanuel Kant—the subconscious, philosophical force driving our culture is envy. This is not true of all people, but it is the basic cultural trend. Envy is merely a part of the feeling I mean; envy is only the common name for it. The actual feeling is: *hatred of the good for being the good*. And here I mean *any* kind of good, according to any sort of moral code. Anything that is a value to men or any virtue that they achieve is hated precisely because it is good.

Newman: *Hated by whom?*

AR: By the people who openly profess the Kantian philosophy, and by all the followers who have never heard of philosophy but have absorbed these ideas and act on them. It is the hatred, predominantly, of man's rational faculty. As a result, those people also hate everything that is rational or strong or independent in men. Normally, it is assumed that one hates somebody—if one hates at all—for some kind of evil, but one loves or admires that which one regards as good. Here, the psychological perversion is that a person is hated precisely for having a quality regarded as good. Such a person is penalized instead of rewarded.

Newman: You said that Kant is the chief destroyer of the modern world. What is it about the Kantian teaching that makes you say that?

AR: I would say: everything. Most philosophers hold mixed premises, and some of their ideas may be wrong and others right. Kant comes as near as anyone could to being wrong on every major point. In every department of philosophy, he has created nothing but evil. Let me give you a basic illustration. He has devised the most ingenious, utterly false but very fancy structure to try to prove that man's mind is impotent and cannot perceive reality. What we perceive is what he calls a "phenomenal" world, some sort of illusion created by some sort of mental structures he calls "categories." Kant claims that we have a collective delusion, which everybody shares, and that's what we perceive. The "real" reality, according to Kant, is the "noumenal" world, which is another dimension, absolutely unperceivable and unknowable. Thus, what we live by—what our consciousness is aware of—is not valid. There is no such thing as reason, in effect. Kant's idea of reason is this guess or this feeling about another dimension. But what we normally call reason is not valid according to Kant. If so, man is defeated.

Newman: I thought your principal objection was to Kant's argument that a moral act is good in itself—not as a means to an end, but as something good in itself. This leads to a flowering of what you call "altruistic liberalism," or "liberal altruism," which you think has deluded a great many people, and has led to many of the troubles you now see at large in the world. I thought that was the center of your objection.

AR: That's right. And it is my next point, but it is part of ethics, which is always based on some view of epistemology. Epistemology is the science that studies what man may accept as knowledge and how he validates it. Any code of ethics needs an epistemological, as well as a metaphysical, base. Kant's ethics, of course, is consonant with his epistemology. Once you declare that man's reason is not valid, you can preach anything you wish. Your enemy is disarmed. You can be arbitrary and mystical, and men have no recourse against you. You have undercut the essential means of man's survival: his rational mind.

Now we get to my point about his ethics. Kant preaches something worse than merely "virtue is its own reward." He claims that any action of yours from which you, or even other people, gain anything is not moral, or is not morally significant. To be moral, an action has to be done out of a sense of duty, from which you derive nothing. If you derive any sort of reward, whether material or spiritual—even simply the pride of being virtuous—your action is no longer moral. Strictly speaking, he is not even an altruist, because an altruist will tell you to sacrifice yourself for the good of others, which is evil enough. But Kant goes further. He says that neither you nor others should profit by a moral action. It should be done for "its own sake," but in the literal sense—with no desirable consequences and for the sake of no goals of any kind.

Newman: *The difficulty I have with this, is that whatever Kant may have said and however strong his influence was, we do live in a period, and have for some time, in which reason, if anything, has been exalted. The scientific method has achieved enormous respect and, in many ways, the technological application of science dominates our lives. Can you say that reason has been destroyed, or even subordinated?*

AR: That is what I say. Everyone today has noted the difference in status between the physical sciences and the sciences of man, or the humanities. In the humanities, we are not only behind science, but we are retrogressing rapidly to the jungle and to primitive man. Science is moving forward tremendously, while ethics and, above all, epistemology have deteriorated. We hear all around us propaganda declaring that "reason has failed," "reason is impotent," "we should be guided by our emotions." We have the hippies and the New Left. We have the entire "back-to-the-jungle" phenomenon, led by people who are anti-science and anti-technology. What are they preaching? A return to the primitive existence of man before he learned to use his mind. Observe the worship of primitive cultures and primitive art. Observe the inarticulateness of so-called art today—and I am using the word "art" here only out of courtesy, because surely modern literature and modern painting are not actually art. Incidentally, it is Kant's esthetics that is the base of today's non-objective art.

Newman: *But apart from non-objective art, which goes back at least a few decades, the other things you cite are very recent. You talked about the hippies, the anti-technology movement, the "back-to-the-jungle" movement. Now, if those things are identifiable as anti-reason, they have occurred only relatively recently.*

AR: But man's mind couldn't be destroyed overnight, fortunately. It has taken the development of decades, actually a century-and-a-half, to reach the ultimate consequences. The fact that we still have the physical sciences is a remnant of Aristotelian epistemology—the Aristotelian view of reason, logic and science. Aristotle is the father of science and, whether scientists recognize him or not, whatever they achieve is on the basis of his logic. And even science, and the whole scientific method, is being undercut enormously by the same modern philosophy, but the process of destruction will take longer there. However, while science—whose purpose after all is to serve man—is still advancing, man is retrogressing. What we haven't discovered is how man should live. What is right and wrong? What is the proper morality? What we see today—the complete, open revolt against reason and morality—is the ultimate consequence of Kantianism.

Newman: In other words, you think the culture has come to a crisis in our time.

AR: Yes, exactly. But if you observe the trend that brought us here, the underlying attitude, or the sense of life, has been intensifying for decades.

Newman: Miss Rand, what is the evidence that the scientific method is being undercut?

AR: Observe the panic created today by rash, unproved conclusions about scientific matters, issued without regard to context or consequences. We see scientists reaching conclusions that are rescinded within a few months. One example is the mercury in tuna fish, initially attributed to today's water pollution, but which we then discovered existed thousands of years ago. A more recent example is the sudden ban on the use of hexachlorophene, which was declared to be dangerous. Within a very short time, there were was an epidemic of infant deaths in maternity wards, because hexachlorophene was the protection the babies needed against certain kinds of infection. The promulgators of these claims are men devoid of a serious, scientific method. They do not know what to regard as proof. They do not know what is required in order to offer a hypothesis, and then to prove or discard it. They predominantly use the statistical method, which is valuable in some realms, but is not the basis of scientific knowledge.

Observe the ecological movement. It predicts that we will destroy the earth. One group of scientists claims that there will be a hothouse effect. Because of the pollution dome, the earth will get too hot and the glaciers will melt. Another group claims that pollution will screen the sun, if I understand correctly, and we will all freeze to death. Now, it is not possible, in rational terms, to hold both hypotheses at the same time, and there is no evidence for either one. Quite the opposite—there is a great deal of evidence to show that we are in no such danger. Yet today the ecologists are demanding, on allegedly scientific grounds, that we stop growing, that we stop existing, that we commit suicide. In order to do what? To protect the earth for the mosquitoes and the birds and the fishes. That's what the demands amount to.

Newman: *If you allow that there is going to be a certain inevitable amount of fumbling in this field, as indeed there is in almost any field, and if you allow for the fact that certain dire predictions will be made that will not come true and that there will be disagreement among scientists, or pseudo-scientists, about what will happen, surely the description you have just given of the ecological movement—making the world safe for mosquitoes—is what's known in logic as a* reductio ad absurdum, *is it not? You're making an absurdity of it.*

AR: Yes. And that's a legitimate, logical method to show the fallacy of a certain line—by proving that if you follow that line, you will reduce it to absurdity.

Newman: *But generally speaking, the goals of the ecological movement are much more modest than those you have set out. Its supporters seek to use, as I understand it, the scientific method and its technological application to bring under control certain excesses that our system seems to have brought forth. Isn't that a fairer way to say it?*

AR: I don't think that's exact, because there are two issues here. One is the nature of the ecologists' goals. The second, which is the one we were talking about, concerns their unscientific methodology. Whatever it is that they claim or invent, if we had a proper epistemological approach to science, they would not take loose hypotheses, proclaim them as proven knowledge and demand political action. In other words, in seeking proper scientific knowledge, one distinguishes a hypothesis from a proven fact. And certainly scientists can disagree. That's proper under free science. We are not infallible and omniscient. But one does not borrow or steal the prestige of science to terrorize man, by making claims that no layman can actually prove or disprove. This approach represents a return to the idea of witch doctors or high priests, who had secret knowledge that other men could not follow, discover or disprove, but had to obey. It is not scientific to scare mankind, even if you have grounds for your claims. It is twice as bad when you don't have grounds. And these so-called scientists certainly don't.

Newman: *You don't object to proposals to bring pollution under control, for example?*

AR: No, so long as it's done by means of objective laws, where proof is offered and where industry isn't made the scapegoat. So long as the rights of everybody concerned are respected and the law is clearly and objectively stated, I don't object to pollution control.

Newman: If the costs are passed on to the consumer, which is the usual way of doing things, then how would industry be made the scapegoat?

AR: To begin with, there is no other way for business to function except to pass on the cost, because business cannot be run at a loss. Politically, though, industry *is* made the scapegoat. Most of the so-called anti-pollution literature consists of open demands for total control over industry—not merely in one country, but across the globe—in order to preserve the environment by means of some undetermined power exercised by some would-be scientists. That is the ecologists' goal. They have said explicitly that the purpose of their crusade is to establish a global state to stop the development of science and technology.

Let's differentiate the two issues. Pollution is merely the fact of visible dirt, such as smog, filthy water or litter on highways. That's pollution, and that certainly should be taken care of. Only it's a job for the sanitation department, public or private. It is not a job for politics, nor a cause for which to enslave mankind. But above all, this is not what the ecologists are concerned about when they claim that industry as such—civilization as such—is threatening the existence of all living species. These are two separate issues.

Newman: We can stay on this a long time and perhaps we should. I happen to have been in London at the time of the so-called "killer smog," which did kill people who had respiratory troubles. There was an obvious increase in the number of people who died from chest ailments at that time, which was 1951 to 1952. The air in London nowadays is a lot cleaner, but it wasn't left to the sanitation department. The improvement came about as a result of laws that were passed through the political processes of the British government. And indeed, we've had laws passed in this country to deal with pollution.

AR: What kind of laws? If they are objective, I wouldn't oppose them. Could you give me an example? In effect, did the laws require industry to install anti-smog devices or burn a cleaner fuel?

Newman: Yes, the laws had to do with the sulfur content of coal or, as in a current proposal, with the lead in gasoline—that kind of thing.

AR: And was the law asking something that was technically possible for industry? Or did it demand the impossible?

Newman: Well, I don't know. In some cases, obviously, it demanded what was feasible. But we now have the question of whether the automobile manufacturers can produce an engine that will meet the stated requirements of the law by 1975.

AR: Now that is a totally improper law. There is no proof that automobile fumes cause pollution or any harm to anyone. I will grant you that smog perhaps does, though I am not sure even of that, according to what I've read. But let's say there may be such a danger. As to automobile fumes, I would need much more evidence, because not much has been given, and there is a great amount of evidence to show that the automobile does not contribute to pollution. On the other hand, when government makes demands ahead of scientific knowledge—if it, in effect, tells industrialists what they have to produce when perhaps it is not possible or when they do not yet know how to produce it—that is an out-and-out violation of the rights of the most productive people in the world, the industrialists. And it is the beginning of the destruction of industry and technology, because nobody can do the impossible.

Newman: That leads us to a subject about which I know you have strong beliefs and that is: what is the proper function of government?

AR: In fundamental terms, only one: the protection of individual rights of the citizens. These rights consist of the right to life and everything that life requires, which means: the right to freedom or the right to the pursuit of one's own happiness. In that respect the Declaration of Independence had it stated beautifully. But the main issue on which we have failed in this country is identifying what constitutes a *violation* of a right. And my view is that the only way in which anyone's rights can be violated is by the initiation of force. It is only by force that you can rob or enslave someone. Therefore, protecting rights consists in protecting individual citizens from the initiation of physical force, either by other citizens or by foreign enemies. That is the only proper function of government. A corollary function is the provision of a legal system of courts, where men can settle their disputes peacefully, according to objectively defined laws—laws that are understood and known in advance, and that do not infringe anyone's rights. But the government should not regulate the economy. There should be a separation of economics and state, in the same way and for the same reason that we have a separation of church and state.

But in the matter of protecting people from physical danger, if certain conditions of employment, let us say, are unsafe and it can be proved that there is a physical risk—I don't say that we have to wait until somebody dies—then the employer who is creating this risk can be sued, and can be severely punished financially. In other words, there can be a law protecting a man from physical injury by another man. In this case, the employer who puts men into conditions of danger—not accidentally, but intentionally or carelessly—can be penalized, because he is infringing the right of his workers not to be injured physically.

Newman: What about a somewhat more difficult matter: the length of a work-week? Should government have a right to say that seventy hours a week are too many, if it believes that working underground for that long is deleterious to the worker?

AR: No. That is not the government's function. The worker has the right to quit if he doesn't want that kind of work. But neither the employer nor the worker nor the government determines those questions arbitrarily. People do not work for seventy hours a week, or under bad conditions, because somebody arbitrarily decides they should. It's an issue of the free market. People take the kind of job they can get, or the kind of job they want, granting a certain kind of choice. At the beginning of industrialization, people were delighted to work under conditions they wouldn't accept today—and don't have to. But all the improvements in the conditions of work, such as the eight-hour day—and today we're reducing that—weren't created by government. They were created by industry. As the productivity of industry rises, as industries devise new machines and labor-saving devices, the productivity of each worker increases. That is what raises the value of his labor and cuts his hours.

Newman: But surely such improvement was also brought about by the coming together of like-minded people who succeeded in putting laws through the political process. The eight-hour-day movement in this country owed nothing to politics?

AR: Actually, in historical fact, no. The productivity of this country owes nothing to politics. All that politics can do is put the brakes on. It can retard progress. It can impoverish a country. But how is it going to raise productivity by passing laws, which means: by chaining you?

Newman: If I understand it, your argument is that the growing productivity of industry made possible what you perhaps would regard as luxuries, such as the laws providing for an eight-hour day, a minimum wage, certain conditions of employment, workman's compensation or whatever.

AR: That's right. And when and if so-called social legislation runs ahead of what an economy can properly absorb—and we have this situation today—who are the victims? The unemployed. Unemployment is created by artificial labor legislation. I am not an enemy of labor unions. Quite the contrary. I think they are the only decent group today, ideologically. I think they are the ones who will save this country and save capitalism, if anybody can. But the one flaw is that the labor unions are government-enforced and thus become a monopoly, able to command higher wages than the market can offer. This union power creates the unemployable. It creates this vast group of people, the unskilled laborers, who have no place to go for work. The artificial boosting of the skilled laborer's income causes unemployment on the lower rungs of society. Every welfare measure works that way. It doesn't affect the so-called rich, if that's what the humanitarians are worried about; it always affects the poor.

Newman: *In that connection, you write in your book* Capitalism: The Unknown Ideal *that "capitalism is being destroyed, without a hearing, without a trial, without any public knowledge of its principles, its nature, its history or its moral meaning." Has capitalism not had a trial, a hearing and public understanding in this country, and in other countries, for many years?*

AR: A trial? Yes, in one respect, you might say that. What we had, particularly up to roughly the period of World War I, was a mixed economy in which the capitalist element predominated. In that sense, capitalism was given a trial— and look at what it created. It led to the enormous rise in everybody's standard of living. It led to the development of science, of technology, of achievement and of individual freedom. That is what a partial capitalism accomplished.

But the other part of the mixed economy—the element of government controls—was slowly growing. In this century it has become the dominant part of the mixture, and we're slowly going down the drain, as all other civilizations have. I don't think we necessarily will be destroyed. I think there's still time to stop this trend. But as it stands today, we are committing suicide by means of the growing controls over the free economy. This point is in regard to the question of whether capitalism has been tried.

But in regard to its being unknown and not understood, capitalism's real problem is that it has never had a moral base. From the beginning of its history and particularly in the United States, where we had the freest example of capitalism, there was a fundamental conflict between the country's economic system and its morality. Capitalism is incompatible with the morality of altruism. Now, one must be clear on what altruism really is. Altruism is the idea that you must live not for your own sake, but for the sake of others—that service to others is the only justification of your life—that you are, in effect, a sacrificial animal existing only for whoever wants to be the collector of sacrifices. Capitalism, however, demands that you pursue your own interests, simultaneously granting the same right to everybody else—which means that you deal with people, not by force, but solely by voluntary agreement and trade. Every man has a right to exist for his own sake. He is not permitted to engage in crimes of violence, which would be a violation of rights and a contradiction, but short of that, his life is his own. You deal with others when you want to, and if you don't want to, each man goes his own way, in pursuit of his own goals. You neither sacrifice yourself to others nor others to yourself. That is the *anti*-altruist view. That is the kind of morality required by capitalism. But that morality never existed, and this country had to come to a crisis, sooner or later. We were split down the middle because of the conflict between capitalism and altruism.

Today altruism is winning, and running amok. Let me go back for a moment to my point about the "age of envy." Groups of any kind that can claim weakness—that can claim a lack or a need of some sort—are now allowed to make demands on the rest of society, which allegedly owes them the fulfillment of those needs. Because they have earned it? No—because they are *weak*. This worship of weakness, which today is crudely blatant, is the ultimate result of the morality of altruism. This morality is what is incompatible with a capitalist economy. This is what has destroyed it.

Newman: Were we ever near what you would consider this ideal society of total capitalism in this country?

AR: Not really. Politically and economically, the freest or most capitalistic society the world has ever known existed in the nineteenth century, up to about World War I. But so long as we didn't have a moral base—so long as a man felt guilty if he succeeded—so long as he was hated and envied for his success—it was not perfect capitalism. That period in history was like a preview given to perceptive people of what is possible to man if he were ever to reach a fully capitalistic society. But the process has to begin with philosophy. When men come to understand that self-sacrifice is morally wrong, when they know why they have the right to pursue their own happiness, when they realize that their greatest virtue is to be rational and to act on their independent judgment—then you will have utopia. In *Atlas Shrugged*, I call it "the utopia of greed." That would be the ideal society.

Newman: You said in connection with Atlas Shrugged *that you were challenging the cultural tradition of twenty-five hundred years. But at the outset of this interview you went back only as far as Kant, which is a matter of perhaps two hundred years.*

AR: Kant was the final destroyer. But it is the broad idea of mysticism—the belief in a supernatural dimension, the belief that reason is not valid and that man's mind cannot perceive reality—that is the cultural tradition I am challenging. And that tradition is much older than Kant. With two exceptions, the whole history of philosophy has been dominated by mysticism and altruism. The exceptions are Aristotle, who was the founder of reason in human existence, and his follower Aquinas, to the extent that he was rational as a philosopher—that is, apart from his religious views. Aquinas was the one who re-introduced the philosophy of Aristotle in the Middle Ages and was responsible, philosophically, for the Renaissance. These two carried the whole development of civilization on their shoulders. But the rest of mankind's ideological trend was characterized by mysticism and altruism. Kant was the culmination. He shaped that trend into its worst, most dangerous form and brought it to a perfect climax.

Newman: Do you classify all religion as mysticism?

AR: Oh, yes. By mysticism, I mean the belief in some knowledge acquired by means other than the evidence of the senses and of reason. And by reason, I mean the faculty that identifies and integrates the material provided by man's senses.

Newman: I believe you've said that on your tombstone you want to have one word engraved: "rational."

AR: As a description of me, that's true. Somebody once said that on my tombstone there should be the word "individualist," and I said no—the word should be "rational."

Newman: Are there courses in Objectivism given under your auspices?

AR: Not anymore. Once in a while there are individual lectures, but no courses.

Newman: I've heard that sometimes in those lectures if the word "God" is mentioned, there is laughter. Is that correct?

AR: No, that is not true. We are not militant atheists. We are opposed to religion as a social phenomenon. We are atheists, but we are not primarily fighting religion. For those who want to have religion, that's fine—only that's a different philosophy.

Newman: I rather got the impression from what you said earlier that you thought religion had an unfortunate effect on the country and on the world.

AR: It does. When I say, "that's fine," I mean politically. So long as it's a free country, they are free to have religion.

Newman: You would not interfere with their right to have it.

AR: I wouldn't interfere with them, and they wouldn't interfere with me. I don't have to deal with them. But I am violently—if I can use that word—in favor of the separation of state and church. When you unite these two, religion is a real menace and is as bad as any other kind of ideology that is imposed by physical compulsion.

Newman: Do you think religion leads people into abandoning the rational method?

AR: Yes, necessarily. The only question is the extent. What does religion mean? It is a belief apart from, or contrary to, your reason. You cannot be rational and at the same time believe in something outside the power of your reason. Now, since nobody can be totally irrational, it is a matter of degree as to how rational a religionist permits himself to be. But in principle, faith is incompatible with reason. You cannot have both in the same system of philosophy.

Newman: Miss Rand, when you speak of "altruistic liberalism," are you using the word "liberal" in a political sense, as it is commonly understood?

AR: I never use the term "altruistic liberalism," because the conservatives are just as altruistic. Altruism is not a monopoly of the liberals. If I use the term "liberalism" at all, I use it in the undefined sense in which is used today, because I have no clear definition of what either "liberal" or "conservative" means. I am certainly in favor of the nineteenth-century liberals, who were advocates of capitalism and of individual rights. Today, however, if you go by the essential trend, liberals are collectivists and altruists. They advocate a welfare state, in which need is the primary claim, and man has no right to exist. That is what today's liberals stand for, although there are all kinds of differences among them..

But I regard the conservatives as infinitely worse and more dangerous. I am not a conservative—I am a radical for capitalism. The conservatives want to reverse this country's direction on the grounds of tradition. A great many of them are trying to connect capitalism to religion, claiming that unless you believe in God you cannot be for capitalism. This amounts to the view that capitalism does not have any rational defense, which implies that collectivism does. It is the view that you need blind, mystical, unsupported faith in order to be an advocate of capitalism. This is as destructive of the possibility of capitalism's ever being understood as any theory could be. It is distinctively capitalism that requires man to function by reason.

The enemies of capitalism, strangely enough know it. Observe the concerted attack on reason in today's culture. Observe that every viewpoint or movement that is collectivistic and altruistic is, without exception, against reason. And the alleged defenders of capitalism, the conservatives—who are not even alleging it too loudly, and certainly not too convincingly, today— believe that they can have a capitalistic system without reason as the guide to human action. They believe they can base capitalism on mystical faith. I think conservatism is as contemptible as any political movement today—about on the level of the New Left. Even the Old Left was more respectable.

Newman: I want to ask you something about that point. You wrote in one of the last issues of The Objectivist: *"The year 1965 marked a perceptible change in this country's cultural atmosphere and an acceleration of its decadence." You went on to say, "Who would care to engage in arguments with grunting hippies, the drug culture or Women's Lib?" You said: "The turning point was the Republican defeat of 1964—not the defeat as such, but the miserably poor intellectual showing made by the country's alleged defenders of capitalism and freedom." Is this why you have less patience with conservatives than with liberals?*

AR: Exactly. I'm glad you read that because it summarizes my attitude on the subject. A political defeat as such is no disgrace, but the Goldwater campaign was the one chance to present the philosophical base of capitalism. And what did we get? A display of bankruptcy by conservatism. This bankruptcy, which the Old Left could not take advantage of, gave birth to the New Left, which openly advocated violence—no mind, no future, no ideas, just: "I want it *now*, and I stamp my foot at reality *because* I want it!" This was the most ridiculous assertion of a spoiled, unintelligent child's psychology. Yet observe how the dominant intellectuals today approve of this attitude, calling it a new morality or a new culture. But it is only the revolt of mindless creatures—creatures who are mindless on principle.

Newman: What about Women's Liberation, which you grouped in here with "grunting hippies and the drug culture"?

AR: I think the members of that movement belong on the same level. They are the extreme, and the caricature, of today's cultural trend. Women have no complaints to make against this country. They are the most privileged group of females on earth. They control the wealth of this country. There is no opposition to career women in America on the scale that exists in the rest of the world. I certainly believe that a woman has a right to a career. She also has the right to be a wife and a mother if she wants to, and if she handles it rationally. I'm certainly a career woman myself and so are all the heroines of my novels. There is no place on earth where a woman has as great a chance to make a career as in the United States.

Now here come these monstrous-looking creatures—who feature their ugliness deliberately, as an insult to everyone else—and they claim they are downtrodden and discriminated against. Here is a group of women claiming that they haven't been given intellectual recognition and that they're not considered as intelligent as men. They want equality and independence. Fine. By what means? By *force*. What are their demands? Free abortions, free day-care nurseries, guaranteed job promotions. To be provided by whom? By *men*—by the very men from whom they claim to want independence. I am astonished that nobody comes out and says openly what is self-evident: that those women project hatred. So do the hippies, of course, but Women's Lib more so. These women project and preach the most offensive hatred toward men. A class war is bad enough—but a sex war?

Newman: *In the nature of things, if the demands are to be made of anybody, don't they have to be made of men? These women would say that it is within the power of the men to grant these things because of the way society is set up.*

AR: But who set up the society for men? Men had to go out into the wilderness and create it by themselves. If women are given all the advantages of this man-made civilization, why don't they do the same thing? Why don't they start on their own and show what they can do? Certainly in a free country there is no law against doing so. A woman who has anything creative or intellectual to offer is still free to do so, in spite of the whole culture, which is set up against personal success and career people in general, male or female. Even so, women still have the chance to succeed. If they want independence, they cannot gain it by starting on a subsidy. One starts by creating one's own achievement. Instead of that, they are setting women back centuries, because the resentment by any sensible person against these demands will be directed against career women and will be with us for a long time.

Newman: *Why would there be such a feeling against career women?*

AR: Because there are many men who feel self-doubt or inferiority, and they fear any successful or intellectual woman. There are men who are afraid of women and prefer little clinging vines, who can seem to be inferior to them. This attitude is old-fashioned and primitive. And it is certainly disappearing rapidly, by the only means by which ideas can change: example and persuasion. Today, however, Women's Lib gives every kind of evidence to support the argument of the men who say that women are irrational, emotional, unreliable and incompetent. Take a look at any Women's Lib demonstration on television. That's the evidence that will be used by any woman-hater and by anyone who believes that women are inferior.

I do not believe that women are inferior—not in intellect, not in ability, not in morality. Not in any sense, except one: they are weaker physically, and in the realm of sex, man is the dominant one and the leader. In intellectual matters, for example, there are women who are more intelligent than men. But man, by his metaphysical nature, is the dominant sex, and should be so—not dominant in terms of using force, but dominant value-wise. I am a man-worshipper. I want to look up to man and I am very disappointed whenever someone falls below the level I expect. But the idea of regarding men as your enemies, and claiming sisterhood with lesbians, is profoundly unfeminine—as well as un-human being—and it destroys the best values within a rational woman.

Newman: What about the regulation of drugs? Should people have open access to all drugs?

AR: Yes, though this would not be the first reform I would advocate on the way to a free society. I am against all controls on drugs—except insofar as sale to minors is concerned—just as I am against prohibitions on liquor. The government has no right to protect a man from himself. If men want to take drugs, that is their political right. Certainly, it is the most immoral action one could commit, because it destroys one's mind. But if a man wants to do it, it's *his* mind. However, under a system that was predominantly capitalistic, we wouldn't have this problem. Observe that the drug problem arises as society becomes more controlled, more collectivized and more irrational. The real cause is that men are trying to escape from an unbearable mental state. They do not know how to deal with reality. Every cultural influence they get, from the progressive schools through the colleges, entails the vicious denial of reason and fosters a cult of hopelessness and depravity. The constant message is: "We're all evil by nature—we are impotent—we can achieve nothing—nothing better is to be expected." When someone hears that day in and day out, unless he is an unusual intellect and an unusually moral person, he will collapse. He will reach for drugs to escape the feeling of his own confusion and helplessness. If any one thing is responsible for the drug problem, it is progressive education, which destroys the child's capacity to think.

Newman: Your novel Atlas Shrugged *shows the American industrial system, indeed the world industrial system, in a state of collapse brought on by government controls and by too much altruism. Is that what you see happening today?*

AR: Not "too much" altruism—*any.* Yes, I see the novel coming true in a more literal sense than I ever expected: the destruction of reason, the orgy of altruism, the demands for sacrifice of everybody to everybody else, complete intellectual chaos, the destruction of the independence of industry. The one thing I didn't predict, because I couldn't have reached that state of imagination, is the ecological crusade. That's the cherry on the cake—the attempt to obliterate industry openly, blatantly, consciously. On a better note, the heroes in *Atlas Shrugged*, who were the representatives of man's creative mind, went on strike. Today, too, most creative people are on strike—not by conscious knowledge or purpose, but in the sense of being given no chance. This comes back to the issue of our age of envy. These people are envied, resented and penalized, and are therefore somewhere in the underground. What I am working for is the prospect of seeing, in our lifetime, at least the beginning of a return to a better world, as we saw one in *Atlas Shrugged*.

· 28 ·

Day and Night, a television program hosted by James Day, 1974

[Reading the works of Victor Hugo] was the greatest literary experience I ever had, incomparable and incommunicable.

James Day: *You have said that your primary purpose in writing is to project the ideal man. For those who may not have read* Atlas Shrugged *and have not yet met Hank Rearden or John Galt, how would you describe the ideal man?*

AR: It took me seven hundred thousand words in *Atlas Shrugged* to do it, so it's impossible to give a full description here. But I can tell you the essential characteristics. Above all else, he is a man guided exclusively by reason, a man of independence and a man of great self-esteem. These three are the distinguishing characteristics of what I regard as an ideal man.

Day: *So a rational man would depend upon nothing except his own reason for determining his actions, with no belief in anything he couldn't see or touch?*

AR: That isn't exactly the definition of reason. Certainly, an ideal man would have no blind faith in anything. But reason is the faculty that identifies and integrates the material provided by your senses; you don't smell or touch with your reason. Sensations are the material that reason integrates into concepts. And certainly an ideal man would never permit himself to act on the guidance of emotions or to act without knowing exactly what he's doing. If he's guided by reason, these will be the first two consequences: he will always know what he is doing, and why. He will not act blindly. He will not act simply because he feels like it. To my ideal man, and to me, one of the most immoral actions

223

anyone can permit himself is to say "I did it because I felt like it." It's quite all right to feel, but feelings are not tools of cognition. They are not guides to reality. Feelings are the consequences of thought, not the primaries.

Day: Well, if I didn't do something because I felt like it, why did I do it?

AR: Because you *concluded* consciously that this was the right thing to do. You rationally decide what goal you want, and you rationally choose the steps you will take in pursuit of that goal. If you take a given action, you do so because you think it is right.

Day: Should man have any concern for other men?

AR: "Concern" is a very loose term. What do you mean by it?

Day: Well, most of us are brought up on an ethics that says we are our brother's keeper.

AR: We most certainly are not, could not be and should not attempt to be. The only concern men should have for others is respect for their rights. A man should never expect another man to sacrifice for him, nor should he sacrifice himself for another. He should respect the independence of others and never take part in any form of political enslavement. But outside of that, he is not responsible for other men and should never permit them to assume the role of responsibility for him. He should neither submit to nor exercise force. He should not ask others to live for his sake, nor should he ever live for the sake of others. He should treat others as traders. That is, if two men want to cooperate, they should trade value for value, voluntarily, without sacrifice on either one's part. They both serve their rational self-interest by dealing with one another. And if they don't want to deal with each other, they should not be forced to.

Day: You place the emphasis upon the rational—i.e., on their rational self-interest?

AR: Certainly. I place that emphasis on everything because the determination of what is proper for you can be made only on a rational basis. All your rights rest on your nature as a rational being. If you want to claim any kind of rights, you cannot claim them for your feelings, only for your mind. And the only actions I regard as moral are the ones based on rational goals and rational motives.

Day: *If actions not based upon reason are immoral, what about charity, which is based upon emotion?*

AR: Charity is a marginal issue. One of my main tenets is that charity should never be a duty. When you want to help someone, it is proper, provided you do it on the basis of his *values*—because he's a good person who suffers through no fault of his own or because he's a friend of yours or because he's a victim of injustice. But granting a man charity not for some accidental misfortune, but for a misfortune brought about by his own evil, is the kind of help I regard as immoral.

Day: *How does the concept of love for one another fit into this philosophy?*

AR: Shall we start with romantic love, because I don't quite understand indiscriminate love for one another.

Day: *Well, romantic love certainly is a part of your novels.*

AR: Romantic love is the most properly selfish emotion there is. You fall in love with a person because you regard him or her as a value, and because he or she contributes to your personal happiness. You couldn't fall in love with a person by saying: "You mean nothing to me; I don't care whether you live or die, but you need me and therefore I'm in love with you." If someone offered love of that kind, everyone would regard it as a deadly insult. That isn't love. Therefore, romantic love is a selfish emotion. It reflects your choice of a person as a great value. What you fall in love with is the same values you choose for yourself, embodied in another person. That's romantic love. Any lesser form of love, such as friendship or affection, involves the same thing. You grant a feeling to those you have concluded are values to you. Your response to others is on the basis of values—and if some people are no good, then you feel the appropriate emotion of contempt.

Day: *Are values absolute? Are they either good or evil? Is there any area in between?*

AR: It depends on what you mean. Values depend on the context of a given situation. There are, unfortunately, too many people who are part good and part bad. What morality demands of them is to struggle to the best of their ability to be good and never to do evil consciously. If a man never commits evil consciously and deliberately, I would regard him as completely good. However, if he takes just one action that he knows to be wrong but nonetheless permits it to himself, then he is absolutely evil. The rest is only a matter of time.

Day: You've written that the concept of God is morally evil. Why?

AR: I didn't say it is morally evil. I said it is false. I said it is a fantasy. Religion can be very dangerous psycho-epistemologically, that is, in regard to the working of a man's mind. Faith is dangerous because a man who permits himself to exempt some aspect of reality from reason— to believe in the existence of God even though he knows there is no evidence for it—will not be rational, or will have a terrible conflict. However, I certainly recognize anyone's legal right to practice any religion he wants to. But morally or philosophically—that's a different issue.

Day: For many people religion is a way of explaining the mysteries and the unknown things of life. Do you recognize no mysteries?

AR: I don't believe that lack of knowledge is a license to start inventing fantasies. Man certainly is not omniscient, and he should stay within the realm of what he knows. He should act on his knowledge and constantly try to expand it. I don't think there are "mysteries"—that's the wrong term. There are a great many things man doesn't know, and that's the purpose of scientific progress: to give him more and more knowledge. But you do not invent explanations for what you do not yet know.

Day: Miss Rand, you're an atheist. Were you always an atheist? Did you grow up with religious training at all?

AR: I had practically no religious training. My parents had their religion but fortunately didn't impose it on me in any serious way. I was about thirteen when I decided I was an atheist, and that was that.

Day: Was there anything in particular that brought you to that conclusion?

AR: No, just my thinking about the subject. My main reason was that it is wrong to believe anything for which there is no evidence. I also resented religious morality, which tells man that he's an inferior being.

Day: He's not?

AR: He is not. As far as he knows, he's the highest being in civilization. The idea of accepting on faith some ineffable being who is superior to you in every way, even though you cannot aspire to that perfection, is just a formula for an inferiority complex and for self-abasement. I saw no reason to accept it. That's what I thought as early as thirteen. I still think so, but I know it much more clearly now.

Day: *What kind of education did you have as a young person? You grew up in what is now Leningrad but was then St. Petersburg. Did you go to regular schools?*

AR: I had the equivalent of what here is called high school—the gymnasium in Russia—and graduated from the University of Leningrad.

Day: *What were your interests in those early years? Were they in literature and in writing?*

AR: I had decided at the age of nine that I would be a writer. That was my one overriding interest. But I didn't major in literature at the university. From what I had gathered about the kind of literary courses being given, I knew I would learn nothing about that subject in school. So I majored in history because I wanted to know the history of mankind as a sort of broad frame of reference for my future novels.

Day: *Were there books or writers you were influenced by in those formative years?*

AR: Only one philosopher and one writer. The writer was Victor Hugo, whom I discovered at thirteen. It was the greatest literary experience I ever had, incomparable and incommunicable. I admired him enormously. The sense of life that he communicated, by projecting the grandeur of man, was so high above anything I had encountered in any other books—and was certainly in another universe compared with the reality of Soviet Russia—that I, to this day, owe a huge debt of gratitude to him. And it is from Hugo that I learned the art of the Romantic novel, in the serious sense of the term: the integration of the plot's action with the theme and philosophical meaning of a book. I don't agree with his philosophy but I admire him tremendously as a writer. The other influence was Aristotle, in philosophy. He is the only philosopher with whom I agree, not on everything, but at least on the fundamentals. I don't agree with the Platonic element in him, but I do agree with that which is originally his. He had a great deal of influence on my subsequent thinking. But those are the only two—Hugo and Aristotle.

Day: *Did you begin writing at the age of nine?*

AR: I began slightly earlier, at eight-and-a-half. I remember that the first story I wrote was signed with my name and "eight-and-a-half" after it.

Day: *Was it fiction?*

AR: Yes. It was a movie scenario. I was very impressed with the screen and I started writing screen stories. I attempted my first novel at the age of sixteen, in my first year in college, and had to give it up. I was growing too fast. It became dated by the time I was in my second year. I didn't start writing professionally until I was in this country.

Day: *When you began writing fiction, did you write within the framework of what you call Romantic Realism—portraying man as he could be?*

AR: Always.

Day: *Were you influenced by living in a Soviet society?*

AR: Not at all. It might have helped me in realizing how evil the opposite of individualism is. Grasping how bad collectivism is in practice might have been a value, but it's a horrible kind of experience. I would rather have arrived at the positive without encountering that negative. But I can proudly say that the experience did not change anything in my way of thinking and in my development. I went to a Soviet university. At that time, there were still some good professors, who were actually teaching legitimate subjects. But there was also a great deal of propaganda and it did not affect me in the least. For that, I'm very grateful to myself.

Day: *You came to America when you were about 20 or 21 years old and you went to Hollywood. Was this because of your interest in screenwriting?*

AR: Yes, though that was not my ultimate interest. I could then barely speak English and certainly couldn't write it. But it was the time of silent movies. I had figured out that I could write a scenario but not yet dialogue. That's why I decided I would start with the screen. But my first ambition always was to write novels.

Day: *You earned your living in the early years in Hollywood in a variety of ways, I suppose.*

AR: Yes, I had a bad struggle. I had to hold odd jobs and even waited on tables. The first day I tried it, I was fired on the spot. But with the last job of that kind, I was there a whole week—so I was learning. This was during the Depression, and times were very difficult. I held all kinds of jobs that were very, very boring. But I was able to write.

Day: *Is it good for one's character to have to suffer that way, to work as hard as you worked?*

AR: No, I don't think so. The only good is later. It gives you a certain self-confidence if you can overcome the hardship and rise above it. But I don't think hardships as such are good for anyone.

Day: *You worked without pay for an architect, out of which experience you first began to write* The Fountainhead. *Is that the reason you went to work for that architect?*

AR: As research for *The Fountainhead?* Oh, yes. I had asked him for the job for that reason. He knew I was doing research for a novel, but no one else in the office knew.

Day: *That was not your first novel, but your third, was it not?*

AR: Yes. My first novel was *We The Living,* and *Anthem* was a novelette. *The Fountainhead* came next.

Day: *Did you have difficulty getting your novels published? I've read that you had some problems with publishers who didn't accept them readily.*

AR: I had bad difficulties with *The Fountainhead.* Twelve publishers rejected it on the grounds that it was too intellectual and wouldn't sell. Of course, it's one of the great examples of a book made strictly by word-of-mouth; it was the readers who made this book. And it's still going as strong as ever.

Day: *How many years after publication?*

AR: It was published in 1943, so it's 31 years.

Day: *Do you understand why it became so popular?*

AR: Oh, yes. Because I was presenting readers with a philosophy that is desperately needed today and that doesn't exist anywhere else. And because there was an absolute desert in literature—both in regard to literary quality and in regard to the genre of Romantic Realism. Practically every serious novel in those years was Naturalistic. But the more important factor was the philosophy of individualism.

Day: Why do you not like a Naturalistic novel?

AR: Because it is an incomplete work of art. It has certain elements of art, such as characterization, and some Naturalistic novels have a good style. But art—and this I can prove philosophically—is a re-creation of reality, not a photograph. Art is not journalism. It is a re-creation of reality according to an artist's metaphysical value-judgments.

Day: Does that mean that you write only about what ought to be, not what is?

AR: Yes, but let me finish. I want to be sure that the audience understands what I mean by "metaphysical." I mean the nature of reality as such. It is his view of man and of the nature of existence that an artist expresses in his art. Romantic art presents to man what he might be and ought to be. That is, it presents an ideal and declares: this is the essential nature of man and you, as a human being, can become that if you wish. In that sense, Romantic art is model-building. However, the purpose of art is *not* to teach. Art should never be didactic. That's a secondary issue, which is pure gravy. The primary purpose of art is contemplation for its own sake. In Romantic art, the purpose is for the reader to see what greatness man is capable of and to be inspired by that sight.

Day: So as I read Atlas Shrugged *and encounter any of the heroic characters— Hank Rearden or John Galt or Francisco d'Anconia—they give me a model of the kind of person I might be?*

AR: If you wish. But, again, that isn't my purpose in writing. My purpose is for you to look at those people and to enjoy the spectacle. As a secondary consequence, you might find yourself motivated to emulate them. That's fine. But fundamentally I want to give you that sheer experience, and that's what I want to give myself. I write for the purpose of creating an ideal man in action, whom you can respect and admire—and whom you don't find too often in life today.

Day: You've said that the ideal man would be productive, and that the most favorable environment for such a man is laissez-faire capitalism. So would you oppose antitrust laws, income taxes and all the other restraints that are normally imposed?

AR: Certainly. But they are not "normally" imposed—they are imposed *ab-*normally. I am opposed to all that. You have to leave men free to function. I believe in complete laissez-faire, not a mixed economy. What we have today is certainly not capitalism.

Day: From what you say about art, I would judge that you do not regard photography as art, since it records precisely what is here. How do you feel about abstract art?

AR: Do you mean non-objective art? I think it's less art than is photography. I think it is an enormous fraud, which is impossible to discuss seriously. It means nothing and it is nothing. The perpetrators claim they don't know what they're doing, and I'm willing to take them at their word: they don't know what they're doing, and neither do we. The ashcan is the proper place for such work. And I mean that seriously.

Day: I suspect that many of your readers wonder whether you plan to write any more novels.

AR: Yes, I'm under contract to write one. But I can't promise you when I will have it done.

Day: How many years did it take you to write Atlas Shrugged, *which is an enormous volume?*

AR: Thirteen years. But my next novel won't be that long. *Atlas* is just once in a lifetime.

Day: I should think so! I want to return for just one moment to religion and to the ethics on which so many of us were raised. Religion is used by some people as a way of facing the inevitability of death. How do you, as an Objectivist, feel about death?

AR: It doesn't concern me in the least, because I won't be here to know it. The worst thing about death, and what I regard as the most horrible human tragedy, is to lose someone you love. That is terribly hard. But your own death? If you're finished, you're finished. My purpose is not to worry about death but to live life now, here on earth.

Day: What are the sources of joy in your life? Achievement?

AR: Achievement, and the love I have for my husband. Those are the two great values in life: career and romantic love.

· 29 ·

Focus on Youth, a radio show hosted by Garth R. Ancier, 1976

I am not against the institution of marriage, but I am much more *for* the institution of sex. . . . It should not be treated as a mere bathroom function, which is the way the moderns regard it.

Garth Ancier: *In* The Fountainhead *you wrote, "I think the only cardinal evil on earth is that of placing your prime concern within other men." Haven't you devoted your life to writing for others, not only to entertain them, but to persuade them of your ideas? Aren't you displaying your own concern for others by trying to educate them?*

AR: No, because it is to my selfish interest to live in a civilized world and to deal with intelligent, rational, moral people. Therefore, I have to spread the right ideas, if I know what they are, in order to ensure a better world for myself—at least to the extent to which I am successful. My doing so helps others incidentally, but it is not for their sake that I am writing or spreading ideas.

Ancier: *You have been called a "radical for capitalism," which implies an opposition to big government. This same sentiment is being expressed by Governor Jerry Brown and, until recently, by Governor Jimmy Carter. Do you think this is a healthy sign of a return to capitalism?*

AR: First of all, I wasn't called a "radical for capitalism"; I called myself that. And I did so in order to indicate that my philosophy of capitalism is radically—that is, fundamentally—different from current theories. It was to indicate a basic disagreement with today's political philosophies that I chose

233

this description. However, Mr. Carter and Mr. Brown say they are for anything on earth and only God, if there is one, knows what they are *really* for—but it is not capitalism. Both of them are mystics. Both are advocates of emotions, not of reason. And you cannot advocate a free society without advocating reason. You need reason as the common denominator among men and as the base of a free society. A twice-born mystic and a once-born Orientalist are not advocates of capitalism, even if they wanted to be, which neither of them does.

Ancier: In Atlas Shrugged, *Francisco d'Anconia says that money is a product of man's ability to think and to achieve. Is that true of money in America today?*

AR: You could not have a society that uses money if there weren't people willing to work and produce. If everybody acted like our politicians, there would be no money, simply because there would be nothing to trade it for. There would just be worthless paper, as in the German hyperinflation. Money as a medium of exchange stands for achievement. But that doesn't mean its use cannot be subverted, particularly in a mixed economy. Today, an awful lot of people connected with Washington do get money they don't deserve. The fact that someone is rich today does not prove at all that he has earned his wealth. His wealth might be the result of special favors from the government, which means that he has gained it not by merit, but by force. However, that's the corruption of money. Money itself, as a social tool, is based on the idea that one receives it honestly and earns it by merit.

Ancier: You have spoken of money as a sign of achievement. Man strives to attain something and then is given a monetary reward. That seems to contradict the idea that a man's self-respect should come from within himself and from his own strength.

AR: What on earth would give you the idea that Objectivism advocates a mind-body dichotomy, and that it leans toward what I call "the mystics of spirit"? The notion that a man should live inside his mind, and ignore the outside world, contradicts Objectivism. Objectivism believes, and proves, that man is an integrated being of mind and body. His values start in his mind, and he survives by the use of his mind. But what does it mean to use his mind? It means to apply his thinking toward the achievement of values in the material world. Thinking is only a tool by which to acquire knowledge, and the purpose of knowledge is man's survival. If man were rewarded only from within himself and did not get any reward from the outside world which was voluntarily dealing with him, he would be living in a Kantian-Christian world. It would be a world in which virtue is its own reward. I have never advocated that, and never will. I say the exact opposite: virtue is the only way properly to acquire outside, material rewards.

Ancier: Do you place any limit on the amount of external satisfaction or material benefits a man would want to attain? In other words, assume that a man reaches a level well beyond sustenance and is living very comfortably. What would happen to his need for achievement and for more money at that point?

AR: To begin with, neither I nor you, nor anyone else, can put such a limit on another man's activity. Secondly, in a free economy you make as much money as your business requires. A manufacturer of some simple, popular product will make much more money than the best philosopher or novelist, because he deals with more people, and more people directly need his product. Consequently, he needs much more money to expand his business than I would, for instance. The purpose of any true industrialist, such as Hank Rearden, is productive activity, not money as such. It's the politicians in Washington who want to get money but not to earn it. A man who wants to earn money has to constantly expand and improve his production. In view of today's scientific achievements, how can anyone institute a limit? If a man has exhausted all his possibilities on earth, which is impossible, he can establish a shuttle to another planet. There is so much that we can do materially, with the proper development of scientific knowledge, that there is no one who could properly put a limit on human development. By proposing a limit, what you are saying in effect is: "Let's stagnate."

Ancier: Whom would you consider to be the top five philosophers in the twentieth century?

AR: In the twentieth century, you would have *minus* five. I couldn't name anyone above zero. In the twentieth century, pick them at random and they are one worse than the other. Perhaps Wittgenstein is the most ludicrous. I would put Bertrand Russell as a close second. In the whole history of philosophy, I'd say there are only one-and-a-half philosophers I profoundly respect: Aristotle is the "one," and Thomas Aquinas is the "half." And by "half," I am referring to his philosophical ideas, which are Aristotelian, and to his development of Aristotelian premises; the negative half of Aquinas consists of his religious ideas.

Ancier: In The Fountainhead *and* Atlas Shrugged, *the scandalous activities of the heroines—of which you obviously approve—lead one to believe that you question the institution of marriage.*

AR: What did you call them? Scandalous activities?

Ancier: Well, they were at the time.

AR: You mean as evaluated by society, outside of my novels? But in that sense, everything I've written is scandalous, because I go against the basic ideas accepted by society. That's why I am a radical.

Ancier: Is society's attitude toward sex, including premarital sex, a healthy sign?

AR: No, very, very unhealthy. To begin with your original question, I am not against the institution of marriage, but I am much more *for* the institution of sex. I regard it as a great value, a very important aspect of human life that men and women should not take lightly. It is a main source of human happiness. It should not be treated as a mere bathroom function, which is the way the moderns regard it. Today, instead of freedom of sex, they endorse the most disgusting, deliberate offensiveness, which will only lead back to some kind of mid-Victorian, anti-sex attitude. The real question here is not: "Are you in favor of permitting free sex or forbidding it?" The real question is: "Do you regard sex as a value or as a low-grade activity?" That's where the line has to be drawn. If you regard it as a value, then you will have an appropriate attitude toward it. That is, you get married when it suits your view of your life or you carry on affairs—but only one affair at a time and only very serious ones, not casual, one-night stands. If, on the other hand, you regard sex as evil, you either forbid it, as the religionists do, or you consider it so unimportant that you go around having sex like animals, as the hippies do. The religionists and the hippies are two sides of the same coin, and represent a fundamentally anti-sex attitude.

Ancier: You seem to hold the view that if man reasons out his values, his emotions will come into perfect accord with them. You believe that he will never have conflicts—an emotional desire to do something that is contrary to his intellectual goals.

AR: That's right.

Ancier: In view of the efforts of behavioral psychologists to alter behavior by un-blocking people's emotions, how can you scientifically support your assertion that emotions accord with reason?

AR: The simplest way would be for me to say, "Here I am." Scientifically test me and you will find that in my whole life—and I am quite old—I have never had an emotion that I couldn't identify or that clashed with my reason for longer than perhaps a day, at most. If it's a very complex emotion, the reason for which I don't readily know, it will take me a day to identify it.

First, however, you have to know the status of the science of psychology. Psychology today is on the level of witch-doctoring. It doesn't exist yet as a science; it is in the stage of pre-science. Whatever of value is being done in the field, it is through guessing, out of which a future science will grow. This future science will require a basic theory. It will requite basic premises that utilize such knowledge as has been discovered. That doesn't exist today. If you are talking about such things as "encounter therapy," where people are supposed to smell each other and rub against each other to get cured, I would say you aren't talking about science. It doesn't take a scientist or a philosopher to figure that out—a truck driver knows that this kind of nonsense is an enormous pretense. And the sole point of the pretense is to destroy human psychology and to destroy science. The only thing psychologists have demonstrated is the monstrous anti-rationality of today's culture. The fault lies with today's dominant philosophy, because psychologists are not philosophers. If today's philosophers stand for it, the psychologists will run wild. And they are running wild, and are creating victims in the process. That is the horrible part.

On the positive side, let me briefly answer your question about how to prove the relationship between reason and emotion. Define what you would take as proof and then conduct any experiment you want in regard to correlating human knowledge and emotional response. Teach people first of all how to introspect, and your experiments will discover the correlation very simply. I will borrow one example from the experience of a very good friend of mine, Dr. Leonard Peikoff. He is a philosopher, and he told me that when he would teach in universities, even to freshman classes, he would proceed to explain the Objectivist theory of emotion. Then, without any warning, he would distribute examination books as if he were suddenly going to give the students a test. They were horrified and indignant, saying, "You didn't warn us that there was going to be an exam." He let them indulge their emotions for a while, and then explained that this incident should prove to them, by introspection, that their emotions come from their knowledge and their values. They thought that an exam would be dangerous to them and so they felt angry and frightened. The moment he told them it was only an experiment, their thinking changed and their emotions vanished. That's a simple, experimental proof.

Ancier: *Do you think that the United States is reaching a point where the men of intelligence will go on strike, as occurred in* Atlas Shrugged?

AR: If enough men of intelligence shared my philosophy, they wouldn't *have* to go on strike. What is happening is not that men are literally going on strike, but that they are going on strike involuntarily, without knowing it. It is becoming so much more difficult for the men of ability to rise, and even just to function, that many of them are giving up before they start. We have this gray, horrible atmosphere of mediocrity, because the better men, or too many of them, are apparently not functioning right now.

Ancier: Your experience as a screenwriter is evident in your books. What do you think about today's films and do you have any desire to write another screenplay for the movies or for television?

AR: I have no desire to write one. But what do I think of today's movies? I haven't been to a movie in probably four or five years. I have cable television at home, but I have not subscribed to any movie channel, because I know there is nothing I would want to see. My interest in TV ended with *Perry Mason*. That's the series I like best; I still watch it whenever reruns appear. But modern detective stories, much as I try to watch them, are unspeakably bad.

Ancier: You wrote in For the New Intellectual *that if we were to ask our intellectual leaders what ideals we should fight for, their answers would be a "sticky puddle of stale syrup," as you put it. Who, specifically, are these intellectual leaders?*

AR: Any professor today, any columnist or anyone to whom you would address a moral question. If you want the most current example, take Jimmy Carter. Did you ever see a stickier puddle than his assertion, "We must be moral," with not a word about what that consists of?

Ancier: Do you think that the Humphrey-Hawkins bill, which has at its roots the belief that every man has the right to a job, is beneficial to society?

AR: No, it's pure, theoretical Communism—not just political Communism, but *philosophical* Communism. If enacted and fully implemented, it would lead to actual Communism because jobs don't grow on trees. To guarantee every man a job, you have to enslave some other men. In order to give something man-made to one group of men, you have to enslave the group that produces it. To guarantee jobs, you would have to enslave the best men, i.e., the most productive and the ablest. In favor of whom? The unemployed. Some of the unemployed may be very talented and may be out of work through no fault of their own, but a great many of them do not care to work. They are parasites on principle—and today's intellectual leaders *teach* them to be parasites on principle. My hope is that we are not yet so corrupt as to sacrifice this country to those men. Humphrey-Hawkins is one of the worst bills ever proposed. It may pass, but they had better repeal it as fast as they can.

Ancier: In much of your writing you demand a completely free society in which men can function rationally. You've said that the United States is the closest thing to such a society, and yet you've pointed out again and again that it has many more governmental controls than it should have. Doesn't this indicate that in fact men do not operate on reason, but on emotion? How, then, is your philosophy relevant to them?

AR: I will argue only by asking you to focus on what it means to be rational. To be rational is to be consistent with reality. Man has no choice about the need to be rational. Either he is rational or he dies—that is the only alternative. To say that men are not rational means that they don't *want* to be. But if they don't want to act in accordance with reality, reality will take care of it. Man cannot survive unless he acts rationally. Now, you quoted me as saying that the United States has more controls than it should have. I want to correct you: there should be no economic controls at all. What I advocate is the separation of economics and state, in the same way and for the same reason as the separation of church and state.

Ancier: Miss Rand, is there anything more to say about your philosophy that you haven't said already?

AR: I'm glad you are not that acquainted with my philosophy, because if you were, you'd know I haven't nearly said everything yet. I do have a complete philosophical system, but the elaboration of a system is a job that no philosopher can finish in his lifetime. There is an awful lot of work yet to be done.

· 30 ·

The Raymond Newman Journal, a radio show, 1980

Individualism is an American concept. . . . The greatest distinction the European can dream of is to serve, or be rewarded by, the state.

Raymond Newman: When I first undertook this series of radio shows, I made a list of the people I wanted to interview They had to be people who had something important to say and who had accomplished things that merited recognition. I immediately put one name at the top of the list. You can imagine the great pleasure I now have when I tell you that my special guest today is that person: Miss Ayn Rand. Like her hero Howard Roark in The Fountainhead, *Ayn Rand is an architect—but she is an architect of ideas, structuring her own unique philosophy, Objectivism. It is a philosophy that has influenced millions of people around the world. Miss Rand, I welcome you to the show. Many people think of philosophy as affecting only a portion of life, perhaps politics or economics or morality. But your philosophy ties together all aspects of human life. Could you speak briefly about the principles at the core of Objectivism?*

AR: I shall try but it is obviously very difficult, because if Objectivism could have been presented briefly, I should have done so. Instead, I have written millions of words, and even at that, I cannot say that I have completely finished. Philosophy, since it underlies everything in life, cannot be presented too briefly. I can only give you the essentials and hope that, if you are interested in philosophy, you can understand what they mean,.

Philosophy has five branches. The basic one is metaphysics, and closely associated with it is epistemology. In fact, the two cannot be separated. In

241

metaphysics, Objectivism holds that there is only one reality—not two, nor four, nor ten—which we perceive by means of our senses, and that the things we see do exist. Our purpose as conscious beings is to gain knowledge of that reality. And this is the province of the second department of philosophy, epistemology—the theory of knowledge. Epistemology tells us what we know, how we know it and what we may properly regard as knowledge. Objectivism holds that reason is man's only faculty for gaining knowledge of reality, and for guiding his choices and actions. By "reason," I mean the faculty that identifies and integrates the material provided by man's senses.

The next branch of philosophy is ethics, or morality. It tells man how to make the basic choices on which the conduct of his life depends. The fourth branch, politics, is the study of man's relationship with other men, and it is based on the kind of morality that a given philosophy upholds. There are certainly evil ideas at the base of most political systems; nevertheless, some theory of right and wrong underlies every kind of political system on earth. The fifth branch is esthetics, the part of philosophy that deals with art.

There is your skeleton. Let's quickly fill it with flesh.

Newman: *Is it true that if a person holds a certain view of metaphysics, he is likely to develop a certain ethics?*

AR: Yes, certainly.

Newman: *If, for example, a person holds the view that life is mysterious and unknowable, what morality would he likely develop?*

AR: Most probably the one that is prevalent today: altruism. He desperately needs someone to guide him. By his belief that life is unknowable, he confesses that he has not made many attempts to learn anything, because life certainly is *not* unknowable. Since he has given up trying to understand reality, he is not able to survive unless somebody sacrifices for him and guides him. He cannot stand on his own. He cannot possibly practice the virtue of independence. This mentality, by logical progression, leads to the culture of today.

Newman: *And what politics would he likely support?*

AR: Collectivism. That is, a system in which the tribe, the herd, the society, other men—or, actually, a dictator—will supposedly take care of him. He will thus get the kind of "care" he deserves.

Newman: Let me extend it one step further and ask what his esthetic preferences would be.

AR: I don't know, but probably the kind of junk that's sold today—something allegedly emotional, with no plot or structure, as far as novels are concerned; something with no intelligible subject matter, as far as painting is concerned. That is what will appeal to him, because he does not want to exercise his faculty of reason. He does not want to think.

Newman: I heard you a couple of years ago say in response to a question: "Don't accept anything without proof. Make me prove everything I say." That was very refreshing to hear from a philosopher, because usually a philosophy will come to a point where it requires you to accept something on faith. Your book The Virtue of Selfishness *caused quite a flurry because selfishness is often thought of as an un-complimentary trait, to say the least, and yet you state that it is a virtue. Will you prove to me that selfishness is a virtue?*

AR: I cannot possibly in the time you would permit me. Half-an-hour isn't enough—an hour isn't enough. But if you read that book, it will give you some idea of why selfishness is the top virtue, equal to rationality. Just to indicate that the proof does exist, I will call your attention to the following point. Man cannot survive without a code of values, which tells him how to act. Man is not programmed with an "instinct" for survival. He may have a desire to survive, but he doesn't have the knowledge. He needs to acquire knowledge of how to live. Man needs to know what actions will further his life and what actions will destroy it. He survives by means of a volitional faculty, reason, which he may choose to exercise or not. He is not forced to think; he can suspend his reason—but if he does, he will be helpless to survive. Philosophy provides the code of values needed to sustain man's life. Ethics, in effect, is a life-preserving discipline which man has to understand and apply to his own life. So it is his metaphysical nature as a human being that requires a morality to tell him how to protect and fulfill his own existence.

Newman: You have logic behind your ideas, and yet so many people adopt opposite principles. Why have people turned away from the concepts you advocate?

AR: They haven't "turned away"—they have never held them.

Newman: Weren't the kind of ideas you present more accepted in the early days of this country?

AR: Yes, but only by implication. Those ideas are implicit in a free, capitalist society, but they are not explicit. The trouble was that altruism, the prevailing morality of centuries of human degradation and misery, was combined with a political system that required an entirely different morality. The politics of this country, as established by the Founding Fathers—who were Aristotelian, and with whom I agree politically in practically every respect—required an ethics that would justify and explain the proper, rational kind of selfishness. By that I don't mean doing whatever you please or indulging every whim; I mean practicing those virtues and pursuing those values that a man's survival requires. Instead, America was split from the beginning. It had a political structure that was unprecedented in world history and, in essentials, perfect—but which rested on a moral base of altruism.

This conflict destroyed America. There was no understanding of a proper, selfish morality—a morality that does not sacrifice you to other men, nor allow you to sacrifice other men to yourself—a morality that holds man as an end in himself and tells each individual that it is right to pursue his own happiness, provided he can justify it in rational terms. For example, you could not justify finding your happiness in the destruction of other men. You could never rationally justify murder, robbery or harm done to other men—nor would you enjoy such actions if you are a rational person. On the other hand, you are not a sacrificial animal. You are not here as a means to the ends of others. It is not in the least bit noble or inspiring to die for another man. Why should you? Now, if it is someone you love, that is a different issue. You may or may not choose to die to save your loved ones—but it is not an issue of duty. It is not a virtue to be miserable or to sacrifice yourself. It *is* a virtue to achieve happiness, because it is a difficult task, demanding consistent rationality from you.

It is enormously easy to give up and sacrifice yourself, particularly if there are collectors of sacrifices all around you. They can smell your willingness to sacrifice. If you want a fuhrer, as in Germany, you will get one. If you want a holy dictator, as in Russia, you will get one. Even in practically every family, there is one strong personality whom everybody depends on, exploits and, at the same time, obeys. Well, that's a mini-dictator. These phenomena—the exploiting family or the whole exploiting nation—all come from the same source: the morality of altruism. They require, on the one hand, people who do not want to be independent and who want to be led and to be sacrificed, and, on the other hand, collectors of those sacrifices: the dictators or the family tyrants. There have been two thousand years or more of this kind of morality. It is the tradition behind all of today's religions, which hold a monopoly on prescribing morality. They are not doing a very good job of it, but still they hold that monopoly. And that is why people do not understand my philosophy or, when they do, are afraid to adopt it. Those who are afraid know it is true but they fear that it imposes too big a responsibility on them.

Newman: Productive work is a virtue in the Objectivist ethics. How do you distinguish between "productive work" and "work"?

AR: Almost anything that is work is productive, unless the one performing it is completely irrational. I don't make the distinction, as a rule. I use the term "work" to refer to productive work, by which I mean any kind of work that creates values. Again, the test is reason. If you can rationally demonstrate why you spend time producing a certain gadget, it does not matter how many customers you have. Sometimes the greatest products are not immediately recognized. The standard by which to determine whether a product is a value, and is therefore worth producing, has to be your own reasoning. And if your product has only a small following, it would be up to you to decide whether to close your business and go into some other kind of work.

Newman: Many people hold regimented or routine jobs, which don't allow a lot of intellectual creativity or individual thinking. Could such work still be productive work?

AR: Of course. Productive work originally involves an act of thinking, but the more complex the product, the more it also requires physical action. On all the levels of complexity that the production requires, every man involved in it must use his own mind. His intelligence and understanding are needed. Even on the lowest kind of assembly-line job, you still have to focus and know what you are doing. Your intelligence is required all along the line of any cooperative act of production. And how productive should you be? As productive as you wish, and as productive as you can be. If the whole of your intelligence can lead you only to being a foreman in a factory and no higher, it's perfectly proper to stay on that level. On the other hand, if your mind can do more, then it is up to you to rise, to develop your intelligence and to take more and more demanding work, until you get a job that utilizes all of your capacity.

Newman: So it is, in a sense, a moral obligation to yourself to find a job that utilizes your full potential.

AR: Certainly, because the use of your mind—rationality—is your top virtue.

Newman: You have said that the expression "Judge not, lest ye be judged" is improper, and that in fact one should judge and be prepared to be judged. But judging other people is extremely difficult. When does one classify someone as immoral?

AR: Only when he has engaged in some immoral action. For what I classify as moral or immoral, I refer you to Galt's speech in *Atlas Shrugged* or to "The Objectivist Ethics" in *The Virtue of Selfishness*. There you will see a short list of the virtues and the vices under Objectivism. It's not an exhaustive list, but at least it gives you the essentials. Once someone acts in a way that you can prove is immoral, you have to judge him accordingly. You never judge a person on mere potential, and you seldom judge him solely on what he says, because most people do not speak very precisely. You would not judge a person as immoral on the basis of one inadvertent remark. If, however, he goes about the country preaching immoral ideas, then you would classify him as immoral.

Newman: There are people who are mixed, in that they hold certain virtues but in particular situations, they may act against them. Is that like being a little bit pregnant—i.e., if you are a "little bit" immoral, you simply are immoral?

AR: In fact, yes. But the important thing here is the degree of knowledge a person has. If someone does not know exactly the nature of what he is doing, he can't be considered immoral, particularly if it is a young person. Also, the action is then correctable. One would have to be guilty of a major crime in order to be judged immoral. For instance, if a person is caught lying, I would never forgive that. I would regard that as a major immorality and would consider the person immoral, irrespective of any virtues he might have. Needless to say, a robber, a murderer or someone who is systematically infringing the rights of other people is immoral, no matter what virtues he might have in other areas. In judging people who have mixed premises, which most people have, you must hierarchically balance the seriousness of their virtues and their vices, and see what you get as the net result.

Newman: One of the most perplexing questions we ask ourselves is: "What is the purpose of life?" For many people the answer seems always to remain mysteriously out of reach. What is the answer, in your view?

AR: I would say that the question itself is improper. It smuggles in the wrong answer. The question should be: "What is the purpose of *my* life?" or: "What is the purpose of some particular individual's life?" But to ask: "What is the purpose of life?" implies that somebody outside of ourselves—some supernatural being—has to prescribe that purpose, and that we should spend our lives trying to discover it and live up to it. There is no such thing as "the purpose of life," because life is an end in itself. *Life* is the purpose of life. And nature has given us a very good way of knowing whether we are spending our lives properly or not—namely, whether we are happy or not.

Your moral obligation is to pursue the highest form of happiness possible to you. Your decision as to what will make you happy is not arbitrary. It is not proper to slaughter whole continents of people, or even one person, and then say, "I did it because it made me happy." You do not have that moral right. You cannot succeed in living if that is the kind of value you pursue. But if your values are rational, then you spend your life on that which gives you happiness. Happiness is the emotional state of having achieved your values, and it is up to you to select what makes you happy. The range of choices—of rational choices—is enormous. It is as wide as there are people on earth. And you have only one thing in common with all the other seekers of happiness: the demand—not of a supernatural being and not of society, but of *reality*—that you pursue a rational purpose. You must use your mind to its utmost in deciding what will make you happy, and you must logically prove to yourself the validity of your choice.

On those conditions, there is no clash between your existence and your enjoyment of life. Your existence is an end in itself. You are not giving it up in order to pursue some goal. You are not sacrificing for your choices. You are saying, "If this is what I want, and it's difficult, everything I do is worth the effort because I want it, and I am going to achieve it." On that formula, you are totally moral and you will live a good life. That is the purpose of your life. But any person who attempts to prescribe—not even enforce, just prescribe—the specific means by which other people should attain happiness, is a monster and has no claim to morality at all.

Newman: *Then the one critical factor in happiness is setting rational goals. Are those long-range goals?*

AR: That depends on your choice. The more complex, the longer the range. Very simple goals can be achieved range-of-the-moment. But if you select a very intellectual, complex goal, it will take you quite a long time. Man lives his life long-range. He doesn't live like an animal, which completes a cycle of life and starts all over again. Man has to look ahead and plan across the range of a lifetime. Therefore, the longer your range, the better.

Newman: *What level of contact with immoral people is acceptable? For example, is it acceptable to trade with someone who is immoral?*

AR: If I know that a given person is immoral—if he is dishonest, if he is cheating me, if he is dealing with countries like Soviet Russia—I would not deal with him. But you cannot spend your life researching and censuring the views of all the people you come into contact with. Unless it comes to your knowledge, you don't inquire into the morality of people with whom your dealings are very simple, such as a purchase from a store. If, however, there is a closer, more long-range relationship—for example, with a potential employer or employee—then you must have more precise standards. You certainly should not want to work for or to hire immoral people. But here again, you have to be careful. You cannot pronounce your employer immoral just because he doesn't agree with you. You cannot set yourself up as his censor. If he has not done anything immoral in his business and does not require any immoral action from you, then you can accept him. If, however, you know that he is, say, a receiver of stolen goods and he wants you to cheat customers, then you do not deal with an employer of that kind.

Newman: Is there any reason to treat family members differently than other people in this context?

AR: None whatever. I am very much against that sense of "family" which makes a small tribe out of family members and ties you to every aunt and second cousin you might have. The only exception, of course, is in regard to your parents, because that relationship is different from any other, and you have to acknowledge that fact. Generally, you would not break with your parents as easily as you would with other members of the family. You have to judge those family members as you would every person you meet: if you don't approve of them, you don't become friendly. But you cannot choose your parents in that sense. You have to give them a long benefit of the doubt and permit them, in effect, more offenses against you than you would allow to friends or acquaintances. You have to give parents a certain credit for the fact that they chose to give birth to you and took care of you while you were helpless. But it's not an unlimited claim on their part, and if you clash with your parents too much, you have to maintain an attitude of polite "duty" and see as little of them as possible. This is probably the only realm in which I recognize such a thing as "duty," which is a very wrong concept as a rule, because it asks you to do something for which you have no reason. But here there is a reason—the fact that your parents gave you life—and it makes you do more for them, or bear more from them, than you would in dealing with any other people.

Newman: I'd like to turn to politics. You have stated that the government ought to be the exclusive agent for the use of force, under objective rules of law and justice.

AR: That's right.

Newman: And yet today we see an alarming rise in violent crimes in this country, and in the number of people applying for gun permits to protect themselves. Do you see this as a dangerous trend? And do you favor any form of gun-control laws?

AR: I have given it no thought at all but, offhand, I would say that the government should not control guns except in very marginal forms. I don't think it's an important issue, because I don't think the fate of this country will be decided in physical terms. If this country falls apart or the government collapses in bankruptcy, having a handgun in your pocket isn't going to save your life. What you need in order to fight for a proper system of government are the right ideas, along with other people who share those ideas—not handguns for personal protection.

Newman: Article Six of the Bill of Rights gives individuals the right to subpoena witnesses to testify in their favor. People who don't respond to subpoenas are subject to contempt citations, fines and imprisonment. Does this deny the freedom of the witness if he chooses not to testify?

AR: Not really. I am in favor of such laws because, presumably, if there is a court case, somebody has been hurt. And if a witness has knowledge relevant to the issue and he refuses to testify, he is the one who is violating the rights of the defendant, or whomever his testimony involves. If either party in the case needs the information he has, he couldn't have an honest reason for refusing to provide it, because he is interfering with justice. He is saying, in effect, "The court may decide wrongly without me, but I still don't want to testify." I don't think that's legitimate.

Newman: The United States is a nation of immigrants, many of whom come from Europe. And yet our culture is significantly different from that of Europe. What do you see as the differences?

AR: The United States, from the beginning, was based by implication on a morality of selfishness, which was the attraction for people who wanted to escape from tyranny in their homeland and to come here to enjoy the responsibility of standing on their own and being free. This attitude is the opposite of Europe's sense of life—its basic, subconscious, emotional understanding of life. Throughout the history of Europe, the values and ideas of its people never changed on one basic point: Europe is a state-worshipping culture. It has always worshipped the power of the state, whether in the form of absolute monarchs or, later, of collectivists. European societies have never understood the importance of the individual and of individual rights. Individualism is an American concept. Obviously, some people in Europe understand it, but they are the exceptions. Because European culture is so steeped in the altruist idea that man must exist for others, the greatest distinction the European can dream of is to serve, or be rewarded by, the state. The state is regarded as an almost supernatural being and the individual citizen as just a serf.

In America, it is exactly the opposite. America is the first country in history that was deliberately and consciously founded on a certain philosophy. It is a philosophy, rooted in Aristotelianism, which respects the individual and holds that society should be based on individual rights. This principle was formulated for the first time in the United States by the Founding Fathers. It is so great an achievement that centuries from now, men should kneel when they think of what their forefathers created in this country.

Yet today, the greatest and noblest country in the world is being denounced and demeaned in every way by its intellectuals. In America, the public is much better than the intellectuals. The poison is coming from the universities, particularly the philosophy departments, whose ideas come from Europe. Today, we are seeing the ultimate climax, the last disgusting collapse of Kantian philosophy. Immanuel Kant is the villain of European history, and the intellectuals in America are trying to sacrifice this country also to his vicious ideas. I don't think they will succeed. In this country, the basic sense of life is pro-individualist. The United States was made by that philosophy, which still functions, even though most people are not consciously aware of it. One of the popular expressions in this country is: "I don't want to be pushed around." Well, that is an eloquent illustration of man's personal independence. Whereas in Europe, people believe that man is born to be pushed around.

Newman: Have you seen any changes in the American sense of life recently?

AR: That's too broad a question. One could not judge that. Within the last few years, the country has certainly turned to the right, by which I mean: anti-collectivism and pro-capitalism, more or less. But without some *intellectual* direction, this won't do us any good. At present it is impossible to foretell what will become of the country. All I can say is that if the right kind of ideas were being communicated, they would win—and, in fact, are seemingly winning today, but they are being misrepresented so disgustingly by political candidates that I don't know whether the country will eventually survive.

Newman: I want to turn to esthetics for a moment. You stated that the purpose of an artist is to bring his view of man and of reality into existence. Does this occur regardless of whether the artist is aware of that purpose?

AR: Yes, because it's in the very nature of art. But "to bring into existence" means to bring into an artistic form, i.e., into the condensation of an artwork which presents the artist's view of life. This presentation takes place whether the artist knows it or not, because he cannot produce a work of art without some idea behind it—an idea that reflects his metaphysical view of man's nature and of man's place in the universe.

Newman: *Why is that important to the artist?*

AR: Because it's always important to know the nature of the feelings that motivate you. The nature of an artistic feeling is to express something of your view of life. Every artist in every form of art will always tell you that he wants to express himself. But what is it about himself that he wants to express? His metaphysical values. Of course, today's so-called art contradicts this principle and does not express metaphysical values—but that is because it isn't art. The horrible, shapeless, purposeless and senseless mess that passes for literature or painting or sculpture today is deliberate, cynical nihilism: the desire to destroy all values and to destroy man. And that also is a metaphysical view, isn't it?

Newman: *You have indicated that one of the goals of your writing was to portray the ideal man. And you certainly did that with John Galt in* Atlas Shrugged. *Is there more for you to write about in fiction?*

AR: Is there more? Oh, now don't ask such a difficult question. Yes, there is more, but as to whether I will do it, I don't know. I would very much like to write more fiction but I don't like costume dramas or fantasies, and it is almost impossible to place a Romantic story in today's world. And by "Romantic," I mean the literary school of Romanticism, not a love story. Today's world is too disgusting, and I could not project a hero in it. If I find a way to do it, I might write another book, but I am not sure.

Newman: *What is the status of the rumors that* Atlas Shrugged *is being made into a movie or a mini-series?*

AR: At present the producer is considering making it into a movie. He has not given up. He still has a contract for it, but what exactly he will do about it, and when, I don't know. The project is still in the works, but inactive at present.

Newman: *Well, speaking for myself and for so many other people, I hope that it comes to fruition very quickly. You've shown that life ought to be glorious, purposeful, joyful and valuable. And for all of that, and for being here today, I thank you.*

AR: Thank you very much.

· 31 ·

Louis Rukeyser's Business Journal, 1981

[Businesses] are supporting universities and every other kind of
organization that preaches anti-businessman and anti-capitalist
propaganda.

*Louis Rukeyser: Ayn Rand has led one of the most remarkable lives of the twenti-
eth century. Born 76 years ago in Russia and educated at the University of Leningrad, she went on to become, in her best-selling novels and her nonfiction works, the
world's foremost philosophical advocate of individualism, capitalism and what she
provocatively calls "the virtue of selfishness." Ayn, in a speech you made here for the
National Committee for Monetary Reform, you suggested that American businessmen have become their own worst enemies. What did you mean by that?*

AR: I didn't suggest it; I stated it openly and firmly. I meant that they have
dropped ideas completely. Businessmen are practical when they deal with any
matter other than the intellect, but for some reason they believe that ideas are
unimportant and irrelevant. As a result, they are supporting universities and
every other kind of organization that preaches anti-businessman and anti-
capitalist propaganda.

Rukeyser: Do you think businessmen are too apologetic about the profit motive?

AR: I don't think they are *too* apologetic; they should not be apologetic at all.
They are apologetic in a dreadful way, when they should instead be proud of
the profit motive.

Rukeyser: I suppose some businessman listening to you might think: "Well, it's all right for her to say, but I've got to sell my product; I've got to woo my customers." What would you say to such a person?

AR: To begin with, he does not have to "woo" his customers. It is much harder for me, as a professional intellectual. I supposedly have to "woo" my readers. But do I? No. I state what I want to say, and those who agree with me will come to me. I don't want the others.

Rukeyser: Is it your view that U.S. businesses should stop supporting the universities?

AR: Definitely. Businesses should go on strike against the universities, demanding at least some kind of "fairness doctrine," on the order of what television used to have, so that every important viewpoint is presented.

Rukeyser: You have spoken of the virtue of selfishness. Indeed, that was the title of one of your books. What would you say to all those Americans who believe they have an obligation to support their weaker fellow-citizens through welfare and similar programs?

AR: Fine. Let them do it—but they have no moral right to force me or any other American to support the so-called downtrodden. They have no right to my work; they have no right to my life. I am free to do what I want. Those Americans who believe in providing for the poor should do so voluntarily and privately—not through government, not through taxes, not through force.

Rukeyser: Some people think that the election of Ronald Reagan and similar political developments suggest a shift toward the ideas you've been proposing. Yet you seem very gloomy about our future. Why?

AR: Because I don't think that Ronald Reagan is a proper advocate of capitalism. He is not for capitalism; he stands for a mixed economy. And he is not a very good politician. I never voted for him—I didn't vote for any Presidential candidate in this past election. But I do believe that a shift to the right is taking place. The public is tired of the welfare state, and would like to return to some rational Americanism. But there is no intellectual leadership at all today.

Epilogue: Leonard Peikoff
and Recollections of Ayn Rand

In her presence, you had to feel—at least, I felt—there is hope, there is a future, justice will triumph. That sense just radiated out of her.

EDITOR'S NOTE: Leonard Peikoff hosted a radio talk-show from 1995 to 1999. On the last program, he was interviewed by his wife, Amy.

AMY PEIKOFF: Today is Leonard's last day on "The Leonard Peikoff Show," and, as promised, I'm going to be asking him questions about Ayn Rand—what she was like, what kind of association he had with her, what he misses about her and much more. Let me start with some background material. Leonard, how did you get to meet Ayn Rand? And what were some of the first questions you asked her?

LEONARD PEIKOFF: I met her in 1951, in California, through a mutual friend who knew that I admired *The Fountainhead*. Ayn was writing *Atlas Shrugged* at the time. Actually, she was just starting the first page of "Part Three" on the day that I met her. I remember that one of the first comments she made to the other people there was: "I can't get Galt [the hero] to talk correctly." He hadn't spoken throughout the whole first two parts of the novel. And she had built up such an expectation in her own mind of what he had to sound like that every piece of dialogue she gave him seemed inadequate. That was the problem she was then wrestling with.

As to what I asked her, I had really only one major question. I told her that I just could not figure out *The Fountainhead*. I had always been brought up to believe that you have to be either moral or practical—you can't be both.

Life requires you to pick one, and I was wrestling with that choice. I said to her: "I don't understand the character of Howard Roark. He's obviously intended as an idealist. He's the man of integrity and honor, the man who won't compromise. And yet he's clearly practical—I can see why his course leads to success, and why Keating is just a passing fad, who falls by the wayside. Obviously you don't intend Roark to be *both* moral and practical, but I can't make out which one he is."

You can imagine her response. Here she is writing *Atlas Shrugged,* one of the sub-themes of which is the false dichotomy between the moral and the practical. So she gave me, estimating conservatively, at least a twenty-minute, nonstop lecture. She ignored everybody else in the room and delivered an impassioned answer on what was wrong with my question. That changed my life right there.

AP: I can definitely see why that impressed you. From that point on, in what capacities did you know her?

LP: Since I lived in Canada for the next two years, as an undergraduate student, I just made periodic trips to see her. She had moved to New York soon after I met her, and that is where I would travel to visit her. Then the time came when I had to make a commitment to a career. I had finished pre-med and was supposed to become a doctor, like my father. But I didn't want to. My father said to me: "Why don't you go to New York, live near Ayn Rand for a year, major in philosophy and get it out of your system? Then come home and live a normal life, like everybody else." So I moved to New York in September 1953—and never came back home, except for occasional visits. From that point on, I saw her regularly, as a student and, increasingly, as a friend.

AP: Describe one of your typical philosophical evenings, when you went to Ayn Rand's apartment and had long discussions with her.

LP: At first, I went only with other people. There was a group of about ten or twelve of us—which was jokingly called "The Collective," because we were all staunch individualists—and we went on Saturday nights. We would get to read the latest part of the manuscript of *Atlas Shrugged,* and then talk about it with Ayn. Gradually everybody established his own independent relation with her, and I did, too. I would go primarily to discuss philosophic issues, particularly ones that came up at school.

I was in graduate school at that point, working on my Ph.D. in philosophy. I was completely confused by everything the professors said, and I took notes on what I didn't understand. I would then go to her, and she would patiently take one point at a time and clarify it for me. Those discussions were legendary—in part, because of their length.

She was in her fifties or more, and she was indefatigable. I'd get there at about eight p.m. We would have maybe ten or fifteen minutes of what you'd call small talk, but she did not care for it much and we would quickly start on some philosophic topic. We would talk nonstop, just the two of us. Her husband might be present; he would just sit back and watch. But the conversation was between me and her. Usually, I would ask a question, she'd give a lengthy answer and I would then have some reply and follow-up question. We would go on like this until about midnight, at which point she would be hungry. We'd go to the kitchen, where she'd fix sandwiches and coffee, and we'd talk again. If it was an ordinary evening, I'd go home at three or four in the morning.

But on a great many occasions, I wouldn't leave until much later. At about three o'clock I would often say, "Well, I guess I'd better go," and it would be four by the time I reached the door of her apartment. I would walk eight or ten steps down the hall to the elevator, and she'd stand at her door and say, "I just want to add one point." I'd already have pressed the elevator button and it would arrive, and I'd have to let it go back down—you can hold it only so long before a bell starts to ring. She would be standing in the hall, making some point, but I didn't go back to her apartment because, after all, I knew I was leaving any second. So we would have this protracted philosophic discussion, at four in the morning, down the hallway. I wonder what the neighbors must have thought—I'm calling out my questions, and she's saying, "Here's a lead for you to think about until next time." Finally, at six or six-thirty, I would rush home, try to get as much of her ideas as I could down on paper and then go to bed.

AP: Do you have all these notes somewhere?

LP: Somewhere, yes, except for the ones I completely used up for [my book] *OPAR* [*Objectivism: The Philosophy of Ayn Rand*].

AP: Tell us about a humorous incident. How did you come to call Ayn Rand by her first name?

LP: She was very formal. She was introduced to me as Mrs. O'Connor—her husband was Frank O'Connor—and that is what I called her for a year or more. One day, she and I and several others were taking a car trip to upstate New York, and I overheard them talking about Dagny [from *Atlas Shrugged*].

I wanted to ask whether Dagny was the heroine. But I was a kid and did not know the correct pronunciation of "heroine." I thought it was pronounced *"hee-roh-ein,"* with the emphasis on the first syllable. So I asked her, "Is that the heroine [hero, Ayn]?" She turned to me indignantly and said, "Certainly not—she's the heroine." She thought I was calling her "Ayn," you see. So at the price of being considered an idiot for seeming to think Dagny was the hero, I got away with calling Ayn Rand by her first name. And I continued doing so from then on.

AP: How did you become Ayn Rand's legal and intellectual heir?

LP: I was the last one left. There was a whole group of people who had surrounded her, not always for ideal reasons. But I fully understood, if I say so myself, what she had to offer. I understood that Ayn Rand was a unique event in history and that certainly nothing would ever equal it in my life. Many people were hurt by something she'd say to them in anger, usually a blunt statement about some immoral behavior of theirs which she had seen. I regarded any anger at me (which was not because I was immoral) as trivial. I was extremely devoted to her and intended to stay so until the end, even if sometimes she was (in my opinion) too indignant about some error of mine.

At one point there were three or four candidates who could have been chosen by her as her heir. But one after the other, they broke with her or she broke with them. I was her last loyalist and so became her heir.

AP: And that means what, exactly?

LP: She gave me all her property—her intellectual property, her copyrights, her entire estate. She left nothing to anybody else. She told me, basically, to do with it what I wanted; it was mine and she trusted me to preserve the spirit of her philosophy. Other than that, the only instructions she gave me pertained to her funeral arrangements, which I carried out. As to her manuscripts, she had agreed, informally, about fifteen or so years before her death, to a request from the Library of Congress to donate the manuscripts of her novels. But she refused to sign the gift papers they sent her or to commit herself. Even so, I did eventually donate them to the Library of Congress.

AP: Since her death, have you been busy with intellectual projects involving her works?

LP: Yes. I've been bringing out her posthumous material; working with her publisher to create the best-quality editions and better publicity for her famous works; evaluating movie proposals; dealing with requests by writers to quote from her; et cetera. Her estate has flourished, and it's a business in itself just to manage it.

AP: What was Ayn Rand's essential purpose, or motivation, in her work? Did she intend to come up with a revolutionary philosophy?

LP: That was not her primary concern. She wanted to project the heroic, ideal man. That's what she had always wanted, going back as far as she can trace her development. But she found that in order to do so, she had to *define* the ideal man. She was not content with generalities like: "He's strong and courageous." She wanted a fundamental understanding of what constitutes the perfect man, in order to be able to project him fully for artistic purposes. That led her into philosophy.

And since she had the mind that she did, it led her not just to values and ethics, but to the foundation of ethics, which is epistemology and metaphysics. She was led to define a total philosophic system. Philosophy, to her, was a means to an end. She was like an engineer who wants to build a bridge, but decides he first has to study theoretical physics.

AP: Why then did Ayn Rand start writing philosophic nonfiction? Why didn't she just keep on with fiction?

LP: She wanted to remain productive. She thought that some of the ideas in her novels needed nonfiction elaboration and development. Her main motivation at this point, though, was that she wanted to write, but could no longer bring herself to write fiction. Her idea of fiction was Romantic Realism, which is fiction set in the real world in which the author lives. By the sixties, she thought that the events going on in the world were so evil and grotesque that she had no desire to set a novel in that kind of reality.

She considered various ideas for historical fiction, she considered a novel set on a space ship—anything to get away from the corrupt modern world. But such escapism was counter to what fundamentally interested her in fiction writing. Consequently, she gave it up. Although she always tried to come up with a satisfying (to her) idea for a novel, she never actually did. Instead, she devoted her energy to short-term, nonfiction projects, clarifying various aspects of her philosophy. She felt that this was a way of supporting her novels, by giving their ideas objective proof. Ultimately, she finished that aspect of her life work too. As to her magazines and her commentaries on current events, she finally felt she was tired of repeating herself, and stopped writing (except occasional pieces, like speeches).

AP: What was her favorite among her fiction works?

LP: Oh, without a doubt, *Atlas Shrugged*. She thought any author's favorite work should be his latest. "If it's not a significant improvement, what the hell's the matter with him?" is what she would have said. If a writer likes his early stuff better than his later stuff, he's in trouble.

AP: What about her nonfiction works?

LP: I think that *Introduction to Objectivist Epistemology* was the most intellectually challenging—that was one of her favorites. Another was the article she wrote on Apollo 11, the 1969 space mission to the moon, in which she describes her live observation of the liftoff. She brought both a philosopher's insight and an artist's use of language to that article. That combination made the article one of her top favorites.

AP: So in nonfiction, she did not think that every new article she wrote had to be better than the previous one?

LP: No, it couldn't, because these articles were short and the subject matter might not allow it. As a cultural analyst, she had to write about whatever was happening in the world. So a later piece would not necessarily be better than an earlier one.

AP: How about her work habits? Was she one of these people who work around the clock, nonstop?

LP: No. She had the view that about six hours a day is the most you can devote to creative work. And by that I mean giving it your total concentration, with no phone calls or other interruptions. She would usually have lunch around 12, and go into her office at 12:30. She wanted the freedom to work late, but she had an arrangement with her cook, who had to catch the subway. In order for her to catch the last possible safe subway, dinner had to start for Ayn at 6:30. So she would finish writing at 6:29 and go straight to the dinner table. She would not go back to writing that evening. As long as I knew her, she worked for those six hours, six days a week. That was her time for creative work—as distinct from all the business that she did in the morning, with publishers, agents, lawyers and so on.

AP: What type of people did Ayn Rand like? Do you think she would have liked the creative people behind today's new technologies?

LP: She would certainly have liked creative, innovative people, if they were decent individuals. But it's possible to be creative—and obnoxious. It's possible to be innovative in a specific field, but be a conformist in every other. She did not go around like Diogenes with his lantern, constantly searching for innovators. She would meet people who were recommended to her as being rational and, above all, interested in ideas. She loved to talk about ideas. With several exceptions, the new people she met and liked were those who wanted to discuss philosophy with her.

AP: How did she deal with them in the first encounters?

LP: She would try to find out about their ideas, which was a virtue on her part, but which also caused her a lot of problems. If the people seemed sincere, if they seemed to understand what they were saying and if she agreed with their views, then she tended in her younger years to take such people at face value. She assumed they were just as straightforward as she was. She assumed that they knew the implications of everything they were saying. She assumed, in effect, that they were genuine Objectivists.

Sadly, she was disillusioned time and again. This was a burning question throughout her life: How do you judge people? She never became cynical about people she'd meet, but since she had been betrayed so many times by individuals she had thought were good, she got to the point in her final years of feeling that she did not really know how to judge.

AP: Was it that feeling of betrayal that led to her having this temper that everybody talks about?

LP: No. She definitely had a temper, but it came in part from her thinking that what was obvious to her was equally obvious to other people. If you see that two and two are four and someone persistently says the answer is five, you get annoyed. You say to that person: "What the hell's the matter? This is an obvious point." All her ideas stood just this way in her mind.

Now, many times, her anger was 100 percent justified, because, as I've said, the person was being dishonest and she picked that up. But on some occasions that was not the case. For example, she was often angry at me when I was, in fact, only confused, not dishonest. Her anger was really the projection of a genius; she was unable to grasp the degree of authentic confusion that I had. She did eventually come to the point of grasping how different she was intellectually from other people, but it was a very unhappy discovery for her. She said to me many times: "I do not want to, and can't, think: 'Oh, Ayn the genius—as against the average person.'" She hated that idea, she hated that sense of herself. She believed she was who she was because of her honesty, not some super-intelligence. So she tended to assume that people who did not measure up to her intellectually were being dishonest. She did not always hold that view about other people, but she had a tendency toward it.

AP: Can you say a little bit about her husband, Frank O'Connor? What kind of person was he?

LP: He was a great guy. He was the strong, silent type, like Gary Cooper—even better-looking than Gary Cooper. He had spent some years acting in silent movies, and doing other things. But he ended up as a painter. In fact, I have some of his paintings on my walls, right now. If you looked at his paintings and Ayn's novels together, you'd see some of what they had in common—that very benevolent, joyous sense of life. He was not an intellectual; he was not much of a talker. But he was very witty, and when he did zing a line in, it was memorable.

AP: Did Ayn Rand travel after coming to the United States?

LP: Well, of course, from Chicago to Hollywood [soon after she first arrived in America], and then she and her husband drove cross-country to New York. After that, to my knowledge, she traveled only on certain vacations or to give speeches, and always within the continental United States. Her favorite place was Ouray, Colorado, which is basically where she got the idea for Atlantis, or Galt's Gulch, in *Atlas*. She thought that was the most beautiful place in America.

AP: Didn't she ever visit Europe?

LP: No, she never went back to Europe.

AP: Do you think she regretted not having the opportunity to see, for example, Michelangelo's masterpieces in Italy?

LP: Europe represented a painful chapter to her. Europe stood for Russia in her mind, and she had been desperate to escape that whole terrible culture. She thought America was the greatest place. In her last couple of years, she expressed a mild desire to go to Italy and France, but it was never a passion.

AP: But it wasn't that she felt scared to go, for fear that the Soviets were going to seize her?

LP: No, not as far as Western Europe was concerned. She wouldn't go to Russia itself, of course, because for as long as she was alive there was an official Communist death warrant out for her there.

AP: Which buildings in New York City did Ayn Rand like the best?

LP: That's a great question. I know she hated the Daily News Building the most. I think she liked the Empire State Building best, for its symbolism and for its structure. I think she liked the Chrysler Building; that reflected her architectural taste. She loved Frank Lloyd Wright, of course, but he doesn't have any skyscrapers in New York. She loved his Falling Water house, in Pennsylvania. Wright was her favorite architect, without a doubt.

AP: A listener says he heard that Ayn Rand accepted the existence of God not long before her death, and wants to know if this is true.

LP: Nonsense. She did once say, many years earlier, that in thinking about the topic she had come up with an argument for the existence of God which was better than any of the standard ones. But she never told me what it was and she obviously didn't accept its conclusion. It never came up again in our conversations. That listener's claim is foolish.

AP: If you could have one more evening with Ayn Rand, what three questions would you ask?

LP: Oh, for God's sake—I have to get down to three? All right. Number one: What do you think of my book *Objectivism: The Philosophy of Ayn Rand*, and did I in any way misrepresent your philosophy? Number two: What is the solution to the problem of induction, in detail? And number three: Do you still think there is hope for Western civilization, without our first having to go back to another Dark Ages?

AP: What do you miss the most about her?

LP: Well, intellectually, I miss what I would call her "omniscience." Whatever you asked her—within the fields she knew—she had not only an answer, but an encyclopedia of knowledge in her mind backing her answer up with identifications, integrations, connections, illustrations. Suppose you asked her what she thought of a movie she'd just seen. By the time she finished her answer, it was as if you had taken an entire course in esthetics, movie-making, dialogue construction, philosophy and art.

Personally and emotionally, I miss her benevolent sense of life; her strength of character; and her friendship and support through every crisis. I miss *her* as a person—quite apart from her knowledge—and I'd need a whole volume to explain that. A tiny example: she had a dislike for a person's conveying some bad news and then saying, "Good night, I'm leaving." You had to leave, if at all possible, on a positive note. She would say, "Before you go, communicate something positive to re-establish the proper view of life." And sometimes it was really hard—especially when you're a graduate student, and all those irrational classes you have to endure are making you miserable—to think of something positive. But she would project the power of being able to cope with anything, of being able to answer anything and solve anything. In her presence, you had to feel—at least, I felt—there is hope, there is a future, justice will triumph. That sense just radiated out of her, and made it easier to leave on a better note, and to live more fully and happily.

AP: Would you care to speculate as to what she would have thought of the world today?

LP: It's really hard to do so, because things are worse in many ways and are getting worse all the time. So a lot of things would sicken her. I think she'd be very happy about the collapse of Communism in Russia. But she would be warning people that Russia is still a cesspool.

I think she would have regarded the whole Clinton saga as unreal. Her reaction, without a doubt, would have been: "It's too broad to put in fiction; no one would believe it." She would have thought that Clinton himself couldn't be put in a novel, because people would say that that's carrying satire too far.

I don't think, in general, that she would have been surprised by the state of the world. She knew that things were getting worse.

AP: What would Ayn Rand have thought of your radio show? Specifically, would she have agreed with all the various positions that you've taken on this show?

LP: What a question! She probably would have thought that the show was a good idea and that it was a noble undertaking to try to spread rational ideas by radio. She liked radio; she thought it was an intellectual medium. I know she definitely would not have agreed with everything I've said, and I will give you an example or two. But I don't want to come across as saying that she's necessarily wrong. That would be ridiculous, because in real life when I disagreed with her, 999 times out of 1,000, she wiped the floor with me. And her arguments were so powerful, I was embarrassed that I had even uttered an opposing view. So it's not fair to take advantage of her death to "get in the last word."

She would certainly have agreed with what I've said on anything in philosophy, but not necessarily on narrower issues, like pornography, for example. She thought pornography, as such, was disgusting. Now, when I discussed its positive aspects on the show, I was focusing on certain tasteful pornography used as a form of emphasis to change the sexual routine. I don't think I ever even raised this subject with her. But it's quite conceivable to me that she would have come up with arguments—I can even hypothesize what they are—that would have blown me out of the water. And she might have disagreed on various other concretes, such as my evaluation of specific people or movies. But she certainly would not have disagreed with me on any major interpretation of the news.

AP: Would these disagreements then represent departures from her philosophy?

LP: I don't think they are departures from her philosophy. A philosophy is a set of principles, which must then be applied to concretes. There can be a lot of disagreement among true advocates of a philosophy when it comes to specific, concrete cases. There can be differences of strategy, differences of interest, difficulties in untangling complex events, et cetera. But with respect to philosophic principles themselves, I don't think I ever said anything on the air that departed from Objectivism at all. And if I did, I certainly did not do so knowingly.

Index

267